PRAISE FOR *SHERLOCK HOLMES AND THE NEEDLE'S EYE*

Unique, inventive, educational, and fun. What's not to like?

—Jerry B. Jenkins
Novelist, Writer, and Owner of the Christian Writers Guild

A phenomenal accomplishment. Every page crackles; every chapter takes my breath away. Bailey's attention to historical detail—whether of London or Jerusalem—is all by itself a major attraction. I can't wait to dive back into it. All I need to write a one-line review of *Sherlock Holmes and the Needle's Eye* is one line from it: "The Needle's Eye is the product of pure genius."

—Ger Erickson
Editor, Brentwood Press & Publishing Company

Bible study leaders are always on the lookout for the "hook"—the original slant that will captivate readers and students to take a fresh look at familiar material. Len Bailey has tapped one of his life passions—the Sherlock Holmes stories—as an avenue to explore unexpected nuances in visits to ten Bible stories. In keeping with the detective story format, each of the Bible passages is formulated as a mystery to be solved. Fifty pages of investigative questions at the end highlight the ten questions and give excellent prompts to reflecting on or discussing the passages.

Profess

SHERLOCK HOLMES
HOLMES
AND THE NEEDLE'S EYE

OTHER TITLES BY LEN BAILEY

Fantasams

Clabbernappers

SHERLOCK HOLMES

AND THE NEEDLE'S EYE

The World's Greatest Detective
Tackles the Bible's Ultimate Mysteries

LEN BAILEY

THOMAS NELSON
Since 1798

NASHVILLE   DALLAS   MEXICO CITY   RIO DE JANEIRO

Published in Nashville, Tennessee, by Thomas Nelson. Thomas Nelson is a trademark of Thomas Nelson, Inc.

Author is represented by the Stobbe Agency.

Thomas Nelson, Inc., titles may be purchased in bulk for educational, business, fund-raising, or sales promotional use. For information, please e-mail SpecialMarkets@ThomasNelson.com.

**Library of Congress Cataloging-in-Publication
Data is available upon request**

Printed in the United States of America
13 14 15 16 17 18 RRD 6 5 4 3 2 1

To my mother, Margaret Ann Bailey, who introduced me to Sherlock Holmes

This book has two parts: It begins with the narratives of all ten mysteries followed by a section of investigative questions for each narrative. If you are reading *Sherlock Holmes and the Needle's Eye* as a Bible study, begin by answering the questions in the back that pertain to the particular week you are in. The mystery to be solved will be displayed below the chapter number. The investigative questions will lead you through specific scriptures, and familiarize you with the mystery's environment, but will not reveal the mystery's solution. Keep in mind that some questions can only be answered after reading the mystery. After that, turn back and read the corresponding narrative in the front of the book where Sherlock Holmes and Watson go back in time to the particular Old or New Testament setting and solve the mystery.

If you want to read *Sherlock Holmes and the Needle's Eye* as a novel or a collection of individual mysteries, simply begin reading at the beginning—and enjoy!

CONTENTS

CONTENTS

ACKNOWLEDGMENTS

I APPRECIATE THE FOLLOWING PEOPLE FOR THEIR HELP IN producing this volume. First, thanks to Dr. Warren Wiersbe for his encouragement and for presenting me with the two-volume set of *The Annotated Sherlock Holmes* by William S. Baring-Gould. Thanks to my wonderful wife, Denise, who endured my repetitive watching of the BBC productions of *Sherlock Holmes*, starring Jeremy Brett. For their advice and patience, thanks to Nina Rosselli, Linda Wiebking, Rick and Jody Prunty, and Karen Vikiras, and to Les Stobbe, my agent. Thanks to my IT technician, Marty Patryn, for keeping me up and running. Finally, to Jack Sorensen, my good friend, DVC aficionado, and brother in the Lord, many thanks.

FOREWORD

ON MY NINTH BIRTHDAY, MY PARENTS GAVE ME MY FIRST "ADULT" Bible, and I have been a student of the Word of God ever since. When I was ten, a librarian introduced me to Sherlock Holmes and Dr. Watson, and reading the novels and short stories again and again over these many years has made me a devout "Sherlockian." But I never dreamed that anybody would combine the Bible and Sherlock Holmes! However, my friend Len Bailey has done it and has done it quite successfully!

Imagine Holmes and Watson unraveling some of the problem texts in Scripture that have puzzled people!

Even if you are not a Bible student or a fan of Holmes and Watson, I urge you to read and enjoy this book. You will especially appreciate the way Len has captured the "Victorian atmosphere" of the original Arthur Conan Doyle stories, and as a bonus, you will also learn more about your Bible and how to study it successfully.

In the first Holmes novel, *A Study in Scarlet*, Holmes says to Watson, "It is a capital mistake to theorize before you have all the evidence. It biases the judgment."[1] That principle applies also to Bible study—so start reading and discovering how Holmes does it!

Warren W. Wiersbe

THE NEEDLE'S EYE

How shall I begin? How might I convey to you, the reader, of a most troublesome circumstance which befell me, whereby I might kindle in you an understanding of the dark misgivings which linger in my nightmares? How might I awaken your pity regarding my anxious tremblings and joys, my mortal fear for my life during the ten adventures which resulted from this event, one following after the other in the seeming interminable march of time? Perhaps you will laugh at me. Or will you wave your hand to read of my voyages into the past as too wonderful and fantastic to be believed?

Let me state it thus: My friend and closest companion had completely vanished. Upon my return from the north of Scotland, I entered 221b Baker St., London, to find our landlady, Mrs. Hudson, in a heightened state of agitation and black grief. "Three weeks, Dr. Watson!" she said to me, three weeks since she had last seen Sherlock Holmes. To her credit she had not contacted the police, given the often dubious and questionable nature of Holmes' work, but had wisely chosen to await my return.

Adding to my dismay, I found a sizable hole now existed

in the wall between Holmes' sitting room and his bedroom. I inspected the charred wallpaper about it and the burnt inner timbers. What foul circumstance had befallen the greatest detective in the world? What disastrous turn of events had overtaken him, a situation so thoroughly against him that he might neither write nor telegraph us?

This question I pondered that same night, sleeplessly, until the hour arrived when the yellow fog arose from the River Thames to choke the city in secrecy. I received at my door a dark visitor, wearing a hat and coat of once respectable broadcloth but now stained and patched. He refused to step inside from out of the fog but bade me get dressed and follow him, for he had information, said he, about my dear friend, which I might find valuable. I dressed warmly, and surreptitiously hid my revolver and knife.

And that is how I came to be sitting in a boat, blindfolded, and being rowed across the River Thames in the dead of night. Of course it had to be the Thames, for no other body of water lay within so brief a carriage ride from Baker St., nor nearly so large for a boat to be rowed for so long. Besides, the Thames possessed a peculiar bouquet all its own, a vintage mixture of rotten fish and sewage, of tar oil and coal, of soot and damp hemp—Holmes would have been proud of my investigative deductions.

I began to comment on the idiocy of blindfolding a man on a foggy night but I thought better of imparting sarcasm to parties unseen, for I perceived as many as three or four men about me, speaking in hushed tones.

The rowing slowed. I sensed something large at hand as a sailor might feel the loom of the land. The oars were shipped, ceased their groaning in the rowlocks, and I heard the water dripping from them. We bumped against something solid and stopped. I was ordered to my feet and roughly turned around, no small feat in a rocking boat.

My blindfold was removed.

Three men stood about me, ghosts in the impenetrable fog which lay over the river's surface, closing in about us. The wooden hull of a ship towered overhead—a paddle steamer—for I could just make out the arched structure on this, its starboard side, and the faint name, *Viceroy of India*.

I climbed the companionway ladder to the deck and stood in the deeper gloom of the paddle wheel housing. Two ornate smoke-stacks poked their tops above the fog, just visible against the stars. Crowning the aft cabin-saloon smiled an immense carved head of a dark-skinned, turbaned man with laughing eyes and a pointed black beard, flanked by a pair of leaping tigers.

From the gloom a gang of men closed in about me, wraiths from a weird nightmare. A brawny man stepped up to me. He had a face like a fist. I could feel his filth, smell the rum on his breath. For the first time I felt real danger, and I thought how unwise I had been to leave Baker St. alone.

Rough hands searched me from behind, down my pant legs to my ankles, inside my suit coat, from where my service revolver and knife were summarily lifted. I went to protest, but the big man anticipated me.

"Name?"

"Dr. John Watson," said I brusquely. "And all this shim-sham had better pertain to the whereabouts of my principal friend, Mr. Sherlock Holmes—"

"Your occupation?"

"I've just stated I am a doctor." I imparted this remark with no little consternation, which made the man growl, either at my impertinence or else to match my temper. "You already know my place of residence—your man fetched me from there. If you have harmed my friend in the least—"

"You keep a civilian tongue in yer head, or I'll serve you out yer guts, just." He brought out a knife. The flat of its blade he tapped against my shoulder. "C'mon with you, Dr. Watson, as you call yourself."

It was dangerous, I deduced, to argue with a man larger than an ape but having a brain the size of a lizard's. He led me below to a cabin, handed me a dim lantern, and shut the door behind me.

Bluebottle flies.

They buzzed and bumbled about my head. My next sense engaged was smell, the sweet odor of decay, while my sense of sight followed up fast on its heels. The room was a shambles, like the tangled wreckage of a ship caught in a gale force wind. Old furniture lay strewn all about: a richly upholstered sofa was laden with rubbish and draped with a sheet; chairs for the promenade deck were piled atop each other in confused heaps; bottles and paint cans were stacked carelessly (surprising in view of the mortal fear of fire aboard a wooden ship); wood posts and handrails leaned drunkenly against each other; and along the far wall lay spars, skeets, small blocks, and cordage for the *Viceroy of India*'s only sail.

From the corner of my eye, I caught movement. I sprang at the couch, lantern in hand, and pulled back the sheet. The debris lying beneath yawned and then gazed up at me uncomprehendingly.

"Holmes!" I said.

The great sleuth stared upward at me for a heartbeat and then sat up, the sheet still wrapped about him. What I could see of his shirt and trousers were dirty and unkempt.

"What have they done to you?" I asked.

Bleary-eyed, he returned my gaze and began to weep. "I should have married the woman."

"Whatever do you mean?"

His hands trembled—they were free, not bound by rope or iron cuffs—and he brought them up to cover his face. His whole frame and visage shook, not with weeping, but with a certain insane energy which found its outlet in a high-pitched whine. I felt sick at heart. How gaunt were his features; how thin were his fingers, like an eagle's claws! The realization hit me, given my years in the medical profession and having seen this same physical and psychological condition of men in hospitals and upon battlefields: Sherlock Holmes was dying.

His eyes focused on me, dully at first. His befogged mind, unlike the enveloping mists about the *Viceroy of India*, seemed to clear. He grabbed my arm in a fierce grip.

"Watson! I am mad with exhilaration. I have made the most stupendous discovery!"

"Holmes," said I, "you must take some sustenance—food or drink." I shot a look to the stacks of plates with uneaten food where the bluebottles buzzed.

He shook himself, as if awakening from delirium, and grinned widely.

"So, you have returned unscathed from the land of mac-Alpin? Any Scots still living north of Hadrian's Wall? Ha! Do they still paint their faces blue?"

"Who are these ruffians, Holmes? Why are you confined to this ship? I'm afraid that they have relieved me of my revolver."

Holmes jolted fully awake. He jumped up, the sheet falling away, his smoking pipe clattering onto the floor. He twitched his shirt into place and began pacing, stopped to take me in as if he mistrusted his senses, as if he had dreamed this sequence before.

"I am not in danger, as you suppose. Incredibly, I am come here of my own asking. These men, Watson, surprising as it may seem, work for me—they are my protectors in this most irregular circumstance. They know me and still like me anyway, ha! They are trustworthy thugs—again, as surprising as it may seem, the best of a bad lot. I have done them favors in the past for which they are heartily grateful."

"Mrs. Hudson is heartily worried about you—"

"Soon, I will return to Baker Street. My research is all but completed—*is* completed, I should say—the most fascinating exploration ever. But this ship—this fortress, if you will—must remain a secret. I posted a watcher at our flat to fetch you hither the moment you returned . . ." Holmes circled his finger in the air.

"From Scotland."

"Yes! From Scotland. This ship I have tenanted—she is grand, is she not? A most elegant mistress hearkening back to the carnival days of the paddle steamers. I chose her, the *Viceroy of India*, in honor of your acquaintance with Afghanistan and India, the exotic lands of spices. You shall feel at home here, for I tell you, it gets hellfire hot down here, just as in Bombay. Oh, somewhere I have misplaced a crude humidor of trichinopolys.[1] Shall we celebrate our ship? It would give me some illusion of calming my nerves with all these paynim statues about—of Sikhs, Tibetans, and Sinhalese, with their dancing elephants and baboons. In the night's middle watch, with the full moon out, I did bump headlong into the Scorpion Man—scared the devil out of me."

I picked through my friend's feverish rant. I fastened onto something he'd said before—*the most fascinating exploration* ever . . . He knelt before me, placing his warm hands on my knees. In his gray eyes I saw the most ardent fire, drawn from the spring of ingenuity or from the deep well of madness—I know not which.

He said lowly: "I feel much better now that my Watson is here. But I warn you—I am in earnest when I say I have landed on a most remarkable shore. I have skirted disaster as upon the knife's edge; I have peered into the abyss, with the wind in my face."

There came a sharp rap on the door, and I fairly jumped out of my skin owing to listening so intently to Holmes. A slim woman in drab clothes entered and set a heavily laden tray on the table, and wiped her hands with her dress.

"Ah, Mrs. Ferguson, thank you," Holmes said, and she left without word. He whispered to me, "She has advantages over Mrs. Hudson, but cooking is not one of them—see here this pinionade of pine nuts. Woe be to her husband (he is the lurid, lumbering fellow who brought you hither) should he ever be so unfortunate as to fall convalescent beneath her. She means to fatten me with bowls of barley water sprinkled with spice powder, plates of blood sausages and brayed greens, examples of which you may find stacked in quantities by the door—she is positively Anglo-Saxon, Watson."

"Still you must eat, Holmes. As a medical man, I'll not vouch for your present state."

"Twaddle."

"See here," said I, turning up the lantern's light and lifting the plate's covering, "a cut of cold beef (or some familiar beast), potatoes, and Scottish wheat bread. I'll hear no more until you have eaten healthily of this, as well as swigging of this cup—it is ale."

I would brook no argument. He sat at the table, eating surprisingly hungrily, grinning. He motioned to a small, metal cube sitting on the only uncluttered tabletop in the room, which lent it some importance. I picked it up for inspection.

"Take care," he cautioned between mouthfuls.

The little box measured seven or eight inches on a side, quite heavy for its size, with a solid top and bottom, and three of its four sides opened. The fourth side mounted a curious metal wheel, a sort of spinning dynamo of amazing detail which floated in the circular aperture. I moved it with my finger. It spun easily but amazingly did not fall out.

"The Needle's Eye!" said Sherlock Holmes, smaking, and shoved a wedge of potato into his mouth, which restricted him to only pointing, with an egg spoon, to a place behind me. Papers, I found, with curiously scribbled numbers and signs—equations written hurriedly, I surmised, not from duress but from fear that the moment of genius should suddenly evaporate.

He went on. "Do you remember the occasion of our first meeting so many years ago, in the chemical laboratory at Bart's? Of course, chemistry is all my passion—solutions, alkaloids, both persistent and fatal . . . yet I have ignored the study of physics and astronomy to my undoing. But Professor Moriarty, he is a different story."

"Do these papers belong to him?" I let go of the unholy pages. I felt an expanding in my chest, for I had involuntarily held my breath at the mention of that dread name: Professor Moriarty, the arch-criminal of London.

"*Did* belong. I found myself, over the years, left unattended in Professor Moriarty's study on three separate occasions. And since one cannot steal from a thief[2] . . . With those equations, however, I have delved into regions completely out of my depth."

Holmes fell silent. He stared straight ahead, his hand still gripping his tankard. I felt the *Viceroy of India* rise gently with a swell, presumably from a passing ship feeling its way upriver in the thick gloom.

"Are you quite all right?" I asked quietly. I feared for my friend in his highly impressionable psychoneurotic state, bordering, perhaps, on a delusional *malade imaginaire*.

"Who am I, Watson?" The voice was Holmes' but his face was of one caught between the realms of Pandora and Mephistopheles. "What have I done? What forbidden gateway have I opened which cannot now be shut?—which I dare not shut? What ominous oracles, what severe sirens have I summoned by my indiscretions?"

I weighed the little box in my hand. I sniffed it—burned carbon. "Does this Needle's Eye have anything to do with the monstrous burn hole in your apartment wall? I could clearly see your iron bed from the sitting room!"

He seemed not to be listening and then he abruptly asked, "Are you up for an adventure, Watson?"

A similar inquiry from any other man might have filled me with trepidation, and truthfully, coming so unexpectedly from Holmes, it left me uneasy.

"Certainly you are!" he said, answering for me. "Why else leave your warm house on a foggy night in the company of a rascally knave to venture to destinations unknown?"

He rose from the table and approached a wall, which I now perceived to be a vast hanging curtain of sailcloth, and pulled it aside to reveal the expansive interior of the aft cabin-saloon. It stood in stark contrast to Holmes' reckless living quarters, with its polished wooden floor, its high roof with hanging lamps of burnished bronze, its far wall dominated by the stern windows. I could almost hear the music from the bygone era, the chatter, the laughter, when the paddle steamers were all the rage on the River Thames, before the *Princess Alice*[3] disaster signaled the decline of these magnificent ships.

But then a chill settled over me. A large cube dominated the far end of the floor, a massive iron structure eight feet on a side, an immense replica of the box I held in my hand except for a long, thin pole rising halfway from the center of its platform. The blue-metal dynamo, nearly seven feet in diameter and resembling the front of a locomotive, floated freely in the aperture.

"As to your question, Watson, yes—the little iron box nearly set my room afire. Originally, I built the Needle's Eye to incorrect specifications, eight *inches* a side, when Professor Moriarty's drawing dictated eight *feet*! Ha! When my small dynamo shot out its bolt of energy, its closest target was my bedroom wall . . . and you know the rest."

"I know the rest of what?" I blurted. Too many questions vied in my mind to be the first asked. I was dumbfounded. I would have thought Holmes entirely mad—his behavior and incredible story—if I had not seen firsthand the destruction in his sitting room. "What does Professor Moriarty's invention mean to accomplish?"

"To travel at the speed of light!" Holmes clapped his hands together, the sound of a whip cracking. "For some mischievous reason, no doubt. Think of it: in a flash he could appear in Europe, commit a crime, and be back in London a split second later. His equations are theoretical postulations enabling objects to accelerate to the speed of light. Of course, his logic must fail for this simple reason: material objects—be they people or inanimate—possess a proper mass greater than zero and therefore cannot accelerate to the speed of light. The equation breaks down."

I simply gaped.

"Imprimis. In order to attain light speed, a man's mass must be reduced to zero, which means he would be—for all intents and purposes—dead. The other related problem is this: as mass accelerates, it expands (theoretically), but it is doubtful the object's mass has the molecular gravity to pull itself back into stasis when returning from light speed.

"The Needle's Eye is the product of pure genius. I am in Moriarty's debt. But his equations, his calculated logic, were utterly doomed to fail in practice."

I heard soft footsteps across the ceiling, one of Holmes' soldiers walking sentry duty on the promenade deck.

"Imagine Moriarty frustratingly testing his invention," Holmes continued, "the rotating dynamo's beam of energy fastening onto what few enemies or useless toadies he compulsorily placed in its path, and as the thing accelerated further, blowing them into smithereens—or into various parts of the universe. I'll not weep for them."

"*Why* did you build this monstrous thing?" I blurted.

He fastened his glowing eyes on me. "Suppose the professor *almost* had it correct? What if light speed can actually be attained by a different route? Instead of speeding matter up, what if we *slow it down*? First, we accelerate the dynamo to its maximum spinning velocity. Only *then* does it connect with the object. As it slows, the object slows as well—at the molecular level. Theoretically, the object's material would not expand, as in acceleration, but *reduce*—reduce so nearly to zero mass as to approach pure energy and able to be transported."

My mind, my mouth, was still trying to formulate intelligible questions when he held out a thin, delicate object: a single golden needle. Of course—Holmes had named this machine the Needle's Eye!

"This needle is placed on end atop the four-foot-high rod rising from the center of the cube's base, aligning the needle's eye to the dynamo's center. At the given time, the dynamo shoots out a beam of energy through the triple-eyed needle to the two portals, linking with any objects found there. Then, as the dynamo winds down, it slows down the objects' mass. At almost zero-mass state, in a flash the object is whisked through the gateway—through the Needle's Eye!"

"But for what purpose?" I persisted. "Where might it transport someone or something—if it really can? Come now, Holmes; this is highly fanciful, bordering on the fantastic. You can't possibly think this oversized gadget might work."

My reasoning failed me, whereby I might defend my assertion. I felt foolish, but Holmes placed a kindly hand on my shoulder. He ushered me to a small table, brightened his lantern, and set it near a microscope. I peered into the eyepiece. I turned the focus dial. What came into view I could hardly believe!

"Oh!" The exclamation popped out of me like a champagne bottle's cork. There, beneath my amazed stare, sat a miniature desk! And atop the desk sat a minute almanac!

"The Needle's Eye *does* work, my friend," Holmes said evenly. "This desk no longer sits in my flat, for it was caught in the dynamo's vortex—of the small version which you held in your hand—and apparently was being reduced when I interrupted the beam to keep my sitting room from catching fire."

"Staggering!" I peered into the microscope again, unable to convince my rational brain of the irrational truth, as if the carved elephants on the wall had come to life and danced across the floor. "But will it work with people?" I scrutinized my friend for a moment, his heavy-lidded smile, his flaring nostrils. "Wait; you mentioned opening doors you might not be able to shut, and peering into the abyss—"

"With the wind in my face," he said dreamily. "Indeed, I did subject myself to the bolt of blue fire, Watson. Light speed is but one side of the coin, old boy. It gets us only halfway there."

"Where?" I said, in a barely audible voice.

"Space and time are indelibly intertwined—a marvelous discovery in and of itself with all sorts of delectable possibilities. What affects the one invariably affects the other. When mass is slowed down and reduces nearly to non-matter, when it enters the speed of light through the back door, the time continuum is also pulled backward. This is the other side of the coin: when light is bent, and mass with it, we have the bending of time." I felt Holmes' intense stare, as if waiting for me to perceive a deeper truth from the evidence supplied. "Have you made the connection, Watson? Professor Moriarty wanted to travel at the speed of light, but what he really invented is—"

"A time-traveler!" I said in a spark of inspiration.

Holmes put back his head and guffawed and then refastened his attention upon me. His voice lowered to a whisper, as if we conversed as infidels in the temple of Krishna, as if the carved Persian and Hindu faces staring down from the cabin's palm-grove cornices might begin spouting torrents of Urdu-ish objections in protest against these unnatural deliberations.

"And now you see, dear friend, why this ship, my hidden lodgings, must remain a secret—why I am holed up on this innocuous, dilapidated ship. An invention with such ominous potential must not become public knowledge, not yet. Though most of the quays are dominated by the enemy—Moriarty's minions, the police, government agents—I can operate here with impunity. How the Needle's Eye came to be built is another story." He crossed his arms and snickered. "But how could I expect Mrs. Hudson to house so large and dangerous a device at Baker Street? Ha, ha! Where might she place it—in the kitchen, for all love?"

I swallowed hard. A certain dread settled over me, as if I were being drawn into something, though not altogether sinister, that exuded danger all the same. I asked the question Holmes kept ignoring, the one question needing to be answered.

"Dear friend, why have you driven yourself so? *Why* have you built this machine?"

"A client!" Holmes reached in his pocket, displayed a calling card, and handed it over.

"Costly paper," I said, feeling the texture. I held it to the lantern. "Royal cream—eight pence a packet, at least. Watermark. Neat hand."

"Strong handwriting," he offered. "The downward stroke signifies confidence; the upward, elegance." His hair shone black in the lantern's light as he turned, tall and trim if a little disheveled—fitness combined with latent—or rather, pent-up—energy. "The note forecasts, upon acceptance, ten Bible puzzles to be solved. Ten adventures fueled by deep mystery."

"Puzzles? Isn't the Bible rather straightforward to be mysterious?"

"I perceive our client wishes to illuminate particular scriptures, and has faith, presumably, in my ability to solve these cases or to at least focus general facts into specific. And you, dear friend, must utilize your talent for accuracy, if not always so properly through embellishment, to lay these essential particulars before the public; but do not write in an emotionally inward point of view, which often is your practice, but outward." He winced sardonically and gestured toward London. "Ah, the ever-vigilant public, at a loss to know the difference between the unpardonable sin and a pikestaff, yet so willing to offer its dubious, if not altogether spurious, considerations on the subject."

"But your disinterestedness in Scripture is remarkable, Holmes. Will you accept this challenge?"

"Ah, Watson—think of the exhilarating situations lying over the horizon—the lands never seen by modern man! I desire earnestly to exercise my mind in study, in harsh meditation. This present opportunity—that is how I must receive it—is a godsend!"

"I can hardly believe this!" I tilted the card to view it in a better light. "Who—?"

"Who was the sender?" he asked, anticipating the rest of my question. "Mrs. Hudson failed to get a clear look at the caller. Our client desires anonymity, for the note is signed K2L2—another mystery. Payment of twenty-three thousand pounds is tangible enough, ha!"

"A godsend, indeed!" I whistled. "A fascinating venture, Holmes, but hardly credible. How might Bible mysteries two or three millennia old come to life again? Or be investigated? Any culprits, any evidence, must be long dead in the dust—"

I stopped short. The Time Traveler filled my whole vision. Of course! This vehicle would allow Holmes to open the gateway to the past and investigate the ten mysteries. I took in the massive dynamo, its thin, iron blades, now motionless, but able to accelerate to a tremendous speed, synchronizing harmoniously with a human body through the focused gateway—through the Needle's Eye.

"One important caveat," said he. "The needle accompanied the note. This golden needle, this singular item, sparked my recollection of Professor Moriarty's papers which lay idle in my wall index." Sherlock Holmes rubbed his hands together eagerly—he was positively beaming. I thought he was quite mad. "Stop sulking, Watson. I cannot abide your sulking."

Holmes had misread me. With complete equanimity I regarded my friend. What a grievous loss it would have been for me, for all of England, to have found Sherlock Holmes dead on board this ship or sick beyond recovery. Perhaps Holmes had read me perfectly, however, and was simply embarrassed at my show of fondness for him.

"As for the safety of this machine," he went on, "and as to our various destinations, we should place our faith in the note sender. Are you not moved?"

I followed him inside the cube. A feeling of latent power came over me, a sense of terrible resolution. I touched the dynamo's blades. Cold. It rocked easily, gently, held suspended in midair by the surrounding opposing magnetos. I turned to find Holmes fixing the gold needle in its place atop the center pole.

"Tell me, Holmes," I said. "Where did the Needle's Eye take you?"

"I saw a man hanging from a tree." My friend looked off, his gaze as detached as his voice. "Who he was, I do not know. How ancient of a setting I visited, I cannot begin to fathom, nor why I immediately, after just a glimpse, returned here. The image of the hanged man has burned itself upon my brain, as with a hot branding iron. The note fails to list the mysteries to be solved, but the first one must involve this unfortunate fellow."

"When will you attempt to go again?"

"When will *we* go?" He smoothed his hair with his hands, looked keenly at me, and laughed in the most unnerving, monomaniacal manner. "As the Americans are so fond of saying, no time like the present! Is my faithful Watson equal to the task?"

I don't recall exactly what I said in response, only that I felt the hair on my neck curl.

ONE

THE HANGING MAN

"**WHAT A GHASTLY SPECTACLE!**" **DR. JOHN WATSON,** A DOCTOR of exceptional import, studied the corpse hanging from a tree: the blacked face, the bulging eyes, the protruding tongue.

Sherlock Holmes, of markedly more exceptional import, stood off, allowing the image of the hanged man to transpose from a vision into stark reality. He walked toward his time-traveling companion and stopped just short of the corpse and said, "Every man's death surprises him—even when he expects it."

Watson shivered. He brushed off his overcoat and hat, glittering as if frosted in diamonds, a temporary consequence of blasting backward through the centuries. "Why must time-travel involve the accumulation of frost, of all things?"

Holmes glanced over the rolling hills. The *Viceroy of India*'s dark cabin had vanished, and with it, the Needle's Eye. Foggy night had given way to sunny day. He reached into a nearby tree hollow to retrieve a folded note. "See here; the same royal cream stationery used by our mysterious patron." He studied it briefly and handed it to his fellow journeyer.

Watson read the cogent facts of their new surroundings and then voiced the question written there. *"Why did Ahithophel hang himself?"*[1]

"The Judean foothills is the place; 1000 BC is the time," announced Holmes. "Our wretched man here is none other than Ahithophel, principal adviser to King David of Israel."

"Regrettable the old fellow hanged himself."

"Now, what machinations of your sinister imagination, Watson, suggest suicide?"

"The Bible says so. And that note."

"Oh, Watson, how you confound my sincere attempts at perseverant patience!"

"Well then, Holmes, allow me to apply your systematic approach to the situation. First, the man's hands are not bound. Second, the items in his house from which I just came are undisturbed. Robbers or a *posse comitatus* would have ransacked the place, surely. Finally, by eavesdropping amongst the locals, I have learned the man, indeed, hanged himself."

"Watson, you are my heart's friend! How well you piece it together. But surely practical clues abound for this conclusion. The stepstool, man! See how it lies nearly beneath him, having been but slightly kicked away—forward turned? Conspirators would have placed it to one side or would have carried it off after completion of their foul deed. And look to the ground. There is but one set of footmarks—this poor fellow's. (You and I leave no trace here, Watson, for we are invisible elements in this ancient time, as insubstantial as moonbeams.) On the other hand, remote suicides such as this naturally encourage suspicions of violence—"

"But there is no instance of extradural hematoma," commented the doctor, "no violation of the frontal, sphenoid, zygomatic, lacrimal—"

"Oh, peace, Watson. Just say, rather, he's not been beaten."

A slight wind nudged the body. The rope creaked.

"I would further inquire as to why he hanged himself out of doors and not in his house," postulated Watson.

"A worthy observation—comprehendible, at least. But had he hanged himself indoors, Levitical law would declare his house unclean, burdening his relatives with cleansing it before handing it down. He loved his family. Passionately. This singular fact may aid us in solving this suicide."

GILOH

In a low room, the intruders from the future stood in the shadows, watching a pair of men reclining before a flickering fire. The older one called out, *"Shushan Eduth!"*

"Why, it is Ahithophel!" whispered the doctor, watching him eat from a bowl with his fingers. "This is Ahithophel's house in Giloh, in the Judean foothills. Somehow we have been transported further back to when he still lived."

"Indeed. And what strange magic has enabled us to understand Hebrew? The big chap is his son, Eliam, a member of the Thirty, David's company of mighty men.[2] One of the potential puzzle pieces, perhaps."

"Counselor to the king sits with a warrior for the king. Heady circles for a father and son to circulate in."

Holmes nodded. "Ahithophel, dressed in his richly adorned robes, jewelry, rides upon his lordly horse and dines regularly with the king—all the honors due the most trusted adviser in the land. Listen to their conversation, Watson. The father comments discreetly on the royal court's political and practical politics; the son reciprocates on how the army is doing, its commanders, its disposition and readiness in regard to future campaigns. The event that turned Ahithophel's heart against King David has not yet occurred."

"But he is learning military principles he will one day use *against* his master, King David."

"Truly." Holmes' nostrils flared. "But why? Why will he turn from loyal counselor to traitor? What nudges him—no, catapults him—into such rashness when he has all the riches and comforts a man may desire? What clues abide for us here?"

Watson felt his breath taken away. A robed woman entered from the courtyard, stroking a ten-stringed *nebel*, or harp. She sat gracefully on a cushioned couch. Her black hair flowed down over a form most lovely, of rarest beauty. Her gold headband and earrings flashed as she delicately strummed the instrument, and her warm, dovelike eyes looked straight through the doctor.

"Ahithophel owns stunning servant girls to boot," observed Watson, glancing sideways at his companion.

"Affairs of the heart are your specialty, Watson (or should I say, your weakness). But please do engage your faculties upon this case."

THE CITY OF JEBUS

Stars winked in the east. The ponderous moon watched Holmes and Watson pick their way atop a high wall. To their left the sheer stonework fell a hundred feet into the Kidron Valley's abyss.

"We stand upon the old Jebusite stronghold, Jebus by name: holy Zion." Holmes anticipated the doctor's question by elaborating, "Otherwise known as Jerusalem."

Watson caught the scent of sheep and cattle on the dark breeze. He tried to gauge the distance in the darkness. "This eastern wall cannot measure but four to five hundred meters long. Can Jerusalem have ever been this trivial?"

"This is Jerusalem in its infancy. King David moved his capital here from Hebron. See how his newly constructed palace dominates the city's middle."

The doctor spied a solitary figure standing nearby. "It is Ahithophel again. What does he do so late upon these walls?"

"Something has changed since last we spied our friend," remarked Holmes. "Observe!"

The royal counselor gazed southeast as the heavens surrendered to the night. It was then that something inexplicable happened: from the Fountain Gate tower, three women peered down at him, whispered amongst themselves, and disappeared with a chorus of lilting laughter. Ahithophel wheeled about and with trembling fists, with angry tears glistening upon his cheeks, raised his eyes to the king's residence.

"How do servant-women dare to ridicule David's personal adviser?" noted Watson. "Couldn't you hear the derisiveness in their laugh? Treachery shines fiercely in his eyes where before glowed loyalty and love. He is nigh unto tearing his hair—his heart. What has happened to instigate such open mockery?"

Holmes put his forefinger to his lips, not that they could be heard, but so that they could listen. He gestured to a hooded man approaching Ahithophel, who passed through the two Englishmen as if they were made of smoke. The Londoners moved closer, undetected even though they stood virtually at their elbows, listening intently until the two schemers split apart, separating in opposite directions in the hushed secrecy of night.

"Did you hear the word?" asked Holmes. "*Betrayal!*"

"Both of them said it," pointed out Watson. "Who was the other fellow, the one so intent on speaking to Ahithophel in the dead of night, so anxious to remain hidden? I perceived a handsome face beneath his hood."

"Not Eliam, his son," said Holmes, "who stands taller, and yet not so lordly as our intrepid conspirator." He thought for a moment, his face flashing with illumination. "Surely, it can be none other than King David's son, Prince Absalom."

THE SERPENT

In the glaring sunshine Holmes and Watson stood atop the tower at the Water Gate at the north tip of Jerusalem. Below them in the city and the surrounding countryside, throngs of people cheered, blew trumpets, rattled tambourines. Watson wiped off his shoes and grumbled.

"I yearn for London. How is it that we are invisible here, and yet I can gather all this dust? When do we return?"

Holmes squinted across to the king's palace. "This is a momentous day, is it not? In shame King David has fled to the east over the Mount of Olives, while Absalom, with ardent support from Ahithophel, has taken over his father's throne. The wound between father and son is fatal: it cannot be healed. There is no going back now, for you see the tent Absalom has pitched upon the palace rooftop? In plain view of all of Israel, he lies with his father's concubines—violates them on a bright, sunny day."

"Good thing the tent flaps are closed at this end."

"My mind is more abstractly engaged. I am reflecting on the dissonance between the sublime and the base, on the happy occasions when heaven and earth diverge from similar paths to different results." Holmes lit his pipe, puffed energetically. "Take Satan: he preaches rebellion in deep heaven in hopes of usurping God's throne. One-third of the angelic host swear him allegiance, but still, he is cast down."

"Be so good as to come to the point." Watson testily brushed off his coat sleeve.

"That one should never war against God."

"This is your point?"

"Now, take Jerusalem," said Holmes. "Absalom, the sly and crafty snake, preaches venomous revolt. Virtually all the people follow him, approve of him usurping the king's throne—the very king who, with God's help, brought Israel from a fledgling nation into prominence. But Absalom is doomed as ever the devil was. Look at them all down there, the leering, unwashed, unfettered, uneducated masses: the weak-willed, so easily swayed, ever-gullible public."

"I gather you miss London too."

"Mankind is but a bland sort." Holmes tapped out his pipe, his terrier ears perking up. "I see movement below in the throne room. Quickly, Watson—follow me!"

London's greatest sleuth and his companion skipped down the stairs and stood back in the crowded throne room. "Look, Watson: it is our man, Ahithophel!"

The royal counselor, dressed in his finest robe, approached the throne and bowed before the handsome man seated there.

"Your advice is like one who inquires of God, my old friend," said Absalom. "Here I sit, king of Israel."

"Yes, my lord," Ahithophel said gently, "but doesn't your father know how to punish those who sit too long? Tonight, set out with twelve thousand men in pursuit of David while he is weary and faint. Strike him with terror. All of his soldiers and family will desert him. Then you may kill him in the manner which seems best to you."

Absalom chewed slowly, wiped the fig juice from the corner of his mouth.

"Hushai? What do you say? What wisdom from the Arkite's lips?"

A man stood forward from the gathered nobles. "Hear me, my king! The rash, the impetuous! These are they which David punishes," replied Hushai, "which David slays in his turn. Ahithophel's advice is not good. Witness Goliath of old and Saul of more recent memory—both of whom carelessly confronted David—unsuccessfully. He knows the wilderness: Is this where you will pursue him tonight? He is a warrior from his youth, and those with him are brave—brave and wary: Joab, Abishai, Ittai the Gittite, the Kerethites, the Pelethites. Pursue him tonight, be defeated, and your people's loyalty will melt like the spring snow. No! Remain in your stronghold of Jerusalem. Gather your strength. Gather Israel's troops to your banner. Only then march against him—yourself as king leading them. Wherever David flees, you will have him."

Sherlock Holmes relit his pipe. His tobacco was particularly tasty, as was this case. He watched the young king lick his lips, too, and then rise.

"The advice of Hushai the Arkite is better than Ahithophel's."

Stunned silence gripped the room. Watson nodded toward Ahithophel's departing form. "Did you see the misery on his face? The indignation? The shame?"

"As pale as death," replied the detective.

Sherlock Holmes motioned Watson out onto the palace balcony, an impressive vantage point. He puffed on his pipe and fell into a meditation.

"Absalom should know better," scoffed Watson. "Hushai is a known confederate of King David's."

"And so, we have come full circle." Holmes pointed down to the man riding his donkey out the gate. "Ahithophel, now but a mere *pedisequent*, returns to Giloh. He will put his house in order and hang himself. A bit extreme?"

"Absalom *spurned* Ahithophel!" charged Watson. "His reputation."

Holmes paced. "Surely, having one's counsel rejected cannot be reason enough to end one's life."

"People have done so for less." Watson fumbled with something in his pocket. "Thousands of years ago, honor meant more."

"Truly? Honor dictates that one must side with one's friend in his hour of need. How honorable is it, in a coup d'état, for Ahithophel to side with the usurper? Another fact bothers me: Ahithophel didn't wait around long enough to witness the inevitable battle between the king and prince."

The doctor pulled out his traveling Bible and thumbed to the appropriate page.

"You're cheating, Watson—"

"It states: '*Now when Ahithophel saw that his advice was not followed, he saddled a donkey, and arose and went home to his house, to his city. Then he put his household in order, and hanged himself, and died; and he was buried in his father's tomb.*[3] There it is, in white paper and black ink. Be content for once, Holmes, with Scripture's account, simple though it may be."

"It's far too uncomplicated; unsophisticated, even. It doesn't *feel* right. Our client, who undoubtedly placed the mystery card in the tree, wants us to know the *real* reason—the hidden reason— why Ahithophel ended his life."

"Holmes!" gasped Watson. His hands began to flicker with a glittery fire. Holmes' face glowed, sparkling from within. The Needle's Eye was pulling them back to London: Jerusalem burned away.

MARY WILLIAMS, HANGED

Watson stared through the large, blackened burn hole into Holmes' bedroom. The miniature Needle's Eye had done extensive damage. The charred interior supporting timbers stank, while—

"—the wallpaper is quite burned away," said Watson, finishing his thoughts out loud. He felt a slight tremor in his spine to realize a similar blue bolt of flame had traveled through his own body.

Beside the fireplace sat the detective, barricaded behind an unfurled copy of the *Times*.[4] A stream of smoke issued up from his black, clay pipe. A rich aroma of a different sort led Watson to the breakfast table. He lifted the silver lid from a platter brought up by Mrs. Hudson and stared, wolflike, at a plate of Scotch eggs and toast.

"Hungry?" asked Holmes from behind his paper.

"I'm always hungry."

"Hmmm. I read here the account of Mary Williams, hanged yesterday for the Townsend affair. D'ye remember? She murdered Hauty Burke, the fellow found innocent in court for murdering her granddaughter. I read the inquest. Chap was guilty, no doubt." He whistled lightly, then added, "Here it says, when they asked Mary on the gallows for her last words, she said, 'I came here to die, not talk.' Ha!"

"Carried out her own sentence, did she?"

Holmes turned down the paper's corner and said, "Just as Absalom avenged the rape of his sister Tamar.[5] You never bothered asking why Absalom rebelled against his father. Since our case concerning Ahithophel's suicide has reached a temporary lull, I have acquiesced at last and consulted the Scriptures—what a merry thought! As it turns out, there were many reasons for Absalom to dislike his father."

Watson had begun loading his plate with a silver spoon, and smirked. "Holmes, you own a Bible?"

"Borrowed. From the basement of Rector Thompson's parsonage, which burned down near Aldersgate—d'ye remember?" He motioned over to the back wall. Near the sidebar sat a squat podium supporting an immense Bible the size of a seat cushion. "The tragic story goes thusly: Amnon, Absalom's half brother, falls in love with Tamar, his beautiful sister. He lures her to his bed, rapes her, and then sends her away in disgrace. King David is furious but does nothing. Absalom bides his time, scheming, planning. Two years pass, and when the time is right, he avenges his sister by murdering Amnon. Absalom flees the country. But after a few years' banishment, King David receives him back again. Curious."

"David loved Absalom, surely," said Watson with a mouthful of toast.

"Or he felt guilty. Perhaps he realized Absalom had carried out the sentence which he, as king, should have executed." Holmes put down the newspaper and relit his pipe. "David, no doubt, thought himself noble in accepting Absalom back into Jerusalem. How often do parents, in trying to remedy an earlier oversight, think themselves saintly as they blunder again? This misstep was fatal, a show of weakness which unmade a king and nearly a kingdom."

"Certainly the Lord's curse hangs over him," asserted Watson.

"Yes!" Holmes jerked up out of his chair, rubbing his hands together. "The curse stemming from his sin with Bathsheba years before—"

"The story is famously lurid."

"Ah! For those stricken with hot passion—from pride or lust—the fall is most grievous." Holmes gritted his teeth. He lowered his face to within inches of Watson's. "One evening, from the palace rooftop, King David spies the form of a beautiful creature bathing—Bathsheba, by name. He watches. His hot, bewitched blood courses through his veins. He paces. He watches again. He desperately attempts to balance insanity with wisdom. Perhaps, he reasons that this beautiful Jewess belongs to a Hittite, a foreigner who, despite his loyalty, is no better than a Moabite, a Philistine, an Amorite, peoples for which David has become famous by slaying."

Holmes stood. "King David perspires. His head pounds. He lunges for the bait. In his passion he sends for the exquisite woman, indulges himself. She becomes pregnant. This heightens his madness, his recklessness. He strikes out insanely, attempts to cover his tracks by having her husband, Uriah, murdered—a better man than himself."

"But God sees all," commented Watson. "I know the rest: David has displeased the Lord, and the son born to him in unfaithfulness, dies."

"You can see the storm coming, Watson, but David does not. A strange despondency settles over his throne—call it inevitability? indifference?—which numbs him from the reality surrounding his palace. Sin in all its forms—rape, vengeance, deception, murder—all the trespasses of which he is guilty, are acted out around him. King David is ripe for picking. Enter Absalom! He begins undermining his father. Atop the wall at night he conspires with Ahithophel. At the city gates he consoles the people in their trials, treats them as equals. When he has won over the fickle populace, Absalom makes his move. He proclaims himself king and marches on Jerusalem. David flees for his life.[6] Absalom seizes the throne. David's kingdom unravels. The Lord's curse has come to pass."

Holmes reached down and gripped the heavy fireplace poker, a sickly flame in his eyes. "The bloody sword poised over David's house falls with a resounding crash!"

Holmes raised the poker claymore-like, and striding across the room, brought it crashing down on the table. The silver platter flipped over and fell, the lid ringing like a bell on the floor. The student lamp wobbled. Watson lunged from his chair and caught a teacup just in time.

"Holmes!—Are you insane?" Watson felt of the splinters in the tabletop and looked up at his friend. Had Holmes relapsed into his erratic moods of his self-imposed confinement on the *Viceroy of India*? Watson had harbored fears of the deleterious affect of

13

time-travel—was this an unforeseen consequence of the Needle's Eye that Holmes must act out the strange lunacy of King David?

Holmes let the poker fall to the floor with a thud. He gripped his head with both hands. "Something I saw! Why cannot I remember . . . or something I heard!" He stopped in his tracks. "Why? Why? Why?"

"*Why* do we need a new table?" Watson mused. "Because this one is damaged beyond all practical use. *Why* do I hear footsteps on the landing? Because Mrs. Hudson will shortly turn you out for damaging her silver set. I should not blame her, Holmes."

THE MYSTERIOUS WOMAN

The wall clock tick-tocked away the afternoon. The windows were a contradiction: curtains halfway parted, blinds halfway down, window halfway raised. Holmes puffed meditatively on his pipe and leaned on the fireplace mantel. The smoke circled about the bowl before ascending, waving an airy-fairy hand before dissipating into oblivion. He breathed out, tapped his fingers near the clock, scrutinized Watson sitting near at hand, reading the newspaper.

"I am pleased you have chosen to be so sedate, Watson. With this investigation at a dead end."

"I'm pleased your violent bate is passed. I shan't trust you with a revolver."

"Oh, I am further from the truth than ever," he said dismally. "I am groping."

"Please solve this mystery of why Ahithophel hanged himself, Holmes, or leave me entirely alone!"

"This is the nearest I have seen you to pouting, Watson."

"And you to raving mad—"

Holmes exhaled another cloud. "What are the facts? Those beyond any doubt?"

"I have the answer, but you will laugh at me—"

"Come, Watson, I will not laugh, really . . ."

"Precisely what I said before—what Scripture states plainly."

"Then I will laugh."

"You act as though it's the stupidest thing you've ever heard!"

"No, but it is the stupidest thing I've heard today. Or maybe even this week."

Watson folded his paper neatly. "The answer, simply, is this: Ahithophel proposes the only effective military action against David. But Absalom takes Hushai's advice, squandering his only chance to destroy the king."

"But Watson, you miss the larger question: Why did Ahithophel follow Absalom *in the first place*? What happened between him and King David to instigate this disloyalty? Why should Ahithophel risk reputation, land, wealth, even his life? What could Absalom promise him which he didn't already possess under King David? A clarence?"[7]

"You're so coy, Holmes. Look: inevitably David will return to Jerusalem victorious and reclaim his throne. Ahithophel ends his life because he knows his days are numbered, along with all the conspirators who supported Absalom . . ."

Watson left off explaining. Holmes had clearly stopped listening, crossing the room to the pedestal and grappling the Bible, his eyes then wafting over page after page, his arms turning like a great windmill. He became still. Then he turned one page more.

"Wait one minute!" Holmes spoke with a low tone. "One

connection remains which I have not investigated. Ahithophel's son was one of the Thirty—do you recall? Surely a strong camaraderie existed amongst these mighty men. They suffered many campaigns together, trained together, fought together, sang together, got rip-tilting drunk together—"

Holmes tapped his pipe's amber mouthpiece against his teeth—*click, click, click.* He stood back from the Bible, and with a flourish, gestured to the doctor. Watson approached the open volume: massive, like the Book of Life referred to in Revelation, except "2 SAMUEL" was written across the tops of both pages.

"Chapter 23, Watson. Read the bottommost name on the list, verse 39."

"Uriah the Hittite also belonged to the Thirty. Fascinating piece of trivia, Holmes. Really it is. So, Eliam knew the man King David murdered. Are you suggesting Ahithophel's son contributed anything to Uriah's death? An incredulous stretch, dear boy, which does you credit."

"On the contrary, Watson—and do not call me, 'dear boy'—Eliam respected Uriah, a Hittite of the Hatti: a Canaanite tribe descendant, surely (not the northern Kizzuwatna, of Hamath or Carchemish), but a Jerusalemite—"

"You're showing off, Holmes."

"Well, Uriah lived as a respectable man, in control of his passions. David recalls him to Jerusalem, ordering him to spend the night at his house with his beautiful wife and to avoid suspicion of his guilt in connection with her pregnancy. But Uriah refuses such personal comfort while his comrades are camped in tents on the field of battle."

"Where is this leading?"

"Hmmm. Let us sift for gems amongst the little things,

the minutiae. For instance, the various places the Needle's Eye landed us."

"At the suicide tree; inside his house with his son; and inside the palace."

"You omitted a place," said Holmes. "Atop the wall in Jerusalem. At night."

"Nothing memorable happened there."

Holmes fell into a meditation. And the more his thoughts deepened, the deeper became the lines on his forehead, and the closer Watson inched toward the fireplace to guard the iron poker. Holmes snapped his fingers. "I remember—you commented on the three women in the tower who laughed at Ahithophel—"

The doctor scratched his head.

"Oh, my fevered brain—wait! You called them servant girls. What made you gather such a thing?"

"I've read on my own, Holmes, concerning biblical customs and dress. I simply applied your laws of observation: the women were attired in ordinary homespun, as best as I could see; they wore no jewels, nor earrings, possessed no royal bearing—"

"One moment." Holmes looked straight at Watson. "Then who, pray tell, was the beautiful woman who, bedecked in gold and an embroidered robe, played the harp in Ahithophel's house?"

"Of course!" The doctor snapped his fingers. "She was no servant!"

Holmes held his pipe behind his back and with his free hand turned the Bible back a page or two, wafting like a schooner's sail. The air smelled musty.

"Ah!" The firelight flickered in the detective's eyes. "At last, Watson, we come to the end of our search! How many countless

mysteries end precisely at the beginning? Sometimes, to understand the final steps, we must retrace to the first steps!"

The Bible lay opened to a new place. Holmes jammed his pipe
back in his mouth, and with a dramatic flourish to the open book,
resumed his place by the mantel, a seraphic smile playing about
his lips.

The doctor's eyes trailed down the page, stopped, and read
where Holmes' finger had rested, at 2 Samuel 11:2–3: *"Then it
happened one evening that David arose from his bed and walked
on the roof of the king's house. And from the roof he saw a woman
bathing, and the woman was very beautiful to behold. So David
sent and inquired about the woman. And someone said, 'Is this not
Bathsheba, the daughter of Eliam, the wife of Uriah the Hittite?'"*

"Good gracious, Holmes—what a find, man!" Watson could
hardly form the words. "The daughter of Eliam, and therefore,
Ahithophel's granddaughter! The maiden playing the harp that
night! She was none other than—"

"Bathsheba!" Holmes proclaimed.

The detective walked to the window, turned, and leveled his
finger at Watson. "And later, as Uriah's wife, living in prosperity
in Jerusalem, she would bathe in her private inner courtyard—
except David could see her from his palace roof."

"But Ahithophel called her by a different name . . ."

"No." Holmes relit his pipe, smiling crookedly. *"Shushan
Eduth* means 'The Lily of the Testimony,' obviously the name of
the harp melody he wished for her to play."

"So, then, her name"—Watson crinkled his brow—"was not
Susan or Edith."

"No, Watson, not Susan." The quirky smile again. "Certainly
not Edith."

REVENGE, SWEET REVENGE

Watson sat opposite Holmes. The detective smiled menacingly and said, "Revenge, Watson. Cold, razor-sharp revenge."

"Ahithophel with the wonderful family, a son and son-in-law to be proud of—"

"And Bathsheba," put in Holmes, "ravishingly beautiful in her womanhood, the pride of Giloh, the talk of the barracks. Uriah the Hittite, highly principled even when drunk. Ironic: his honor cost him his life."

"King David. Murderer," sighed Watson. "What a scurvy thing he did to Uriah! How beneath the greatest king of Israel, the man after God's own heart!"

"And Ahithophel enraged. His granddaughter of famed beauty, violated by the shepherd-made-king—as if David didn't have enough wives already! All this while Ahithophel's noble son-in-law is away fighting, being murdered by his own king! Oh, to have to endure the whisperers in the palace, the gossiping, the giggles, conversations ceasing abruptly when he happens by. To top it off, Ahithophel's great-grandson dies in infancy. Oh, how Bathsheba wept! How Eliam and Ahithophel wept!" The light of illumination flared in Holmes' eyes. "Remember the night atop the city wall. Both men said the word *betrayal*. Absalom said it because he planned to betray his father. Ahithophel said it because *he had already been betrayed* by King David."

"And so Ahithophel bided his time," Watson said, just above a whisper. "It makes sense, now, why he instructed the new king to lie with his father's concubines on the rooftop in broad daylight—don't interrupt me, Holmes, let me contribute—to expose in the light of day what David did to his granddaughter in darkness."[8]

"Brilliantly vindictive!" Rage lit up in Holmes' face and then vanished. "To lie with a monarch's concubine's was tantamount to usurping the throne. But David's suffering could not be enough for Ahithophel: he wanted David dead."

"Instead, he killed himself," said Watson sadly. "When his advice was spurned in favor of Hushai's, he realized he would never exact his revenge on King David for the dishonor perpetrated on his family. How fascinatingly morbid."

"Mary Williams trumped Ahithophel in that respect, did she not?" reflected Holmes.

"But not Absalom. They both hung for their murders."

"You were right, Holmes, Ahithophel's passionate love for his family did turn out to be an important clue."

They sat in silence for a moment. Faintly, they could hear children playing in the street below, the clip-clop of horses, the rattling of passing carriages.

"It came to my mind," Watson said finally, "how the Lord used Absalom's revolt to smooth the way for Solomon's ultimate approach to the throne. Not only Ahithophel, but Mephibosheth, another disloyal subject, was flushed out—not to mention removing Absalom himself, the most formidable threat to the throne."

Holmes nodded. "Yes. Solomon could deal with his older brother Adonijah, conniving and ambitious, fatal qualities when not chaperoned by common sense." Sherlock Holmes chuckled deeply. "Very insightful of you, good doctor. We shall make a first-rate detective of you yet."

TWO

DIGNIFIED HARLOTS

THE LONDONERS STOOD ATOP A FLAT-ROOFED HOUSE SURROUNDED by other flat-roofed houses for as far as they could see. Watson was about to comment on the lack of chimneys, of soot and chugging smoke, of enormous buildings and spires, when he became alarmed.

"Holmes! What has happened to us?"

Watson stared, openmouthed, at Holmes' attire. The robes they wore—Watson's of a bluish tint and Holmes' of black—were of strict biblical fashion, supplied magically, presumably, by the Needle's Eye.

"The clear implication is this, Watson: we are visible to our surroundings."

"What? Are we in danger? How can you remain so calm?"

"I am in steep meditation, considering the Needle's Eye and how it chooses to clothe us. When our modern clothes are exchanged for those biblical—as we wear now—you and I are able to be seen by ancient peoples: we become alive to our setting."

"No doubt, this is true," groused Watson.

"But did you notice before when we were transported wearing our nineteenth-century finery that we were all but invisible, passing insubstantially amongst legendary biblical heroes like a dream? We must take great care as to what we do and say."

Holmes, shadowed in his black hood, remained pensive, presumably wondering why the Needle's Eye would allow him possession of his silver-headed walking stick. With this he pointed down into the narrow street and shouted, "Watson, look!"

A woman waved her hands about her head in a frenzy as she ran, her cries drowned out in the hollering crowd hounding her down the narrow city street. A brute force of men hit her, grabbed at her hair, shoved her along. Rips opened in her robe's fabric, no more than a dirty and sagging bedsheet which she clutched to herself, exposing her shoulders and legs. A blow from the side sent her sprawling in the dust. She was dragged to her feet by her hair, shaken violently in a chorus of laughter, and pushed on her way.

"Her head's bleeding, for goodness' sake!" cried Watson.

The detective ignored him. Or else preoccupied himself on a plan.

"Oh! That frantic woman! Who are those ruffians set about her?" Watson was nigh unto tugging Holmes' sleeve. "Can we not assist her in some way?"

"I presume we are wearing this biblical attire for precisely such a purpose," growled Holmes the hawk, staring down from his perch at the surrounding network of streets and courtyards, of alleys and stairways. "There! There is the place we can head them off. Follow me!"

Holmes took off at a dead run, with the startled doctor trying to keep up. The houses were so close together one might run to the horizon without touching ground. Watson's heart went into his throat as the detective hurdled over a wall and fell from sight, but his hooded head appeared again, a little lower.

"Are you not fascinated," called back Holmes, laughing madly as he ran, "to know where the Needle's Eye has transported us? And when? And why?"

Watson went to answer but tripped over a tent of palm branches and went sprawling. He clambered up, looked about just in time to glimpse Holmes hopping over a mound of baskets. They scampered over a wider roof, where a kneeling man, milking his goat, just had time to glance over his shoulder before the robed pair disappeared onto the next house. They crossed yet another roof, then another, each time glancing below to the street at the shouting crowd.

They came to a roof which stretched out before them. Holmes lengthened his stride, accelerating to a fantastic speed. He lifted off the roof's far edge, launching himself, cane and all, across a wide street. He landed on a lower balcony, rolled into a table, smashing a score of clay dishes and scattering a pot of hot coals, before rushing through the house and out its open door. Watson was right behind him, having followed him over the precipice like an unwilling sheep, landing on top of the hot coals and the shards of clay with a shout, and then hollering again as the housemaid struck him twice with a broom on his way through. She screamed at him again, hit him again, and forced Watson to scamper down a staircase. There! He saw the detective's fleeting figure disappearing down the narrow street. Watson took off in pursuit, the street growing narrower so that his arms touched either wall. He rounded the corner to find Holmes pushing a cart laden with palm branches.

"This is Jerusalem, my dear friend, in New Testament times!" Holmes leaned heavily forward, inhaled deeply. "The fortress to the west is Herod's palace. But it is eastward, I fear, where they are bound—grab hold, Watson! We're just in time!"

"Yes, I see!" panted Watson. He wiped his forehead and grabbed onto the rough planks.

Here came the mob, single file along the narrow street, pushing the woman along. Nearer they came, their shouting growing louder, harsher. One man passed by the cart, then another.

"Now!" shouted Holmes. Watson had anticipated him, heaving madly at the cart with a deep growl. The wheels creaked. The cart lurched forward just as the woman passed, cutting off the mob. The first man pivoted around just in time to have his feet knocked out from under him by a sweep of Holmes' stick. Watson swooped up a squabbling chicken and handed it to the other man, bewildered at the flapping bird in his hand.

The two Londoners whisked the woman away, a hand beneath either of her arms. Down a wider alley they capered, her feet barely touching the ground, and then along another street and through a crowded marketplace adorned with hanging fruits and vegetables, tables of breads, and cages of cooing birds. Down yet another passageway they ran and ducked into a broad doorway. Holmes closed the heavy door behind them and latched it, listening. Watson patted the kindly woman on the shoulder before he collapsed nearby, breathing like a bull.

After a moment Holmes relaxed. He helped the woman drape her dress over her shoulder, signaled her to keep silent. He began searching the room, crowded with rows of earthenware jars. From nearby, perhaps from next door, emanated a low, rhythmic hum.

"Grinding grain," remarked Holmes, giving his best guess. He dipped a hand into a tall container, smelled of the brown grains, and let them cascade down. "Barley. A few months past its prime."[1]

"Lacerations with possible hematoma of the left orbital

structure." Watson had begun to attend to the woman's injuries. She smelled richly of perfume, he noted, as he tucked a rebellious lock of her black hair behind her ear. "Oh!—a patch of hair has been torn from her scalp—this requires immediate attention! Who were those dastardly men?"

His question was directed as much to Holmes as to the woman.

"Teachers of the law," she spoke up shakily. Her voice, smooth. Her skin, smoother. "Holy men."

Watson snorted. He dabbed blood away from her nose—not much else he could do here. He caught Holmes in the tail of his eye, ascending an interior staircase. The doctor found a strip of linen and instructed the woman to hold it tightly against her head. He followed Holmes up the stairs which opened out onto the roof.

"I am fascinated to learn," Watson stated, adopting the posture of Holmes in shading his eyes and looking out over the city, "what this poor woman did to incur such hostility from these religious men. And I suppose any medicine—particularly iodine and sutures—would be too much to ask for in this primitive time?"

"Medicine is not so highly regarded in New Testament Israel,"[2] Holmes simpered, "nor doctors, for that matter. Prayer, rather, and offerings to the Lord on the infirm's behalf are acceptable. But in a more pressing matter, I am pleased to report the absence of pursuit from our gang of holy men. You would do well to pull your hood up."

"We'll have to move her soon, Holmes. These thugs may search house to house—sooner or later we'll be discovered. She needs hospitalization. Oh!—those violent, reckless, intrusive, arrogant, self-serving, profane bullies hiding behind their religion! Cowardly, antagonistic, disallowing, treacherous, murderous rascals!"

"Don't mince words, Watson, it is unbecoming you. But, please be attentive to your first question: What might this woman have done, indeed?"

Watson choked back a cry as he looked down the side of the wall. The woman! She had slipped out a side door to scurry discreetly down the alleyway.

"No," Holmes said, with a firm hand on Watson's shoulder. "Leave her. She is not so foolhardy nor so unobservant. We may frighten her more than her pursuers. Take our absence of beards, our ignorance of the Pharisees and scribes, my walking stick. She knows we are not Jews, Watson, and not from this place. Perhaps even not from this time. Her chances are better, she reasons, relying on her own wits."

THE CONFRONTATION

"Magnificent!" Holmes stopped dead in his tracks and hid his pocket-sized history book within the folds of his robe. He pointed eastward with his stick to a massive building with golden parapets twinkling in the sunlight, adorned in rich scrollwork, and surrounded by cream-colored crenellated walls. "Wonder of wonders! Behold, the shrine to the Idumaean king. Behold, the temple of Herod the Great!"

Watson squinted. "What are those spikes on the roof?"

"To shun the *Columba livia*! Pigeons must not foul the Lord's dwelling, surely. The fortress Antonia—do you see it?—standing left near the Tadi Gate. It is the procurator's residence, where a

Roman garrison is stationed to keep the peace. The high priest's garments are stored there as a sign of Roman dominance—ha! At the southwest corner stands the Royal Stoa, the superb portal with its grand staircase. From here we can view the colonnade's top over the partition, and the open courts beyond. The temple's far side drops off sharply into the Kidron ravine."

"Yes, marvelous!"

"The construction of Herod's temple, begun in 19 BC by holy masons, is not yet complete—as you can see. But let us traipse across yonder valley in Tyropoeon fashion, to the temple gate, which stands open for our convenience, where we shall see what we shall see. Forward!"

Holmes must have appeared ludicrous to the city inhabitants, in his black robe, twirling his walking stick as he traipsed along with Watson huffing along behind.

They entered the immense temple grounds, bright in the sunlight, by way of the Double Gate. Watson stared openmouthed from the shade of the vast roofed pavilion surrounding the square, which was supported by over a hundred pillars, each over fifty feet high, each capped in luxurious blue and gold leaf and bordered by intricately painted and tiled designs of the roof's inner surface. From their tables, money changers hollered and yammered to passersby, offering the exchange of Roman coinage for the proper silver Tyrian shekel.

The Londoners made their way across the courtyard toward the massive temple complex of Herod the Great. But Watson's awe was cut short, for as they passed through the soreg, a five-foot stone fence, he noticed inscriptions in Greek and Latin threatening death to Gentiles or to the ceremonially unclean found trespassing into the temple complex's holier courts.

By way of the Eastern Gate, they hurriedly entered the Court of Women, a large open court with majestic lampstands flickering at each of its four corners. Two unroofed chambers fronted by pillars stood along the north and south walls.

"Holmes, look!"

To their right side stood the woman, disheveled and downcast. She had been recaptured, apparently, and appeared to have suffered for it. Watson lunged forward angrily, and only Holmes' timely grab by his collar kept him back. Two contending crowds hemmed her in: to one side the furious men in purple robes who had driven her mercilessly through the streets; to the other, a pedestrian gathering of men, women, and children clustered about a solitary man.

"Teacher!" said the spokesman for the religious leaders. His voice echoed in the cavernous court. He was a thin man with a thin beard and pointed a thin, accusing finger at the woman. He smiled with even teeth. "This woman was caught in the act of adultery. In the law of Moses, it commands us to stone such women." He smiled wider, serpent-like, as Satan might have done when proffering the apple to Eve. He gestured dramatically to the man. "Now, what do *you* say?"

A rumble of conversation broke out. People gathered from around the temple grounds to find what all the fuss was about. Many of them had never seen this many important religious leaders in one place before.

Unexpectedly, the white-robed man squatted and wrote on the ground with his finger. The thin man questioned him again, his voice becoming shrill. Many of his purple-robed confederates joined in, jostling the woman in their midst. The man in white stood up. He proclaimed loudly, "If any one of you is without sin, let him be the first to throw a stone at her."

"Holmes! That is the Christ—!" began Watson, but the detective put his forefinger to his lips.

Once again, Jesus stooped and wrote on the ground. The treacherous men grew oddly silent. They stood back and, inexplicably, began to file away, one at a time, the older ones first, followed by the younger, leaving the woman standing alone.

"Woman, where are they?" asked Jesus. "Has no one condemned you?"

"No one, sir."

"Then neither do I condemn you. Go now and leave your life of sin."

Jesus spoke a few words to the crowd, and they dispersed, still bubbling excitedly. At last, when the courtyard was empty, Holmes cast aside his walking stick and sprang forward on all fours to where Jesus had stood, tracing his hand an inch above the ground.

"Why are we here, Sherlock?" inquired the doctor, using his Christian name. He picked up Holmes' cane. "I cannot think of any mystery here worth investigating."

The detective held up a cream-colored calling card, wiped off the dirt, and began searching again.

"What are you looking for, Holmes?"

"Oh, the clumsy, clop-clumping cows!" the detective growled. "The ground is utterly ruined by the herd! We are left to our own devices to find the answer with whatever evidence we may gather piecemeal, in shreds, or by inference."

"Evidence? Evidence of what, dear friend?"

221b Baker St., London

The doctor traced his hand over the newly applied plaster that patched the gaping burn hole in Holmes' wall, and grunted his approval. He passed into the sitting room, added coal onto the dying fire, and nuzzled into his favorite armchair before the fireplace. He dusted off his hands and said, "Certainly, the woman walked away unharmed. Bravo!"

"No other concerns?" questioned Holmes, picking up some manuscript papers from the floor. "Nothing in the temple circumstance struck you as odd?"

"You strike me as odd, Holmes. And unconscionably untidy."

"No, impudent fellow—"

"Wonderful people, the common Jews, gathered about the Master's feet to learn! Did you see them? Men, boys, girls, women. And the infants, so cuddly—"

"Simply because they're not old enough to be hated."

"Holmes, you are a petulant tyrant. You need spiritual counseling. Really, you do." Watson thought for a moment on Holmes' prior question. "I think it's odd how these mystery cards appear in such a supernaturally timely fashion."

"You miss the point. Did you not attend how the Pharisees' demeanor changed after their confrontation with the Lord?"

"Oh, that."

Holmes sighed. "Did you not note their temper, their disaffirmation, as they filed out one by one? What shame! What indignity! The same humiliation they heaped on the young woman was, instead, heaped upon them."

"It is the Lord's way—repaying the wicked in their own coin."

"But how did this humiliation happen, Watson? By what

means?" Holmes extended his fist with two fingers raised. "Two times Jesus took the time, in the midst of the hot deliberations with the Pharisees, to stoop and scribble on the ground with his finger."

"That is why you were searching on the ground, and in a most undignified posture?"

"Whatever he wrote immediately affected the Pharisees and teachers of the law, to the extent that they quit the temple court in shame."

"But the Scriptures are silent on what Christ wrote on the ground. It is unsolvable."

"It had better not be." Holmes reached out. From between his fingers peeked out the note of familiar stationery which he had recovered from the dirt.

Watson took it. He deliberated on the graceful handwriting in which this question was penned: *What did Christ write on the ground?*

THE WAGER

"Ponder the circumstances in which the religious leaders brought the woman into the temple, Watson." Holmes lit his brier pipe and gestured with it. "During the seven days of the Feast of Tabernacles, the Jews are required to live in booths made of branches and palms in remembrance of the Israelites' exodus from Egypt (which explains the untidiness we saw in the city's avenues and roofs). In addition, multitudes of bulls, sheep and rams are sacrificed at the temple for the people's remission of sins. It is a festival of sorts. A celebration of joy—"

"Not for the animals, surely." Watson crossed his legs and looked at the empty table. It often held piping-hot food brought up by Mrs. Hudson, but now, only a solitary pot of coffee.

"So, Christ is teaching in the temple courts—"

"With those wonderfully attentive people—"

"When it happens: enter the Pharisees and the teachers of the law with the adulterous woman in their custody. It could not have been difficult for them to locate an example of infidelity in a citywide time of celebration. All the food being consumed. All the drink being drunk. All the people living, sleeping in leafy, scanty huts. Convenient timing that on the next day after the feast they would challenge Christ with what they believed was a hopeless puzzle. A dilemma he could not wiggle his way out of."

"They planned this confrontation, then?" asked Watson.

"Possibly. Probably. These are arrogant fellows with little to recommend them but their passion. Recall, they confronted Christ on an earlier occasion."

"I'll wager three guineas they lost that argument as well."

Holmes put back his head and let out a cloud of smoke. "Certainly. The religious leaders complained that Jesus' disciples violated the elders' tradition by eating food with unwashed hands.[3] Jesus' response is predictably scathing. He castigates them for observing their own laws and traditions which directly violate the laws handed down by God himself, thus nullifying the word of God.[4] And Jesus concludes by saying, *And many such things you do.*"

Sherlock Holmes got up and walked to the window, looking down on Baker Street. "The Pharisees and teachers of the law were intent on stoning the woman. You noted the hatred in their eyes? And in their attitude toward Jesus, a certain smug condescension?"

"I was there, Holmes. Remember?"

"Interesting how the religious thugs just walked away and left their prey unharmed."

"Jesus' response did them in: 'You without sin can cast the first stone.' And since they had all sinned at some point—"

"No, no, no, no, no. Once again, Watson, I would point out your shortcomings—"

"Something you do all too handsomely—"

"—in that you haven't read the applying scriptures sufficiently. Nor inquired into them thoroughly enough." He puffed weakly on his pipe. "You jump to take the easy way out, the obvious explanation. Truthfully, as I have studied the temple's history, so I have scrutinized this story from John chapter 8, the *pericope de adultera*, at length: not exclusively in English (nor only in Sahidic or Bohairic), but in the founding language. I am no scholar in Greek, but I might easily enough put down your notion of past sinning."

Holmes tamped and lit his pipe for the etymological journey ahead.

"The root for the Greek word used for 'sin' is *hamartanō*. However, only once in the New Testament is it cast in the negative, 'without sin' (*anamartétos*), and it is here in verse 7: '*You without sin,*' *means to miss the mark.*'"

"But who amongst the religious leaders could claim they'd never missed the mark in the past?" persisted Watson. "Even the Pharisees and scribes must have admitted, in their heart of hearts, to have committed sins. They were ill-suited, therefore, to throw the first stone. That is why they let her go."

"But they are not going to let Christ dictate false standards to them, dear boy. Nowhere does the law stipulate that only men sinless from birth may stone a guilty party—what a thought, Watson! So, the point that they had all sinned at some point in the past is superfluous. They would not let such a fact stay their hand. If anything, having newly celebrated the Feast of Tabernacles, they probably felt inordinately sanctified."

Watson sighed. "I am hungry, Holmes."

Holmes seemed not to hear. "There is a Greek word for past trespasses. It is *proamartanō*. But it is not the word used here. *Anamartētos* is used here, suggesting a current state of sin, an active, present condition—to be in the act of missing the mark. In essence, Christ said to the teachers of the law, 'You who are *not* in the act of sinning right now—you cast the first stone.'"

"Meaning, the Pharisees and scribes were actively sinning at the moment they were confronting Christ with the woman?"

"Yes! Oh Watson, these fellows were a self-righteous lot. They believed themselves blameless in regard to the law. Remember what Saint Paul, a former Pharisee, related in his letter to the Philippians? . . . '*If anyone else thinks he may have confidence in the flesh, I more so: circumcised the eighth day, of the stock of Israel, of the tribe of Benjamin, a Hebrew of the Hebrews; concerning the law, a Pharisee; concerning zeal, persecuting the church; concerning the righteousness which is in the law, blameless.*'"[5]

Watson nodded. "So, even if Jesus had meant, 'You who have never sinned cast the first stone,' it would have fallen on deaf ears?"

Holmes nodded. "But something stopped them in their tracks.

These shameless men were shamed into submission. Somehow, Christ condemned them, convinced them beyond any doubt that they were actively sinning. Caused them to file away from the court in complete humiliation, *beginning with the oldest*—a singular fact to keep in mind. Christ must have written something quite amazing on the ground with his finger. The crucial question remains: *What did he write?*"

"Probably the commandments—"

"All ten of them? On the ground? With his finger? Ha! Why stop there, pray? Why not inscribe the book of Leviticus word for word, or the Pentateuch entire? No, no, no, Watson (or should I call you Lestrade?). As you so aptly pointed out, we were there. We saw him write but a few words. Alas, they were trampled by the cheering crowd, delighted to see the Pharisees so humiliated."

"But the Scriptures say the Pharisees, upon hearing him, left."

"Watson, you are so tiresome." Holmes slouched back in his chair. "Yes, they heard Christ's accusation. But they needed proof. An explanation of his condemnation of them. Something was needed to *show* them they were sinning. Remember, they left one by one, filing past Jesus."

"I await the great Sherlock Holmes to make a fool of me. But he cannot. This time the doctor will trump the detective! I repeat, we cannot possibly know what he wrote."

"Previously, you mentioned three guineas as a wager amount." A light flickered in Holmes' gray eyes. "Is that inducement enough for you that I can discover these mysterious words?"

"Done." The doctor leaned forward in his chair and shook Holmes' extended hand. "I'll not let you off this one, Holmes, were it but a shilling."

MISSING PERSONS

Watson closed his Bible. Across from him sat Holmes, dressed in his smoking jacket and silk cravat, sipping coffee from a teacup and staring into the purring fireplace. Beneath the detective's calm exterior, Watson detected an impatient agitation like the undertow of the River Thames, edgily waiting for his friend to reach the same conclusion as himself: the only conclusion.

"Holmes, you'll be pleased to learn I've decided to approach this problem contextually."

The detective jerked to awareness and leveled a stare at Watson.

"So, I studied the scripture passage leading up to the adulterous woman account, in the book of John—I do not see how you will win this bet, Holmes; really I do not. The reading is fascinating, yet it only yields more of the same confrontational arrogance. The Pharisees are angry with the temple guards for being entranced by the very man they were sent to arrest: Jesus. The Pharisees interpret this phenomenon as some kind of delusional curse which has fallen on the people—this "mob," as they term them.

"The Pharisees are the mob," countered Holmes.

"Next, the Pharisees become agitated with one of their own members, Nicodemus, who has the audacity to suggest they follow the law's prescripts, that of hearing out Christ first before definitively condemning him. They pummel Nicodemus verbally by using scripture incorrectly as a proof text."[6]

"Do come to the point, Watson."

"When confronted with the law's requirements, the teachers of the law become abusive. So, instead of heeding Nicodemus's warning, they justify violating the law by pointing out that Christ is a lawbreaker himself. Therefore he cannot be the Messiah, so they become a law unto themselves. If only they were to hear Christ out, perhaps they would learn he was born in Bethlehem! But they jump to bad decisions based on bad assumptions—typical of a gang with a collective hubris."

"It is what foolish leaders do, Watson, when pressed with undeniable fact. They insult. They misdirect. They deflect. They become sullen and vengeful and blame the people. Full steam ahead until the enemy is ground under, bludgeoned, silenced. And even then they do not repent of misappropriating the law—"

A change came over Holmes. He sat for a moment, glanced about the four walls as if he had misplaced something, and shot out of his chair. He tweaked his cravat, a good indication he was lost in thought. He approached the large, open Bible lying on the pedestal and smoothed the pages with his palm, as if comforting a friend.

"Misappropriation of the law, yes." Holmes smiled, his eyes glittering. "It is the edge upon which everything balances. Excellent investigatory methodology, Watson, but I'm afraid your thoroughness may cost you the bet."

"With bated breath and upturned eye I await the riddle's answer!"

"Indeed, just as in the instance with the disciples and the washing of hands, the scribes' opinions on the law and how it should be interpreted trumped the law itself—even when diametrically opposing it. Take Christ's charge against them in the matter of Corban."[7]

"But isn't the case in the temple different from the others, Holmes? Not that I agree, but weren't the scribes and Pharisees justified, according to Mosaic law, in having the adulterous woman stoned?"

"Ah!" exclaimed Holmes. "The law, the law, the law!"

He towered over the Bible, and yet the Bible, situated lower, seemed to tower over him. He grabbed whole handfuls of pages and heaved them backward to texts written over a thousand years before Christ, just as the Needle's Eye, in its own way, transported people. Finally, he let the Scriptures lie open, departed to the mantel, and stared into the simmering coals.

"The Mosaic law: it is the anchor, the support upon which the Pharisees built their house of cards. Remember what they said to Christ, *'Now Moses, in the law, commanded us that such should be stoned.'*[8] Really? Does Moses really say this in regard to adultery?"

Watson opened his mouth to answer—

"Before we take a look, a singular point to keep in mind is this: typically, when the religious leaders or the Pharisees confront Christ, they fall into their own trap. This incident of the adulteress woman is a case in point. The Pharisees are caught in the very web they wove for Christ. They hang themselves with their own admission: *'Teacher, this woman was caught in adultery, in the very act.'*"[9]

Watson scratched his head. He approached the immense Bible, found it opened to the Old Testament, to Deuteronomy: the law.

"Read Deuteronomy 22:22," intoned Sherlock Holmes, "or if you prefer, Leviticus 20:10. Do you see it?"

"*'If a man is found lying with a woman married to a husband,'*" Watson read aloud, "*'then both of them shall die—the man that lay with the woman, and the woman; so you shall put away the evil from Israel.'*

"The Pharisees and teachers of the law were correct, Holmes. The woman was guilty of adultery, and according to the law must be stoned."

"But?"

"Adultery takes two. Her partner, according to the law, should be stoned as well. Makes you wonder . . ."

"Wonder what?"

Watson thought for a moment. "Where's the man?"

"Watson, what did you say?"

"Where's the man?" he replied.

"You've done it!" With his hands on his hips, Holmes put his head back and laughed. "Those are precisely the words Christ wrote on the ground!"

THE POOR

Dr. Watson, sitting at the desk near the window, lifted his pen from his journal.

"I wonder if she did," said Watson reflectively, "leave her life of sin, I mean. Her transformation was wonderful, was it not, Holmes? Her shame and guilt vanished in a flash, replaced by a shining radiance! Did you see her face? She knew beyond any doubt she was forgiven and yet had done nothing to warrant it. Even the fabric of her gown seemed brighter—like a bride."

"It is a fact: God is merciful."

"Oh, Holmes, must you be so academic?"

"The fact that Christ let the Pharisees go—that is more shocking. The religious leaders weren't interested in the woman's spiritual state or in the sin of adultery. Their sole aim was to trap

Christ, and to that end they would misuse the woman or the law to do it. That was their real sin."

"The eldest Pharisees left first." Watson bit on the end of his pencil. "Once they read Christ's words, they recognized instantly they were misappropriating the law, that they were in a present state of sinning."

Holmes reached over with a pair of tongs, extracted a burning coal from the fireplace, and lit his pipe. The soothing aroma filled the room.

"They were defenseless, Watson, by their own admission. How could they maintain that the offending man was absent when they apprehended the woman? They couldn't say, 'We had it *on good report* she'd committed adultery.' No, no, no. They already had said they caught her *in the act*. Therefore, they had let the man go free. The command in Deuteronomy even cites the man as the first one to be stoned, followed by the woman." Holmes gazed at the ceiling, thinking. "So much for Christianity being a religion prejudiced against women. Christ, by his actions, turns that notion on its head."

The doctor, lost in thought, stared from his desk at the purring fire. "We'll never know if the man involved ever repented, will we? His sin was concealed from his wife, his family, perhaps from himself. Shame is man's only hope, and he had no opportunity to feel it."

"There is a deeper current here, Watson. These older Pharisees were a wizened group. Perhaps they recalled a deeper theme as portrayed by the Old Testament prophet Hosea. God depicted Israel's fallen condition and spiritual adultery, particularly the priests', by instructing Hosea to marry an adulterous woman. The Lord said through Hosea, '*I will not punish your daughters when they commit harlotry, nor your brides when they commit adultery, for the men themselves go apart with harlots, and offer sacrifices with a ritual harlot.*'"[10]

Watson chuckled. "These Pharisees—oh, they were much too proper to consort with prostitutes, and yet, their hearts were hardened toward their first love: the Lord himself. Didn't the Pharisees actually believe they would acquire eternal life from observing the Scriptures? Talk about self-righteousness!"[11] In a flash of inspiration Watson exclaimed, "Why, it's as if they divorced the Lord—and *married the law!*"

"Marvelous insight," pointed out Holmes, and grinned with the pipe between his clamped teeth. "In Malachi 2:9 the Lord says this of the corrupt priests: *'Therefore I also have made you contemptable and base before all the people, because you have not kept My ways but have shown partiality in the law.'* Both the woman *and* the Pharisees were adulterers. Therefore, Christ let them both go."

"The Pharisees, in their purple robes, phylacteries, and flowing beards—they cut impressive figures, didn't they? Rather dignified harlots?"

"To my mind, their brand of adultery was far worse," postulated Holmes. "In the Bible, no matter where the rape took place (or the adultery), the man was always guilty and paid with his life. But the Pharisees' example becomes intolerable: In punishing the woman but setting the man free, they were hearkening back to pagan laws, the hated Assyrians, during the time of King Tiglath-Pileser I in the twelfth century BC: 'If a man seizes a woman in the mountains, it is the man's crime and he will be killed. But if he seizes her in (her) house, it is the woman's crime and the woman shall be killed.'"[12]

Watson sighed. "Who knows what drove the woman to consort with a married man? Her illicit act was at least professing a need—emotional, financial . . . The Pharisees, though, divorced their faithful God for their own bold self-sufficiency, which they showcased by obeying the law, by standing in the busy marketplace and praying, by sitting in seats of honor at banquets and the synagogue, by being addressed by the masses with admiration and respect.[13] Oh, yes, I agree; they were the worst adulterers."

"Did you notice, Watson? Jesus didn't bother commanding them to depart from their way of sin. The hearts of fools are stone. Hosea says, '*They do not direct their deeds toward turning to their God, for the spirit of harlotry is in their midst, and they do not know the* LORD.'[14] We Londoners have our own rhyme:

> *A man convinced against his will*
> *Is of the same opinion still.*"

"And later," pointed out the doctor, "the Pharisees would violate judicial law on several counts in actually condemning Christ to the cross, though they could find no fault in him."

"The fault, rather, is yours, Watson." Holmes stood abruptly and walked to the table, glancing over keenly at his companion as he refreshed his coffee.

"My fault? Whatever do you mean?"

Holmes took a deep, loving sip. "I refer to Christ's particular wisdom as recorded in Matthew 26:11."

"Stop being so tedious, Holmes. Come out with it."

"'*You have the poor with you always,*'" recited the detective.

Watson put back his head and groaned.

Holmes smiled resiliently, walked over to where he sat, and stretched out his hand, palm up. "Three guineas, please, my good doctor."

THREE

RIGHTEOUS BLOOD IS RED

JOASH, KING OF JUDAH, LOOKED NORTH FROM HIS ROYAL PALACE in Jerusalem. He surveyed the temple grounds with a heavy-lidded glance, like a sleepy lion, but with active, attentive eyes. In high politics, as in the savage wild, it served well to appear other than what you were.

He caught movement at the head of the temple stairs between the two massive pillars. A gray-bearded priest raised his arms, pleading with the crowd gathered below, calling out, "This is what God says: 'Why do you disobey the Lord's commands?'"

"Come down, Zechariah!" shouted a large man, standing near the bronze Sea,[1] with a sword belt draped over his shoulder. "The king has passed sentence on you!"

"Hear the Almighty's sentence for you!" retorted Zechariah. "You will not prosper! Because you have forsaken the Lord, he has forsaken you."

"Step down!" clamored the mob.

The king nodded to a group of troops, who snapped sharply around and set out for the temple courtyard. After all, even in the wilderness, others do the lion's hunting for him.

"These people look got at," stated Dr. Watson, from behind the priest.

"It might help you to know we stand upon the porch of Solomon's temple," replied Holmes. Both he and the doctor were robed in gray, and therefore, visible to this ancient time of which they were trespassers. "These two renowned pillars beside which we stand are named Jachin and Boaz. This priest is none other than Zechariah son of Jehoiada. He castigates the Israelites for worshipping Asherah poles and idols—for turning away from the Lord." Holmes went for his pipe but thought better of it. "As for these people—yes, they have been worked upon. Quickly, Watson!—or all will be lost for our man, Zechariah!"

The priest went to descend the stairs and address the people closer, but his feet would not touch the stairs. He felt himself lifted by either arm by strangers, turned about, and carried into the temple's dark confines.

"This way, Holmes!" huffed Watson. They veered quickly into a side storage room in spite of Zechariah's exclamations and protestations, the priest struggling between them.

"Fortunate that he's shorter than us," said Holmes, wincing, "though I think I have the heavy side."

"Stop your tussling," Watson grunted to the man. They slipped through another storage room filled with garments and utensils and out the back of the temple. Still carrying their writhing burden, they passed through the Middle Gate out into the city.

"Without our assistance, your days are surely numbered," remarked Watson. They stood in a vacant house, perhaps a former stable, for empty chambers lined both walls.

"The Lord is my help," replied Zechariah. "And I will admonish all to return to him."

"Holmes, we should make for the Benjamin Gate," instructed Watson, ignoring the little man. "If it's closed or barred against us, then the Ephraim, or the Corner Gate."

"It is too late—they are all watched!" came a high voice, feminine and authoritative. They dropped the priest. Holmes wheeled about, brandishing his walking stick. A contingent of guards crowded both doorways, and others marched up behind them. They were trapped.

From out of the crowd of soldiers, approached a purple-robed figure. A beautiful face appeared as she put back her hood, a thin circlet of gold encompassing her brow. Zechariah bowed.

"Who are you strangers so intent upon saving my friend Zechariah? I've seldom witnessed this degree of loyalty from foreigners. You have shaved your beards—are you in mourning? In circumspect grief? Certainly you are not Jews. Geshurites, then? Canaanites? Ah!—Ammonites!"

"Er . . . Londonites, madam," stammered Watson, blushing.

"From Hittite territory, then?"

"A little further west, Your Majesty," replied Holmes, smiling warmly. "You are the queen of Jerusalem, are you not?"

"Indeed," she said, and passed a hand over her stomach. "And although I carry the king's heir within my womb, I cannot betray those once friendly to the throne. You see, when my husband was but an infant, Zechariah's father, Jehoiada, saved his life from the murderous rampage of wicked Queen Athaliah, daughter of Jezebel. He raised King Joash within the secrecy of the temple—"

"Then in a coup d'état," filled in Holmes, "he brought the boy out of hiding, in health and vigor, and restored him to his rightful throne."

"Yes," she said. She looked carefully at their robes, Holmes' walking stick. "Furthermore, Jehoiada picked me as a wife for the new king."

"But now, His Grace—" said Holmes.

"Joash is not your king, that you should revere him," she stated, a strange mixture of severity and sadness marking her tone, "nor a man of grace that you should regard him. My husband and his officials have led Judah into idolatry. A man short of memory forgets his proper loyalties and allies. This priest you have rescued, Zechariah, played with King Joash in the temple during the dark years, but now is accounted as an enemy."

"It is double betrayal," spoke up Zechariah. "King Joash has betrayed God with his idols, and he has betrayed those of his youth who brought him to power. However, I may still reach God's people with his message to—"

"Indeed, you will not," replied Holmes quietly, addressing the priest. "I strongly caution you, Zechariah, against such a course. Your very life hangs in the balance. Righteous blood is as red as the most ardent pagan's, and flows as freely when shed."

"We must go," admonished the queen. "A passageway exists between the royal palace to the temple. The king's soldiers will be coming."

"My companion and I will take our leave, Your Majesty," replied Holmes. "Do not place yourself in more danger, nor your unborn baby, Amaziah, by harboring two Gentiles who have violated the temple's sanctity."

"I do not know how you both got so deeply into our kingdom, our city, our temple," she said inquiringly, "nor how you come to know the name I have inwardly chosen for my baby, but I must warn you: run as fast and as far as you may go. And do it now!"

"That will not be necessary," said Holmes calmly. His hands

were beginning to tingle, to glow. An aura rose and formed around the two time-travelers. The queen stepped back, looking at them both as if they were from another world—which, in effect, they were.

"I bid you good journey," she said as they faded away. "The Lord shield you."

REGENT'S PARK, LONDON

"Well, my good man, I've found you!" said Holmes, dressed splendidly in a black topcoat; leather shoes and gloves; starched white shirt; golden cuff links. His satin topper towered over his head, sheltering the cerebrations of the world's greatest detective. He sat down in a jerky motion on the park bench next to his physician friend and stared with him over the Zoological Gardens at the north end of Regent's Park near Primrose Hill.

"I'm no one's good man today," Watson replied glumly.

"I know you may not be anyone's joyful man, no one's carefree man, perhaps no one's optimistic man. But surely, Watson, you will always be a *good* man—unless I took your words for too weighty a meaning."

"You understood me rightly."

"Let's go sit by the lake," prompted the detective.

"I don't sit by lakes."

Holmes crossed his legs and lit his pipe. "I understand they have over a thousand birds in the garden yonder, five hundred quadrupeds. We could walk about and make some mischief. They feed the lions at four o'clock—what d'ye say? A pleasant opportunity to see the latest fashions of London nobility."

No response.

"I am here for you, dear heart. It is a difficult thing that Zechariah ended up brutally murdered between the temple and the altar. Although it happened thousands of years ago and though we tried to prevent it, it cannot set one in too fashionable a mood."

They sat in silence for a moment, and then Holmes said, "I would live at the zoo someday. What d'ye think, Watson? Me and the chimps living together in one happy cage, sharing biscuit and tea like Christians? I might even pass around my pipe. I can make a splendid monkey face."

"Are you doing it now?" muttered the doctor.

"Ha! How delectably wretched you are today!"

"Why don't you go be happy somewhere else, Holmes? In truth, I am an angry man."

"You have a right to be, Watson. If I awoke every morning and saw what you see in the mirror, I'd be angry too—ha, ha, ha! Why do you look at me so?"

"How did you find me here?"

Holmes heard the distant melody of a clarinet playing a rhapsodic tune, which set him to dreaming. He said: "Special eyeglasses which I have developed, when adjusted to a subject's heel-to-toe signature, as well as to his weight and, therefore, to the particular atomic disturbance of the surface upon which he walks, allow me to track virtually anyone in London. I have them in my pocket—d'ye believe me? Imagine, Watson! Imagine such an invention—its considerable impact for the police as regards hunting down known villains!"

No response.

"Actually, it was a more crude and deductive process. Mrs. Hudson observed you walking north on Baker Street—which rules out the Strand, Piccadilly, or the museum—and York, which dead-ends near the Regent's Park, does it not? You were carrying your walking stick, and so, not likely to summon a cab. In a mood desirous of peace and solitude, Hyde Park would hardly answer, nor Green nor St. James Park—Mycroft's territory and lying southward as well—certainly not Hanger's clowns. And I then recalled the Zoological Gardens were your chapel of choice when Mary died."[2]

The doctor sighed. He looked off at the white marbled complex to the backdrop of rich foliage. Proper men and ladies with parasols and hooped dresses nodded politely their way as they strolled past, but Watson's temper simmered as fixed as any star. "I have a beastly admission to make."

Holmes tilted his head and imparted a quirky smile, all reminiscent of a scarecrow—if not a rather fashionably dressed scarecrow. "Let me serve as confessor."

"Holmes, it is not poor Zechariah's murder—"

"Bound to happen, the poor fellow—"

"—awful as it must have been—"

"—his mind so irretrievably set on his own destruction—"

"—which has me so perplexed. No, I refer to the discrepancy in Matthew."

Holmes took a deep breath and lowered his eyebrows. "Go on."

Watson handed him a cream-colored card. "I found this tucked in the pages of your Bible, at Matthew chapter 23, where Christ rails on our old friends, the Pharisees, in rare form, as only he can. But in verse 35 he says, '*that on you may come all the righteous blood shed on the earth, from the blood of righteous Abel to the blood of Zechariah, son of Berechiah, whom you murdered between the temple and the altar.*'

"Don't you see? Christ made a mistake: he cites Zechariah son of Berechiah as being stoned to death between the altar and the temple, not Zechariah son of Jehoiada, the priest we attempted to rescue. The text of Matthew plainly states it in black and white, and plainly wrong."

Sherlock sniffed. "Oh, don't make too much of it, Watson— tempest in a teacup."

"How can this oversight mean so little to you? Let me repeat the problem: Jesus alludes to Zechariah son of Berechiah as being the one murdered between the temple and the altar. But it was actually Zechariah son of Jehoiada, hundreds of years earlier."

Holmes shrugged. "Jesus simply misspoke. He said, 'Berechiah,' but he meant Jehoiada. Or the gospel chronicler got it wrong—or a copier of Matthew's gospel further down the line. These errors occur frequently in manuscript production—the occasional con-flagration, harmonization—subrogation, in this case. Think of it: a story like Zechariah son of Jehoiada being so often told that the one Zechariah is transposed for the other. Simple, really. Not *too* messy."

Watson looked off at the zoo's double staircase. "I noticed it straightaway, Holmes. As did you."

"Yes, I suppose I understand your objection. So obvious a mistake should have been caught somewhere along the line."

"It's thrown me into a spiritual crisis."

"Oh, Watson, just because the Bible lacks perfection doesn't mean it loses authority. Mistake-prone Scotland Yard still bears the weighty authority of law. Let that example answer for you. I myself have failed on occasion—you remember the matter of Violet Smith?[3] Now and again certain unforeseen elements alloy the metal and combine them to make my investigatory efforts futile. But is my good reputation, undeserved as it may be, thusly tarnished? Indeed not. Clients flock to my door, though no longer with as pretty a case as I could wish."

"I knew you wouldn't understand. The Bible is the very Word of God! If Christ made a mistake about Zechariah, how do we know he didn't err in other places? I'm not talking about superficial errors or slight differences in our earliest manuscripts (I know we don't have the autographs—the original writings). One copy might read, 'The Lord,' while the other reads, 'The Lord Almighty,' a cosmetic difference with no doctrinal impact." Watson bit his lower lip. "Matthew's error isn't just a difference in observation—one witness sees one angel at the tomb of our risen Lord, and another sees two. Even that is explainable—"

"Even preferable," interjected Holmes. "I expect varying accounts from eyewitnesses at a murder scene. I would not trust the gospel accounts if they agreed in every minute detail. Yes, but I see your point. The deliberate stipulation of Zechariah son of Berechiah is an issue of credibility—"

"Of contradiction. You must get to the bottom of this, Holmes. It is serious. My mind is overwrought with suspense and worry. Sleep escapes me. The bedrock of my faith has been shaken."

"Never fear, Watson. The answer, no matter how hidden, awaits the unearthing. And *we* shall dig it out."

NEVILL'S TURKISH BATH

"This is the particular place?" inquired Watson. "This is where we are to meet him?"

Holmes remained silent. Speaking required too much effort

in the stifling humidity, and conversation might break the unwritten code of temperate silence peculiar to the men's bath-house. He and Holmes sat opposite one other on white marble benches, naked except for towels draped about their waists. Sweat beaded up on the detective's aquiline forehead as he accepted iced mint-water from a porter, Watson, a hand towel to wipe his face. The doctor put down the *British Medical Journal* and looked far overhead, measuring the expansive stone and glass dome housing the Turkish baths.

Holmes smiled dreamily. A massive man approached them, draped by a towel the size of a mizzen sail, and squatted on a stool. His sleepy eyes looked out from beneath black curls which clung wet and lank to his forehead. Clearly, he had been soaped, washed, massaged . . .

"Nevill's[4] is heaven, is it not?" he grunted. "Received your note, Mr. Holmes. Many thanks for paying my entrance fee."

"Dr. John H. Watson," Sherlock Holmes said by way of introduction, "Dr. Cyril Norberton, professor of Old Testament Studies, Cambridge."

"Retired," he added, shrugging. "What, Dr. Watson? Expecting a dwarf?"

"I'm expecting you might be well up in the matter of the two Zechariahs," said Watson.

The professor's eyes fastened onto a small dish-like object on the marble shelf near Watson's shoulder. He sniffed the air. "Will you hand that diminutive object to me?" he asked. "If my eyes aren't too long unaccustomed to ancient artifacts, I believe it is an oil lamp—Iron Age, specifically? And if my nose doesn't cheat me, I smell myrrh."

Watson shrugged and handed it over, much to Holmes' shock

and consternation, and explained, "I didn't want to leave it in my clothes. It is valuable to me."

Norberton looked at the item closely, the shallow dish, the outward pinch of the rim, where the flax wick would be laid. "Melting unguent of myrrh," he said, sniffing, "not requiring a flame. Very nice copy. Authentic. The lamp was a powerful image in ancient times: a symbol of prosperity, of joy, of guidance. So, guide me, gentlemen. Where did you get this?"

Watson took it back and said, "Do you have a theory? About the two Zechariahs?"

"I have the answer, plain and simple, gentlemen. Nor might my delayed response hope to accentuate my stay here in paradise, for I have imbibed the frosted raspberry ice—excellent!" Norberton yawned like a hippo in the tropical heat. "First, the best of Matthew's manuscripts mention only the name Zechariah. They do not stipulate Zechariah's immediate ancestor. The addition of 'son of Berechiah' might be a copyist's addition."

"No, no, no," said Holmes, his eyes drooping in the heat. "By 'best' do you mean those manuscripts without the mistake? Do you mean the Alexandrian manuscripts over against the Byzantine or the Latinized Western texts? And why, pray, would an overeager scribe choose Berechiah as Zechariah's father instead of the more famous and contextually consistent Jehoiada?"

"Agreed," Norberton said with a shrug. "Christ's indictment of the Pharisees would be more comprehensive if it spanned the entire Old Testament period, starting with Abel in Genesis and extending all the way to Zechariah son of Berechiah in 480 BC. Unless, that is—" the professor cleared his throat, "Christ meant to span only the first man in Scripture *recorded* as murdered, Abel, to the last *recorded* martyr, Zechariah son of Jehoiada, who lived about four hundred years earlier than Zechariah son of Berechiah, in 800 BC—"

"Which he assuredly did," affirmed Watson, simply. "Holmes and I were there."

"Ha! Certainly!" laughed the professor. His initial look of mild irritation at being interrupted evaporated in astonishment at Watson's remark, and he regarded both Watson and Holmes as a pair of cracked pots. "And so, in defense of Matthew's gospel, Zechariah son of Jehoiada is not a logical candidate for Christ's example, if we've correctly assessed his intent—"

"Go on," put in Holmes, impatiently. His mind, having catalogued the facts, hungered for more raw data.

"There are twenty-eight different Zechariahs in the Scriptures," pointed out Norberton. "It's a priestly name. Remember the priest Zechariah in the New Testament? He was expected to name his son after himself (instead of calling him John) or we'd have twenty-nine. It is not difficult to imagine Zechariah son of Berechiah being slain near the altar. So, Christ was probably correct: Zechariah son of Berechiah—"

"But the book of Zechariah doesn't tell us *how* the son of Berechiah actually died," protested Watson. "Or even if he *was* murdered. *Probably* and *imagine* is all conjecture. And there are no other witnesses in the Old or New Testament which bear your story out." He swallowed hard. "Which bear Christ's story out."

The big man wiped his brow, cleared his throat again. "Weigh the cumulative evidence. In Matthew 23 Christ is railing on the Pharisees and teachers of the law—"

"Yes, we've bumped into them before," blurted Watson.

"—for killing the prophets, wise men, and teachers, just like their forefathers." Norberton finished his statement pedantically, as if part of a lecture, giving him freedom to scrutinize the incredulous substance of Watson's interruption. "Zechariah son of Berechiah was a prophet and fits better into the Christ's example about persecuting the prophets. Zechariah son of Jehoiada was a priest."

"Oh, please," said the doctor testily. "And what about Abel, whom you mentioned as beginning the span? I suppose he was the archbishop of Canterbury—"

"Do you see our dilemma, Professor?" interjected Holmes hastily, sipping from his cool drink. "Christ must not confuse us this way. He tells us a fact of history which only he knows, and which the Old Testament does not openly corroborate, and which can be easily confused with an earlier account of a man with the same name."

"There is more evidence. Zechariah son of Berechiah lived at the time of the temple's rebuilding—"

"The second temple," offered Watson.

The doctor became the sole recipient of Norberton's frown. "Yes. The altar was built before the wall's construction even began. So, what I mean is this: the altar existed when Zechariah son of Berechiah preached, as well as the temple grounds. Zechariah outlived Haggai, and was probably slain at seventy years of age or more."

Holmes spoke up: "But did Zechariah son of Berechiah preach prophetic warnings for which he might have been killed, as Zechariah son of Jehoiada had?"

"I'm coming to that, Mr. Holmes. Zechariah chapter 13 is not pretty, sir; no, it is not! The Lord warns of a future time when all prophets and prophecies in the land will cease." Professor Norberton adjusted his bulk on the stool. "History bears this out:

the prophetic word fell silent after the time of Zechariah son of Berechiah."

Watson crossed his arms. "Meaning?"

"Prophecy had been withdrawn from the Jewish people. By the Lord."

"So?"

"Prophecy had already fallen into disfavor with the Jews. The truth, God's truth, became singularly unpopular with a populace just returning from exile in Babylon for seventy years."

"Meaning?"

"Ha!" chortled Holmes.

"Gentlemen," announced Professor Cyril Norberton, rising from his stool. "Read the minor prophets—from Hosea to Malachi—and you will note God's proclamation of judgment. But it is directed primarily against his chosen people. Zechariah son of Berechiah proclaimed such a message. Read Zechariah 14:2. He might have easily perished in such an openly hostile environment." He smiled broadly at Watson. "That, sir, is my meaning."

THE MESSAGE

Holmes leaned against the sideboard located outside his bedroom door and drew in on his brier pipe. "How do I feel after this morning at Nevill's?" he asked in response to Watson's question. "Refreshed! Except for discovering my fellow traveler is a thief. What do you mean by pilfering objects from the past, Watson? Did you see Norberton's face when he laid eyes on your little oil lamp?"

"Don't be upset with me, Holmes, but I took it from Ahithophel's house to remember Bathsheba—even though I didn't know her identity. Remarkably beautiful woman!"

Holmes studied him for a moment. Watson cut such a miserable, repentant figure that he snickered aloud. "Well, let's say no more about it. Some brandy? The Lud[5] for dinner—some of your cherished smoked rarebit?"

"Infuriating man, your professor." The doctor stared out the window onto Baker Street. In the evening shadows he spied a new hat and glove shop on the corner of George Street.

"You found him unconvincing? Be not dismayed, Watson, we shall progress in this investigation, though Norberton's evidence lacks . . . thoroughness. Completeness."

"Worse. It lacks heart. We've reached a dead end. How my view of Scripture has fallen!"

"The Lord must not judge you too harshly."

Watson shook his head. "One thing you should never do is tell the Lord what he must do."

"I told the Lord what he must *not* do," corrected Holmes. "But why do you cry *Pax*? Give way? Yield? Granted, this case does possess a certain obscurity, even dullness."

"Except it is Christ's own testimony which is on trial."

"Oh, yes, Watson. I know the depth of your passion. It is why I have labored extensively in the Scriptures all this afternoon."

Watson looked back from the window. "You've discovered something, then?"

The detective smiled a winning smile. He tapped out his pipe's ash and repacked the bowl.

"Holmes, tell me: Do your findings incriminate the Bible or exonerate it?"

Holmes lit a match and with a flair of his hand, said,

"Norberton commented that the best manuscripts of Matthew contain only Zechariah's name; no reference to Berechiah, which does little for us, and I'll not trifle with your emotions. What matters is that Berechiah's name found its way into Holy Writ, but for what reason? It cannot be to start some new heresy or to deny the saving blood of Christ. What cause, then? Why clarify the text by using a name so obviously obscure to the circumstance that you end up muddying it, instead?"

Holmes began to pace, puffing away like an aimless locomotive. "Norberton did hit on the truth. He just didn't follow up—which is why I stated he lacked completeness. How many of my own cases would have fallen through the cracks, unsolved, had I neglected to be thorough? How many of your patients, good doctor, would have ended in disaster and grief if you had not attended to the details?"

"No wonder he retired from his post at Cambridge—or was let out!" scoffed Watson.

"Norberton did call attention, however unwittingly, to the 'nub of the matter' as the crass saying goes. I asked myself, *why* was Zechariah son of Berechiah killed? Or Christ, for that matter? Or any prophet? Because of their message—it has to be so. The professor also admonished us to actually *read* the other minor prophets—another point for him."

Holmes strode over to the massive Bible waiting patiently upon its pedestal. A cloud of smoke rose from his pipe to enshrine him, and he waved it away.

"I will read four scriptures, Watson. For shame, if you cannot detect a theme!

"Second Chronicles 30:6, 9: '*Children of Israel, return to the* LORD *God of Abraham, Isaac, and Israel; then He will return to*

58

the remnant of you who have escaped from the hand of the kings of Assyria. . . . For if you return to the Lord, *your brethren and your children will be treated with compassion by those who lead them captive, so that they may come back to this land.'*

"Nehemiah 1:9: *'But if you return to Me, and keep My commandments and do them, though some of you were cast out to the farthest part of the heavens, yet I will gather them from there, and bring them to the place which I have chosen as a dwelling for My name.'*

"Hosea 6:1: *'Come, and let us return to the* Lord; *for He has torn, but He will heal us; He has stricken, but He will bind us up.'*

"Malachi 3:7: *'Yet from the days of your fathers you have gone away from My ordinances and have not kept them. Return to Me, and I will return to you.'*

"*'Return to Me!'*" growled Holmes, his teeth still clamped on his pipe. "The passage in 2 Chronicles comes just a few pages after Zechariah son of Jehoiada is killed. And if you pay close attention, Christ is saying the same thing at the end of Matthew 23: *'O Jerusalem, Jerusalem, the one who kills the prophets and stones those who are sent to her! How often I wanted to gather your children together, as a hen gathers her chicks under her wings, but you were not willing.'*"

"Disobedient and stiff-necked," muttered Watson.

Holmes flared his nostrils, like a bloodhound catching a warm scent. He turned the pages over and over, saying as he did so, "I came across two verses in Jeremiah (remember, he lived just seventy years before Zechariah son of Berechiah), one where judgment is pronounced,[6] and another where the message has much the same theme—'turn from your evil ways.'[7] Interestingly, the Lord commands Jeremiah *to stand in a specific place* as he delivers these messages to the people—"

"Let me hazard a guess," Watson said with awakened excitement. "The courtyard of the temple."

"None other than," answered the detective, with a smile. "The Lord wanted to caution his people as they entered his house to worship. Perhaps then they would listen. Jeremiah 26:2–3 reads: '*Thus says the* LORD: "*Stand in the court of the* LORD'*s house, and speak to all the cities of Judah, which come to worship in the* LORD'*s house, all the words that I command you to speak to them. Do not diminish a word. Perhaps everyone will listen and turn from his evil way.*"'" He turned the pages again. "Now let us hear from our man, Zechariah son of Berechiah:

"Zechariah 1:1–4: '*In the eighth month of the second year of Darius, the word of the* LORD *came to Zechariah the son of Berechiah, the son of Iddo the prophet, saying, "The* LORD *has been very angry with your fathers. Therefore say to them, 'Thus says the* LORD *of hosts: "Return to Me," says the* LORD *of hosts, "and I will return to you," says the* LORD *of hosts. "Do not be like your fathers, to whom the former prophets preached, saying,* . . . '*Turn now from your evil ways and your evil deeds.*'"'"'"

"A similar message to the passages before," said Watson resting his hand beneath his chin. "Sounds much like Christ in Matthew 23, doesn't it? This is fascinating, Holmes. Really it is. But how does this address the problem? How may we prove Zechariah son of Berechiah was slain as Christ said?"

"By common theme and circumstance. The book of Zechariah is silent on its author's death. But we have not exhausted all the minor prophets, have we? Let us visit our man Joel, chapter 2, beginning at verse 12: '"*Now, therefore," says the* LORD, "*turn to Me with all your heart, with fasting, with weeping, and with mourning." So rend your heart, and not your garments; return to the* LORD *your God, for He is gracious and merciful, slow to anger, and of great kindness.'"*

"How is our mystery solved?" Watson's voice trembled. "How does this furnish the key? This means a great deal to me, Holmes."

Holmes took a methodical draw on his pipe. "Just a few verses later, in Joel 2:17, something fascinating awaits us: *'Let the priests, who minister to the* LORD, *weep between the porch and the altar.'"*

"It's the exact location, Holmes—between the temple and the altar—just as Christ said in Matthew! Joel reiterates it. Jeremiah confirms it."

STAND OVER HERE, PLEASE

"Joel's passage amounts to a mandate," nodded the Sleuth of Baker Street. "He instructs priests to call the people together when proclaiming the message to return to the Lord, but more importantly, *where* to stand when delivering it. Christ was correct in his assertion. Zechariah son of Berechiah would have been found standing between the altar and the temple, weeping before the people, calling them back to God. And as Professor Norberton indicated, he would be inciting an already hostile crowd who had just returned from Babylon after seventy-plus years of captivity."

"Isn't it true, though, that no one knows the exact date of Joel's writing?" responded Watson.

"If the book of Joel was written before Zechariah's murder, Joel would amount to an instruction for the priests where to stand when delivering God's message. If after his murder, Joel would be alluding to a long-established precedent set by Zechariah son of Jehoiada and reinforced by Jeremiah during the time of the temple's destruction, to Zechariah son of Berechiah during the temple's rebuilding."

Holmes turned back to Jeremiah 26:15. "The clincher is the warning Jeremiah gives the people if they kill him: *'But know for certain that if you put me to death, you will surely bring innocent blood on yourselves, on this city, and on its inhabitants.'*"

"The same language Christ uses against the Pharisees in Matthew 23!" exclaimed Watson. "And it would explain why Christ follows it up with weeping for Jerusalem!"

Holmes closed the Bible solemnly and laid his hand on the cover.

Watson looked off. "And now, I can only be ashamed for doubting the Lord. It is I who need to return to him." Though a physical barrier of Holmes' making had long stood between them, breached occasionally by the merest handshake, the doctor could not contain himself. He patted Holmes affectionately on the shoulder. "Thank you, my dear friend."

"Oh, Watson," Holmes replied testily. He slumped upon the sofa to finish his pipe, and grimaced. "Your anxiety about Scripture perplexes me. I still hold to the loose relation between perfection and authority, and ultimately, to loyalty."

"A logic that may apply particularly well to friendships as well, Holmes."

"But will you not admit that parts of the Bible must be fabricated—or at least in error? Example: the tale of Jonah. Do you actually believe, John H. Watson, a large fish intentionally swallowed a man whole? That for three days this same man remained *plene tutis*[8] only to be calculatedly vomited out on dry land to grudgingly continue his mission?"

"Sarcasm is not befitting you, Holmes."

The detective leaned forward. "But do you believe the story of Jonah?"

"I do believe it. And when I get to heaven, I shall ask Jonah myself."

"But Watson, what if Jonah's not in heaven?"

The doctor's eyes twinkled mischievously. "Then *you* ask him, Holmes."

The detective's grin widened, exploding into a guffaw. He put his head back and laughed outright. "Oh, Watson! How I do love it when you get the better of me. Ha, ha, ha!"

FOUR

THE DEVIL'S ENTERPRISE

UNTIL THIS MOMENT, WATSON HAD KEPT HIS COMPOSURE. BUT Sherlock was getting on his nerves. It wasn't like Holmes to frequent so many shops, especially since it was high time they make their way to the *Viceroy of India* and investigate a new case for the Mysterious Client. Normally, when Holmes wanted to purchase something, he ventured forth directly and bought it directly. There directly and back again, directly, with perhaps a foray into the restaurant district for lunch. But this morning's stroll along the Strand had become quite maddening, darting into this hat shop or tailor's, that cigar or boot shop, yonder gift emporium. With an occasional preoccupied grunt, Holmes would peruse the items displayed within each shop only to make his way outside again. On to the next shop.

Umbrellas began popping open, like down-turned flowers, and the sky was beginning to darken toward evening. Both men, resplendent in black toppers and overcoats, paused before a cascade of flowers displayed prettily on the sidewalk, with the cottage-like shop peeking out from behind.

"I refuse to go in there, Holmes. I'm drawing the line."

"We must."

"What I *must* do involves my patients, my personal hygiene, church, and cigars. It has nothing whatsoever to do with flowers."

"This shop has a back way out. And in a few moments, a tour bus will stop here and flood this place with visitors."

"And your point?"

"We are being followed, tracked since we left Baker Street—don't turn around!"

"Followed? Surely you're joking. By whom?"

"The police, undoubtedly. Moriarty's men would be shabbier-dressed and better at their trade—I asked you not to turn around, Watson. Certainly they are not intent on arresting us, or they would have done so."

"Why would the police be interested in us? Do you think one of your men was arrested, and he talked?"

"My thoughts mirror yours, though I have other suspicions. That is why this shop—"

Watson frowned, and Holmes waved his hand dismissively. "All right then; have it your way."

The detective led the way at a fast pace, tapping the sidewalk with his ebony walking stick—*tick-tick-tick*, with Watson in tow. He stopped abruptly before the large window of Boxton's, one of the Strand's most venerated restaurants, and waved to an astonished man who sat at the window table. Amid Watson's feeble protests they entered the restaurant and passed the surprised maître d'. Holmes headed directly for the kitchen, removing his hat before plowing through the swinging doors. Watson did the same, just in time as they passed directly beneath a dangling roof of pots and pans. A line of surprised cooks looked over at them as they passed—someone shouted at them from behind—but too late. They burst out the back of the eating establishment, hats back on, walking rapidly south toward the river.

"In answer to your next question," said Holmes when he had slowed their pace, "I waved at the stranger at the window table knowing full well the police would think us joining a dinner appointment, and hanging back a while longer before sending in a scout than had we entered a flower shop. I must say, Watson, the bête noire of your sensibilities, aghast at all that is frilly, flowery, and frivolous, has purchased us ten minutes' head start!"

"To the embankment, then, Holmes? And from there, downriver—"

"I have an off feeling about this case, Watson. A sense of disquiet, of reluctance. The *Viceroy of India*, in this particular instance, might not be a necessary vehicle of time travel for us."

THE GOAT CREATURE

"Oh, what a dreadfully damp place!" exclaimed Watson. "I should rather venture to the Olympic by way of the Strand."[1]

They stood at the bank of the Thames River, Southwark side. The clouds had cleared, and the fading sunlight reflected murkily on the river's oily water, where broken barrel staves bobbed and scraped against the boat loaders.

"It was down this river that the iron beams were floated to the *Viceroy of India* for the building of the Needle's Eye," said Holmes, remembering. "Yes, and the delicate magnets with them. An old bloke from Skibbereen who helped build the Tower Subway, an expert in the binding together of iron girders—he followed Moriarty's drawings exactly and built the frame, while his young brother from Midland, an electric point engineer who wired Holdernesse as well St. Luke's, constructed the dynamo."

"The hole in your wall is now wallpapered over nicely," commented Watson, meaning the plastered hole between Holmes' sitting room and bedroom. "You would hardly notice the accident which nearly reduced our block of flats to smoldering ruins."

Across the water, Somerset House and further east, the Temple sat sullen in the Victoria Embankment's mist, aloof from the sooty cottages and smoky tar fires hemming in Holmes and Watson on the river wharf. Horse-drawn buses, hansoms, and four-wheelers rumbled across Waterloo Bridge above. Just that short elevation rendered it a world away.

"Holmes," Watson said lowly, "*Pseudomonas pseudomallei* must be rampant here! Do you not fear the resultant melioidosis?[2] Septicemia? I should rather be at Baker Street with my evening tea. Your accompanying cigar would be preferable to this stench."

Holmes answered without drawing his eyes away from the wharf. "Can you not sense it, Watson, the delectable undercurrent of malice's beating heart? Of enraged hatred the color of tannin, rising, falling, flowing, coursing? Tell me that you do not perceive sinister intrigue in the air."

"You feel entirely too much. And enjoy it too much. What I sense in this atmosphere would fit comfortably in Pepy's diary."

"Watson, my good, faithful, patient doctor, clearly you are in danger of losing these, your attributes." Sherlock Holmes' gaze did not waver, directed toward the bridge. "Do you remember the account of Moses confronting the magicians of Pharaoh? Darkness has its own magical wiles which imitate all too well the genuine article. And so with time-travel, for Evil may have its own effective means upon this two-way avenue."

"Why are you whispering, Holmes—?"

The detective motioned for silence. A crippled figure issued from the direction of the bridge, tall, gaunt, with a limping prance. "Be quite still, Watson. The world gathers its wings darker about us, and life's bustle is choked out in dreadful anticipation. If ever you valued your life, hold your tongue now."

The creature drew near. With shaggy fur, it walked upright on cloven hooves. It stared from a shimmering mask fashioned of burnished copper or bronze from which spiraled two gazelle-like horns. Eyes of alien yellow with black pupils shone from the twin slits as it strutted by unsteadily with a flickering tail. Watson pressed his handkerchief more firmly to his face, not against foul odors, but in horror, at a present loathing which consumed his senses. Holmes' icy stare tracked the goat-man as he passed. The detective fell in step well behind him, breathing *fallentis semita vitae*,[3] and signaled to his companion with his silver-bobbed walking stick. Watson reluctantly followed.

THE WASTELAND

Darkness dissolved into blistering light. The frostiness of night-time London yielded to intense heat. The doctor coughed through his handkerchief against a howling desert wind. Sand gritted in his teeth, and he hurriedly adjusted his top hat's brim lower to shield his eyes.

He stumbled blindly into Sherlock Holmes, standing tall and statuesque.

"Here stand I, and dressed in my favorite Shingleton[4] against this unforgiving climate," announced the detective. "This is the

Wicked Land, Watson, not the Valley of Jericho so touted by scholars as this trial's stage. Here the oracle of God falls heavily, a haunt of jackals, where the murderous Herods were bred, spawn of the Edomites."

"This heat, Holmes—it's nigh unto an oven!"

"Nevill's bathhouse without the steam, eh?"

In the distance an emaciated man sat propped up against a boulder; he cracked open his eyes as the goat creature came to stand over him. It lowered its face, its cruel-nailed fingers lifting its mask to reveal its leprous features, as removing a coffin's lid exposes all manner of writhing filth. Its toothless mouth gaped, the red tongue, wormlike, forming this challenge: "*If You are the Son of God, command this stone to become bread.*"[5]

"Ah! See the man there in direst need!" cried Watson. "See how pronounced are his cheekbones! Dehydration is unmistakably present—he should be brought in from the sun as soon as may be—not to mention the ever-present danger of plasmato-chemical imbalances—blood poisoning—and possible arrythmias! As a medical man, I must protest standing idly by—"

"All for naught, my good doctor. We cannot help the man. You remember the case of the adulterous woman—how our efforts went for naught? And with poor Zechariah? Besides, this man's condition is self-imposed. The Holy Spirit of God has led him here, and he has obeyed."

Watson fell speechless. Surely he had heard multitudes of sermons on this event in the life of the Lord. But yes, Holmes was correct: Christ was led into this awful situation by God's own Spirit.

Holmes continued. "Over the prone man looms the Archfiend; the Adversary; the Accuser. Do you not recognize him from books?

From your disturbed dreams? Abaddon, so named; Apollyon; Beelzebub; the Satan."

"Then, the man lying there—?" Watson choked back his earlier deliberations. "Can this be the Christ?"

"He has no lordly aspect. Remember your Scriptures. Especially in this present circumstance: forty days ago being baptized in the Jordan, and since, fasting here forty days in the wilderness."

The doctor's top hat nodded.

The wilted man struggled to open his parched lips, croaking an answer. *"It is written, 'Man shall not live by bread alone, but by every word of God.'"*[6]

The scene disappeared in a vortex of swirling sand. The wind whipped about Holmes and Watson and they hunched over, their coattails flapping like a ship's sails in a squall. When the tempest moderated, the Londoners found themselves atop a mountain peak. At their feet the whole world lay revealed, the kingdoms of man supernaturally displayed before them as if at a bazaar; the Roman Senate's marbled halls; the shimmering palace domes of the Persian lords at Persepolis; the gleaming white-pillared Parthenon; and the hidden treasure rooms of Queen Hatshepsut's temple at Thebes.

"See, Watson, how the goat creature gestures, offering Christ the splendor and authority of earth's marvels—if only he would worship him. But listen!"

They could just discern Jesus' response, a desperate prayer amidst the howling tempest: *"For it is written, 'You shall worship the* Lord *your God, and Him only you shall serve.'"*[7]

The storm descended again so violently that Watson and Holmes grabbed hold of one another. Holmes shouted something, but the shrieking wind carried all away. In the whirling wind Watson witnessed strange, airborne specters—horned creatures with elongated necks and limbs, with twitching fingers, dancing, twirling, laughing maniacally as if the elemental world hinged and creaked upon this momentous event, terrible in its consequence.

Like a curtain closing, the air fell silent and the sunlight returned.

The time-travelers, hidden intruders upon the scene, beheld two figures standing atop the temple. Satan, having cast aside his true form, stood robed in bejeweled finery. Beside him, Christ swayed side to side, weak, and barely conscious.

"We stand upon the loftiest point of Herod's temple wall," stated Holmes, "high upon the southeast colonnade which looms over the Kidron Valley."

Watson looked down over the edge into the rocky ravine, shivered, and felt the roof of his mouth tingle. "This is a terrible height," he whispered.

"But it is the temple, the Lord's house," quipped Holmes, "and Christ has been brought here to see if he will test the Father's love for him—a double insult."

"*If You are the Son of God,*" came a smooth, compassionate voice, "*throw Yourself down from here. For it is written: 'He shall give His angels charge over You, to keep You,' and 'In their hands they shall bear You up, lest You dash Your foot against a stone.'*"[8]

"*It has been said,*" Jesus answered, "*'You shall not tempt the* LORD *your God.'*"[9]

"Holmes! Look!" breathed the doctor.

Then Satan's image shimmered, expanded. Like a dark cloud, it hovered over the Savior, but a wind arose and carried him away over the valley. His form grasped at Christ even as it dissipated into the thin, crisp air. But this is not what had so amazed Watson, but rather the company of angels appearing all about the Lord, cajoling him, comforting him, attending him, lest he should fall and strike his foot against a stone.

AN OPPORTUNE TIME

Watson had stopped over each of the last three days, knocking on Holmes' apartment door. No answer. Strange. Three days. Three journeys of the sun through the sky since they returned to London, three squares in the calendar of "Watson the Physician" catching up on his practice, looking in on his patients, checking off the list with a pencil (often the same writing tool he had used to chronicle these recent scenes of Christ's temptation). Ever and always, however, a locked door had stared back at him.

No Sherlock Holmes.

Watson deliberated. This familiar feeling nudged him like an old friend seated with him at the same theater seeing the same play. Yes, this was precisely how he felt on his return from Scotland to find London's greatest detective missing. Had Holmes embarked on some fantastic journey by himself? Could it be Holmes, recalcitrant, diabolical Holmes—

And that is how the doctor came to be clopping hollowly across the deck planks of the *Viceroy of India*, having been discreetly rowed out to the ship from shore. He skipped down the stairs to the aft-saloon cabin, flung open the door, and strode in.

"Hello, Watson!"

There sat Holmes comfortably on the couch, grinning broadly. But surely Holmes' exuberant manner, his cheerful disposition, his boorish smile, were not what arrested Watson's attention. It was the knowledge that, except for the colorful cloth wrapped around his midsection, Holmes was stark naked.

"I must apologize for my appearance, and for the light which accentuates rather than underplays my delicate . . . situation. The broadening of sunlight in the room is due to my tearing down a curtain over the windows of the stern to wrap my—"

"I can see for myself. The sin laid against you is that you felt compelled to charge nobly off in the Time Traveler. Without me."

"Why so petulant, Watson? Just a little exploring. I spent two days readjusting the magic cube, and upon arriving in the past, I found my biblical garment to be of a lighter linen than the hot robes normally furnished for us by the Needle's Eye. But upon my rematerializing here, I found my clothes missing."

Watson brushed off a chair and lit a cigar, partly to kill the room's mustiness and partly to do something other than gawk at Sherlock Holmes' *ridicule võtement*.

"I was worried about you, Holmes, again. I stopped by now and again at Baker Street to see if you would turn up. You mustn't travel alone—it isn't safe." He looked down his nose at the detective, who smirked, waiting. Finally, Watson could hold it in no longer. "Where did the Needle's Eye transport you, after all? And where are your clothes?"

"While you puff away, I shall make an observation about the Needle's Eye and how it chooses to present us—yes, I know it's implying a bit much for a machine, Watson, an inanimate object. I do not know how the process of our wardrobe exchange takes place."

"Much less how these timely calling cards keep popping up—"

"Oh, Watson, may I draw from that cigar?"

As the doctor handed it over, Holmes winked and slipped him a small card the color of Guernsey cream. "Of course, you need not ask: that card showed up in the usual manner." The detective took a deep draw on the cigar and added, "If you notice, I used the word *exchanged* in reference to our wardrobe. For it seems that if I perchance lose my ancient garment which is supplied to me, there remains nothing with which I may barter on my return to the present. I come back without—well, you can see for yourself. In my case, the loss of my linen garment has cost me my finest broadcloth suit—as well as hat, shoes, handkerchief. They are lost forever! Or perhaps they may show up, magically, in an untidy pile on the battlefield between the contending Romans and Carthaginians!"

Holmes took another puff.

"As touching the location of our most recent foray into the past, there is a curious comment made by the good doctor at the end of his temptation account. (I do not mean you, Watson, but rather Luke, the physician.) It is the mystery's very crux."

Watson agreed. "I was speculating why the Time Traveler transported us to witness Christ's three temptations: from the desert to the mountaintop to the temple." He opened the card, upon which was written: "Luke 4:13—*Now when the devil had ended every temptation, he departed from Him until an opportune time.*"

"'*Until an opportune time*'? What an extraordinary summation! What circumstance could be more conducive than this for the Son of Man to be tempted? What time more opportune for the Son of Man to sin?"

"That is the mystery," stated Sherlock Holmes. "If Christ would not succumb during his temptation, then when? What could Luke possibly mean by *'an opportune time'*? Furthermore, when we find this more opportune time, we must show proof, not buttress our conclusion with hyperbole or supposition."

"You've not answered my question, Holmes. Where did the Needle's Eye whisk you away to? Was your solitary excursion a success? Have you solved the case?"

"Narcissus would sooner achieve the sun; Sisyphus, the summit with his Jovian burden." He took a long draw from the cigar. "In short, no. It seems a simple enough puzzle, yet nothing nudges me. I started down a rabbit trail, likening the first temptation in Eden, fruit acting as the bait, to Christ's first temptation with the bread. Christ's second trial in refusing the world's grandeur I paired with Job's reduction as the East's richest man. It didn't feel right. Didn't line up prettily, so to speak, and it must line up prettily. I also theorized that Christ accomplished in forty wilderness days what the Israelites couldn't in forty years, which sent me off on another hare's trail." Holmes blew two perfectly rounded smoke rings. "Think, Watson. What did we see in the wilderness? Dispense with all subtleties. Think in obvious terms. We saw two players on the stage: Christ and Satan."

"And the most obvious thing of all—temptation."

A ship's horn sounded in the distance to the faint chugging of an engine.

"What about suffering?" Holmes tapped the side of his Roman nose with his forefinger.

"What about returning my cigar?"

"Certainly suffering is more visible than temptation. Suffering gave Christ's temptation more vigor. Perhaps suffering must always be present if the temptation is genuine, or at least must come as the result of it."[10]

Watson nodded. "Not to mention weakness.[11] Satan waits until the end of the forty days before approaching Christ, when he is weakest."

"Very good, Watson. Suffering, temptation, and weakness. These three will serve as signposts in our search for the *more opportune time*."

"So, when does Satan come at Christ again? Through Peter, certainly, when the apostle tells him he must not go to the cross. Through Judas, most assuredly. But no suffering accompanies those encounters. No weakness. Therefore, no real temptation. What about Gethsemane? There is a real possibility."

"No," Holmes said with a knowing grin, "I should say not." He handed back the cigar and readjusted his sheet to cover his chest as well. "Fascinatingly, we followed the devil directly from the pier into the past—not by way of the Needle's Eye. Satan is alive and well in London."

"Yes," mused Watson grimly. "He's alive and well everywhere."

LEICESTER LOUNGE, LONDON

Sherlock Holmes, fully clothed, sat within a thick booth in a secluded corner at the Leicester Lounge. His tankard before him held a diabolical potation somewhere on the other side of ale, and although after a few sips it had lost status as the object of his focus, still it remained a necessary prop for deep thinking.

"It haunts me," said the doctor, sitting across from him.

"How much more unlike deity could our Savior appear? So shabby and worn!"

"And yet there is another instance in which he must," Holmes breathed.

"Could the temptation in the wilderness be the first act, and Luke's strange statement pointing to some mysterious second half?" Watson took a drink, his eyes glinting over the rim of the tankard. "By the way, you never explained where you went in the Needle's Eye, and your . . . appearance upon your return."

"Gethsemane: that is where the Needle's Eye landed me—amazing! I witnessed Christ's agonizing prayer, oh!—and Peter cutting off Malchus's ear. A handy fellow, Simon, with a sword. But in Gethsemane I perceived no link with Christ's tempta-tion, nor could I say Christ suffered more, even as Satan, through Judas, betrayed him. My fault came in approaching too closely!"

"Come again—?"

"And in so doing, I exposed myself—in more ways than one. Christ's disciples suddenly scattered. I ran with them, Watson, like I have never run before! A group of disputatious fellows—unkind spectators—set upon me like a pack of hyenas! I struggled mightily with them (I was without my walking stick), and while tearing myself from their grasp, my superb tunic was ripped from my body."[12]

Ale spewed out of Watson's nose, ending in a cough and a rough laugh.

"Amuse yourself, Doctor. The Needle's Eye has a sense of humor not unlike yours, for it would not bring me back directly. For two full days and nights thereafter, I pranced about the gar-den, darting from hedgerow to bush, from bush to thicket, in such an exposed condition. An incident arose wherein I caused no little consternation and panic—involving a group of elderly women shouldering large baskets of olives. You've heard the phrase 'spilling the beans'? Well . . ."

"Ha, ha, ha! White as a sheep—and bleating like one too!"

Holmes had told the story in good humor, expecting some measure of ridicule. A man reappearing from the past completely naked must own up to a few lumps. However, even for Holmes' generous nature, Watson was enjoying himself a smidgen too much.

"But let us analyze Christ's temptation," went on Holmes curtly. "Satan posits three questions. In so doing, he questions Christ's credibility, no, his very identity each time—*If you are the Son of God . . .* Each time Christ responds from his center, from who he really is, and quotes from the Old Testament—"

"From the book of Deuteronomy,"[13] said Watson, drying his eyes. "The encouragement is this: If I'm tempted, I need to remember who I am in Christ, but I must also memorize my Bible. If Jesus himself quoted the Scriptures, I should be prepared to do the same. Otherwise I am doomed to succumbing."

"I've never considered Scripture in such a light," replied Holmes, and coughed lightly. "It has always struck me as a cold, removed thing."

"But it has power to combat the devil," mused Watson. "Maybe you should put a few verses to memory, Holmes—clothe yourself in the Scriptures—ha, ha, ha!"

"Very good, Watson," he responded drolly. "I am tired for this evening. All the verses run together in my head like disobedient locomotives, crashing headlong."

"Maybe you're on the wrong track, old man, ha, ha, ha!"

The detective winced. Pulled at his collar. Sniffed.

"What's got you so put off, Holmes?"

"Besides your unsuppressed, yokel humor?" he asked. But with a wry smile, he confided, "Oh, what a shabby fellow Saint Luke is— an opportune time, indeed! Why couldn't he have left off teasing us and ended his temptation narrative a half sentence before?"

"And deprive us of this delectable riddle?" chuckled the doctor.

"I am fascinated with the nature of the devil's attacks and the scriptures chosen by the Lord to parry them," stated Holmes in that characteristically reflective look suggesting that the pub about him had disappeared, the diners, the plates, forks, glasses, lanterns, and Watson with it, leaving him alone to synthesize his thoughts. "First, Satan charges him to change stones into bread. Now, what can be wrong with that?"

"It's making me hungry—"

"Only that Jesus' hunger and thirst were part of God's plan for his life at this time. Satan wanted him to take the easy way out of his situation. But Jesus quotes from Deuteronomy 8:3 where Moses had explained to the Israelites that God had led them into the desert to humble them, and satisfying their hunger with manna from heaven, teaching them that 'man shall not live by bread alone.'[14] Satan was doubly deceived—wasn't he, Holmes?—to think he might demand Jesus to do anything, much less demanding him to coax bread from stones. Christ would later ask his disciples: 'Or what man is there among you who, if his son asks for bread, will give him a stone?'[15] But the Father *had* given his son a stone. Why would Jesus ask for bread?"

"Well put, Watson. And then Satan stages his next temptation on the mountaintop by appealing to vanity and the lust of the eyes—to tempt Jesus to switch his allegiances. In short, he wanted Christ to worship him.[16]

"But Christ's answer is short and focused, a brilliant response from an emaciated man—oh, Watson! Do stop your fidgeting! You should attempt the beef and kidney pie. Kickshaws are to your taste; are they not? Made dishes?"

"But what of the final temptation atop the temple, Holmes?" asked Watson. "It is that which makes me squirm."

"In suggesting Jesus jump from the temple's high point, Satan tempts Jesus to demonstrate he is God's Son by having the Father act in a dramatic way to save him. The devil even quotes Psalm 91 to bolster his claim that God would keep him from harm. But this would force God to do what the Son wanted, not the other way around. This would put God to the test, which was Jesus' curt reply.[17]

"A rather odd and direct way of going at Christ," commented Watson.

"Yes, indeed. This last temptation seems to me a rather weak summing up of things for the devil, suggesting to me that he was the one losing steam; he was the one succumbing to weariness; Christ was wearing him down, for the devil's sustenance is derived from weakness, vacillation, surrender."

"Speaking of suffering and an opportune time," spoke up Watson, "I am in dire need of relief! Does this pub have a lavatory?"

"Of course."

"Do you know where it is?"

"Yes," Holmes said simply.

"Can you tell me where it is?"

"I can."

"Are you going to tell me?"

"It depends."

"On what?"

"If you ask me."

"This teasing does you no credit, Holmes."

"Hitting back with a little humor of my own, Watson, be it ever so adolescent as yours. Besides, you broke my line of thought. My imagination is the fuse awaiting the flame; attuned to the off-whisper; glancing for the gleam of gold in the grotto."

A burly waitress, wearing a wimple and an apron the size of a flag, sashayed up to the table, tapping it with a ladle. She said, "Delicacies abound 'ere at the Leicester, gennelmen."

"Perhaps she qualifies?" said Watson under his breath, eyeing Holmes.

"I am not averse to digging for troves among the common lot," he said discreetly. "After all, the Leicester Lounge is not San Sebastián."

"Something light," said Watson, addressing her, "rather like a tomato soup?"

"Superb choice," the detective chimed in, "perhaps tinged with *allium sativum*, the Akkadian *šūmu*? Garlic, I mean, with the hint of cucumber, onion, sherry vinegar?"

"We'ms got as such, zur. *Gazpacho*, as says the Spanish; *potague au tomate*, the Frogs. And the Germans—"

"Do you hear her, Holmes?" laughed the doctor. "Three languages!"

Holmes looked narrowly at her. "A sailor's wife?"

"No, but I worked the Admiral's Alehouse, did I, down Portsmouth way, zur," she said, blushing. "Learned me French, Portuguese, German, not counting genteel-like English."

"Impressive!" beamed Watson.

"From down Grimpen Mire way, am I," she explained, as if to give greater celebrity to her accomplishment. "Fernworthy, speaking exactly specific, zur."

Holmes stood up violently and knocked over his tankard. The pub grew deathly quiet, Holmes' ale dripping from the table onto the floor. It was then that Watson saw it in the detective's face, the contorted features just short of madness, the massive brain making connections of fact and coincidence faster than the eye could blink.

"Aha!" he shouted explosively, with the violence of an iron ball being fired from a cannon.

London's greatest detective studied the woman, her rounded features, her missing and misshapen teeth, her scraggly bangs. Monomaniacal humor lit up in his eyes and traveled, by way of an alarming smile, across his face, and he came to stand over her. She cried out like a frightened cat until she caught sight of a golden guinea twirling in his fingers. This he placed in her open palm, leaned down, and gave her a smacking kiss on the cheek.

"Holmes! What's gotten into you? Everyone is looking at us!"

"The riddle, Watson. Don't you see? She's given us the answer!"

"Splendid," Watson replied tepidly. "But might I inquire: Where, after all, is the lavatory?"

The Number Three

Sherlock Holmes stood before his familiar Bible, turning the mammoth pages, while Watson peeked over his shoulder.

"I owe you an apology, Doctor," Holmes said, puffing on his pipe.

"Yes, that in my presence you gave the waitress one of my three gold guineas from our Zechariah wager?"

"No, rather you rightly concluded that the first temptation

must have its counterpart, its bookend, somewhere else in Scripture. Insightful, and yet I ignored you. But have you not perceived the substantive pattern of our puzzle? It centers on the number three. First, I asked myself, when would Christ be weaker than when he was tempted? When would he suffer even more?"

Watson followed his finger trailing down to a passage and stopped.

"The crucifixion. Of course!" Watson exclaimed. "All the world's sin descended upon Christ. For the first time in eternity, the Father turned his back upon the Son. Add to that the cross's enormous, excruciating pain; the nails; the crown of thorns; the shame! But how can we be certain this is the event that Luke was referring to—the more opportune time?"

"Listen for the same pattern of three in the crucifixion which we saw in the wilderness." Holmes took a deep breath to read the entire passage, but Watson waved an impetuous hand, leaned over the Bible, and read the text silently, for himself:

And when they had come to the place called Calvary, there they crucified Him, and the criminals, one on the right hand and the other on the left. Then Jesus said, "Father, forgive them, for they do not know what they do."

And they divided His garments and cast lots. And the people stood looking on. But even the rulers with them sneered, saying, "He saved others; let Him save Himself if He is the Christ, the chosen of God."

The soldiers also mocked Him, coming and offering Him sour wine, and saying, "If You are the King of the Jews, save Yourself."

And an inscription also was written over Him in letters of Greek, Latin, and Hebrew:

THIS IS THE KING OF THE JEWS.

Then one of the criminals who were hanged blasphemed Him saying, "If You are the Christ, save Yourself and us."[18]

"Yes—I see it, Holmes! Three times Christ is challenged to come down from the cross just as Satan challenged him during the Temptation: first, in verse 35, by the people gathered there. Second, in verse 37, by the Roman soldiers. Third, in verse 39, by one of the criminals crucified next to him. Such scurvy treatment!"

Holmes flared his nostrils, exhaled a cloud of pipe smoke.

Watson continued. "Each time Christ's identity is called into question, just as Satan did in the wasteland—'If you are the King of the Jews'; 'If you are the Christ!' But Holmes, something is missing: Christ's response to his attackers must be the same as to the devil in the wilderness. But I suppose I am stretching the analogy too much."

"Not at all, Doctor. Rather, I am impressed by your eye for detail. In fact, if the three attacks against Christ were the only link to his temptation, I'd not have considered them. Luke's narrative contains a verse you skipped over entirely. But I cannot be impatient with you, my faithful chronicler, for I had glossed over it myself. It was the effervescent gushing and bragging of our waitress which sufficiently jolted my lugubrious memory.

'And an inscription also was written over Him in letters of Greek, Latin, and Hebrew:

THIS IS THE KING OF THE JEWS.'

"You see, Watson? Each of Christ's three tempters was rebuffed by the written notice which hung over his head: JESUS OF NAZARETH, THE KING OF THE JEWS. The Jews requested Pilate reword it, but in typical Roman indifference, he refused, ha! Oh, but the Jews knew the title was tantamount to a claim: *I, Jesus, am your king!* Everyone could understand it (Satan in all his disguises was confronted with it and could go no further) written in Hebrew (Aramaic) for the Jews; Greek for the Gentiles; Latin for the Roman soldiers. The message atop the cross countered Christ's devilish assailants just as he did in the wilderness: It is written! It is written! It is written!"

"Phenomenal," Watson said, rubbing his forehead as if trying to massage the amazing evidence into his brain.

Holmes' smile broke the surface for a split second. "As I mentioned, our waitress unwittingly awakened this scripture from the deep recesses of my memory by mention of *three languages.* Jilted my muddled thoughts enough to piece the thing together. Well worth a guinea—"

"My guinea."

"And to think I nearly spoiled her outburst with my ill-timed recital of Latin and Akkadian."

Watson seated himself before the fireplace. He sighed. "I cannot celebrate. To actually see the Christ again is a blessing I never dreamed of. But to witness him not only so meanly treated but murdered—and by the religious authorities, no less—is unbelievable."

"That Jesus is the only true God is difficult enough for man to swallow," said Holmes contemplatively. "But that he is the only true man is intolerable. That God should out-pace us as God is disagreeable but comprehendible, and our pride allows for it.

But that God should out-man us as man, we cannot and will not endure it."

"I will never dispel it from my memory—the awful temptation in the desert. The cross and all its cruelties. Are you not moved?"

"It is a case, Watson, a mystery: singular in its aspect, yet only a matter of facts laid out, of cerebral deductions set in a row. A vigorous rational exercise unadorned, and despite your efforts by emotional illuminations, empty of all else."

"Have you not found the source of your emptiness? Unlike the Samaritan woman,[19] have you left the well, unsatisfied?"

"Perhaps the well was dry to begin with. Or dry for me, anyway. Or perhaps there really is no well to begin with, or perhaps I am not nearly as unfilled as I seem. Or I am as filled as I will ever be."

"You have a healthy cynicism. Robust, even." The doctor shook his head. "You lack faith, Holmes."

"Oh, Watson, you're so heavenly minded you're no earthly good. I will not jump out of the window, expecting God to catch me."

"Nor did Christ atop the temple." Watson stood up, his back to the fireplace. "That is not faith, as you are well aware—a timid, childish prank on your part. Faith is not acting *despite* the evidence but *because of* the evidence. Might I add, you are never as acrimonious as when you smoke that particular pipe!"

"No, Watson, *you* are never so acrimonious as when I smoke this particular pipe."

Watson would not be sidetracked by humor. "The point I am anxious to make, Holmes, is this: real faith has substance. It has evidence. Faith is acting on what we know to be true about God."

"And preaching is what you are doing now."

"But are you not moved by the Temptation? Or has Reade[20] so conditioned your morality? Captured your common sense? Not only your objectivity but your heart? Can you not believe in the martyrdom of God—?"

"Respect is due Christ; there can be no argument. Though he was far weaker and suffered far more on the cross than in the wilderness—oh, Watson!—Christ was somehow the stronger for it. Certainly it is the cross Luke intimated, the more opportune time for the devil. And yet, there was present no white-knuckled panic, no excruciating anxiety that God's master plan would fail. No, if anything, Christ held even more fast. And the manner in which he responded from the cross to his murderers, his haters—"

"In love, surely."

"Remarkable love," stated Sherlock Holmes, and tapped his pipe's amber mouthpiece against his lapel. "Unfathomable really—for to quote Donne: '*Si scirem quid Deus esset, Dues essem.*' (*If I knew what God was, I should be God*)."[21]

Watson sat forward. "Speaking as a medical man, I marvel at what I witnessed at Calvary. Amidst the torture of separation with his Father and of bearing the weight of our sins, Christ gave up his soul in his own timing: death could not command it, nor hail his soul away. Nor was he concerned to outlast the two thieves on the cross, as if a mere show of endurance could add to the cross's wonderment. Rather, he died well before them. Indeed, no one ever died in the presence of Jesus. The moment the requirements of his Father were met, Christ bowed his head in reverence to him and gave up his soul voluntarily in an act of his will: '*Father, "into Your hands I commit My spirit.*'"[22]

The doctor sniffled into a handkerchief. "But had the Father utterly forsaken him, Holmes? Truly? Even in this, Christ's most agonizing hour of dejection and separation with God, the Father gives his son the gracious gift of a child. Through his pain and darkness, Christ hears a small voice: *'Lord, remember me when You come into Your kingdom.'*[23] The thief, a most wretched representative of mankind, reminds our lonely savior of his mission and dispels what little of the hopelessness and doubt which had begun to creep into Christ's divine soul [God, forgive by reckless speech!]. And how could the thief, condemned and strung up for dead, know that in this, earth's most evil hour, at the hour of his own death, that the Father would appoint him to breathe comfort into the savior of the world? To bestow upon him the honor of suffering with his son, of rejoicing even as his legs were broken to know his savior had already hastened away *for him*, to prepare him a place? That he, a lowly criminal, would be counted the first of a multitude of thieves and murderers and prostitutes to follow Christ—of kings and queens and earls and dukes, the forgiven of God in paradise?"

Watson stopped short. The look on the sleuth's face was transcendent, as if the room, indeed, the whole of London had been supplanted by the singular image of the cross, haunting in its terrible efficacy.

"As I stood on Golgotha," said Holmes in a hushed tone, "a question formed in my mind: *'Is it nothing to you, all you who pass by?'*[23] Only now do I remember that it came from the book of Lamentations; for never was there a more lamentable event in all of history, never was mankind at his lowest than when he nailed Jesus to the cross."

After a moment Holmes rose, feeling his way across the room, as if dreaming. He gripped his bow, paused, and then laid his violin beneath his chin. He faced the wall so that his face could not be seen, and to Watson's mind, played the most lonely, the most sorrowful piece he had ever heard.

PAIN, LOCKS, AND ROMANS

Pain.

It is commonly held that pain (the excitation of nociceptive neurons) is simply the overstimulation of the sense of touch.

But this is not so.

Pain and touch, at the neurological level, use unique peripheral sensory receptors (first-order neurons) to transmit their surface signals to the brain along the spinal cord's anterolateral system.

Pain.

People assume that signals of pain, the body's frontline warning system, are beamed fastest to the brain.

But this is not so.

Though neurons coated in myelin travel the quickest to the brain, signals associated with sharp or intense pain, called A-delta fibers, are but mildly myelinated and travel, on the neurological spectrum, relatively slowly.

Pain.

Before modern scientific techniques in the experimentation and evaluation of pain, people believed the power of expectation had no effect on the pain experienced.

But this is not so.

The "cognitive set," or a person's expectation of pain, changes the way the brain processes stimuli. A subject's anticipation of pain makes the realization of it far more dramatic.

PHILIPPI: THE TOWN SQUARE

The Philippian magistrates, gathered in their ancient town square, were men holding to the old-world notion that a flogging was a flogging, that the anticipation of such in no way heightened the actual experience. And as Dr. John Watson's arms were tied around a thick, vertical post and his robe yanked down by the collar, exposing his bare back, he watched the shadow of a flying bird wavering along the ground, only to be swallowed up in the larger shadow of a Roman soldier readying his whip. The thin skin over his shoulder blades twitched. His breathing increased. His brow began to sweat.

His brain was on high alert.

Holmes had intimated that something like this would never happen, and the part of Watson's brain left to process rational thought, agreed. The fact that they were dressed in biblical garb, that they could be seen and therefore, apprehended, had always played at the fringes of Watson's fears, but he had reasoned that the gap in time somehow shielded them, that because they were not naturally of this time—

The whirring of leather thongs through the air brought him out of his deliberations. He heard the slap, felt the sharp bite of metal tips into his flesh. There was a split second delay, like the sea pausing before gathering itself and crashing angrily on shore, before the locomotive of pain plowed through Watson's head.

Before the second blow fell, anguish had supplanted antici-pation. Watson gasped a breath when the crack of leather sounded again and a new surge of pain jolted him, seared hotly around him, allowing only a tortured moan to explode through his clenched teeth. His sunlit world fragmented into a kaleido-scope of raw, searing pieces as the pain rushed to the front of his brain, usurping all else. His knees wobbled, and he swayed. Numbing walls closed around him as a wave of nausea washed over him.

A third blow never fell. Watson found himself leaning heav-ily against the whipping post like the rough, wooden mast of a ship. The borders of his pain slowly yielded to a sound, but not the crack of a whip. Someone called out. Watson felt the crowd gather around him. He could breathe now, barely, in shuttered gasps, and felt his wrists being loosed. His lip hurt where he had slammed his mouth against the post.

He staggered free and leaned against something soft and yield-ing. Felt a strong arm encircle him, support him. He smelled stale pipe smoke carried along by the quiet, urgent voice of Holmes. "Watson, my dear, dear fellow, can you stand? Lean against me—I must help you out of here!"

JAIL

Locks.

Some people assume locksmithing is a relatively new craft, while others, congratulating themselves on a firmer grip of his-tory, speculate it began in the Middle Ages.

But this is not so.

Locking devices, with their accompanying keys, were known as far back as ancient Nineveh and predated the pyramids in Egypt.

Locks.

One might presume ancient locks were crude, unsophisticated, and therefore, somewhat ineffective.

But this is not so.

Egyptian locks, as with their Roman counterparts, employed an array of tumblers requiring intricate keys—an efficient model which modern locks still emulate. In some cases, to unlock a door from the inside necessitated reaching into a hollow in the door and inserting a large wooden key having projecting pins which matched the bolt's tumblers, which, when lifted, freed the bolt to be drawn back to open the door.

Locks.

Even if they were effective, believe some, ancient locks were clumsy, dull, and unattractive.

But this is not so.

Some locks were fashioned from iron or bronze and richly inlaid with pearl, gold, and silver, with elaborate etching and scrolling. Roman keys could be fashionably small, tiny enough to wear as a finger ring. Greek keys might be as large and thin as a farmer's sickle, which doubled as a weapon against would-be trespassers.

Philippi: The Jail

The ponderous parchment moon rose over the city wall.

Holmes whispered, "I'm sorry, Watson. Too late did the city proconsuls realize they had arrested the wrong pair of men." The two time-travelers stood before the door of a stone structure, silver in the moonlight. Watson could barely make out Holmes' face as he inserted and twisted a wire-thin piece of metal into a small hole. "As they began to whip you (and were about to string me to the grating), soldiers arrived with two other men in custody—the pair for which they'd mistaken us. They flogged them unmercifully—a gruesome spectacle—and threw them inside this building. More dead than alive."

"How are you coming with that lock?"

"The keys of heaven and hell which Christ gave Saint Peter—I could make use of one of those. But we're in luck. This particular lock is not a cumbersome bolt-slider—a gaping hole requiring a substantial key—but rather, a warded lock,[1] a Roman trademark."

"So, we are in ancient Philippi after all."

"Indeed."

"And we are resolved to breaking into this jail?"

"Indeed."

"The two men who were flogged—are we rescuing them?"

"Indeed."

"So, when we are caught, I shall be flogged again—legitimately this time—yes, I know your answer: indeed."

An impatient twitch in Holmes' cheek, which Watson could detect even in the moonlight, as well as an accompanying huff, advised him to leave off questioning. He placed his hot, lacerated back against the stone wall, felt the cold spread over his wounds, and sighed.

"In the absence of our client's calling card," mumbled Holmes as he probed the lock, a spare picking wire protruding from between his lips, "as to why we were transported to New Testament Philippi, I must assume it is to contact these two men—"

Click!—a soft but satisfying sound. Holmes grinned and

almost petted the lock. He pulled the door open, and warm, humid air hit them in the face. Their feet clattered down a stone staircase where a faint glow emanated. The damp walls hemmed them in—like a corridor leading to burial vaults.

The stairs ended. Light danced on the pavement from the torchlight, the walls to either side pocketed with doors. Watson heard it: faint moaning and cursing. They happened upon an open room. An ugly, squat man slumped over a table, asleep. He was dressed in a leather jerkin and leggings, with a dagger thrust in his belt.

The jailer.

Watson heard something odd, something that didn't fit the backdrop of misery.

Singing.

As he and Holmes followed the wall's curvature, he perceived the melody came from the innermost cell. A small shadow scuttled across the passageway, a rat passing inward—and the two Londoners followed. Watson couldn't see in the blackness at first, but he felt the chill of cold water seep into his boots, smelled the dank dampness of human sweat and filth. He stopped at a door, looked inside the cell. As his eyes adjusted, he saw two men sitting in the center, their feet set wide apart in the stocks. One of them yelped as the rat rose up and bit him savagely on the foot. But still they sang on.

"I could imagine us amongst the foundations of the Metropolitan Police building," said Holmes coming back to him.

"But the police would not allow for singing, surely, nor such a beating," said Watson, indicating the lacerations on the men's backs, grotesque and ugly in the dimness. He felt his back tighten.

"Theirs amounts to a hymn, ancient in form, but I cannot make out the words. Do you have an opinion?"

"Given that we are in Philippi, the two singing prisoners can be none other than Paul and Silas," replied Watson. "They were flogged together and occupy the jail's inner chamber just as the Scriptures profess, their feet bound in stocks. The jailer whom we saw bears the *machaira*, the Roman short sword."

"I'm awed by you, Watson."

"The scene is famously biblical. I'm surprised that you're surprised."

Watson stopped short. The ground began quivering. The rat scampered away. What started as a shimmering in the floor, in the walls, in the ceiling, increased with such fervor that the lone stool in the cell overturned. The wall chains dangled idly, dancing and clinking like black skeletons. Stones and pebbles on the floor skipped and shimmied over the pounding floor.

"Holmes!"

The detective followed Watson's gesture. The prisoner's stocks had shattered, and the cell door was violently thrown open with a resounding clang! The two prisoners staggered out, for the whole building rocked like a doomed ship. With a rumble, the near wall collapsed in a heap of tumbling stones.

"Stop there!" came a gruff shout.

The jailer!

Sherlock Holmes fled up the dust-clouded staircase, with Watson fast on his heels. The doctor had just caught the scent of fresh night air when an alarm went off in his head, the part trained in the Indian Wars, a mental partition linked so sensitively to self-survival that it detected a soft whistling, a tremor on the edge of his awareness. Watson didn't stop to ponder the sound, to think of the implications. He ducked. The whine passed just over his neck, followed by a dull thud. A dagger's hilt quivered in the doorpost near his head.

Philippi: The Escape

With the pitter of hooves in the darkness, the little wooden cart made its way along the road leading out of Philippi. The detective and doctor towered monstrously over their pitifully small cart and pony, which plodded along, patiently pulling them around blocks of stone from fallen pillars and archways. The inhabitants, stumbling out of their houses in the semidarkness, were too dazed from the earthquake to notice.

The main gate tottered drunkenly, and honked as Holmes got down and pushed it open. "Say!" Watson urged the pony onward with the whispered word—the small whip mounted near him stayed in its place. It seemed comical, and besides, Watson had acquired quite an aversion to whips of any size.

The Macedonian countryside opened up before them, the hills lying silent beneath the rising moon. Still the pony panted along the Roman road, Philippi falling away behind them with agonizing slowness. A long straightaway opened up before them, and the cart whined and groaned as if it would burst apart at any moment. At a rise in the road, Watson glanced back over his shoulder once or twice. The third time, at the sound of a distant trumpet, he gestured in alarm. In the distance galloped a regiment of horsemen.

The cart would go no faster—no amount of goading might make it so. Every lurch in the road slowed them dramatically, the clumsy wooden wheels creaking and protesting, sounding as if at any moment they might roll away or that axle might snap in two.

Watson perked his ears. Heavy galloping. The clinking of harness. These had just become discernible when Watson stopped the cart.

"Quickly!" urged Holmes.

The Londoners scrambled off. Up an ugly hill with a rock formation resembling a grumpy old man, they picked their way. Watson reached the crest first, completely winded, and looked below. The soldiers—he could see the dim glitter of their swords and spears in the moonlight—had already dismounted at the cart. With a shout they began clambering double-time up the slope.

"This way!" panted Holmes as he ran past him and grabbed him by the sleeve and propelled him into the old man's left eye. Rasping, gasping for air in the darkness, Watson pressed back against the cave's wall, and his lacerated back itched and twitched.

He could hear the soldiers now, jostling up the steep crags, sounding like an entire regiment. How had they responded so quickly to the town bells? Then it dawned on him: these were legionaries, men who even after retirement to the country would react quickly in an emergency—even out of a dead sleep. Holmes, following the same track of logic, said, "See their horses below, lacking bridles or cover blankets. And the soldiers have no spears or shields, only their quick, handy swords."

The first soldier reached the cave's entrance, weapon drawn, and locked eyes with Watson. The doctor remembered all too well that crooked nose, the simpering mouth—the same swarthy soldier who laid the cat to his back. Those same maniacal eyes grinned eagerly at him, now, as the man ran his thumb along his blade. Searing pain lanced across Watson's back as his cognitive set kicked in. No doubt the brute relished finishing the punishment previously deprived him. But his face went blank as he saw Watson's face begin to glow—like a god's.

"Say good-bye to the nice soldier," he heard Holmes say, even as the cave filled with shafts of light. Watson found himself rejoicing as the world dissolved into a flood of electric blue. The soldier would have the devil explaining *this* to his commanding officer.

What's in a Game?

"Mrs. Hudson, how fares the good doctor?" Sherlock Holmes, dressed in a finely tailored suit, draped one leg over the arm of his fireside chair. "Is he much discomfited from the whip?"

The landlady ignored him, and confined her reply to a curt movement of her lips. But presently she found her voice. "My great-uncle sailed as warrant officer aboard HMS *Colossus*, and he dished out such beatings, as I can tell you. The Lord repay you, Mr. Holmes, in the same coin as what my Dr. Watson got."

Watson lay on his stomach and grinned, enjoying the attention his bare back received at her gentle hands, not to mention the upbraiding his friend was experiencing by her not-so-gentle tongue. "*My* Dr. Watson," she had said. Now, that was pleasant, to be sure.

Holmes waved a copy of the *Standard* and rattled open the newspaper. "See here—an article on the chess grandmasters, Tchigorin and Teichmann."

"They played matches here in London," said Watson, with a wince, not really listening. "In 1883."

"In 1899," Holmes corrected, tracing the page with his pipe's stem. "Here's a sample game—what a novelty! They say the Two Knights' Defense is a popular, extensively analyzed opening, already known by Greco,[2] here, employed by Teichmann. Presumably he is playing the black pieces. He lost in twenty-eight moves."

Holmes tapped his empty pipe on his knee. He shot out of his chair and rummaged through a wall bureau, opening and closing index drawers, pulling out and scattering papers on the floor.

"A pox on you, Mr. Holmes," said Mrs. Hudson, "and fie on your mess!"

"Ah! Here we are!" he cried triumphantly, and held forth a large folder. He shot a disconcerting look at the breakfast table and said, "Mrs. Hudson!" and when she faced him, exclaimed, "Can you not clear this mess?"

"The clutter atop the table or beneath it?" she grumbled. She got up from attending the doctor; she stacked plates and stacked cups and stacked the saucers on a side tray. She laid the silverware beside them and pulled up the tray just in time as Holmes, in its place, unfolded a large map of Eastern Europe during Paul's time.

"The world, as God sees it!" Holmes waved his hand over the map's surface. "Like a great grandmaster—all the pieces in full view upon the board."

Watson sat up. "Why the map? Did you finally receive it?"

Holmes smiled, twirling a cream-colored card between his index and middle finger. "*Why was Paul's Macedonian campaign begun in Philippi?* I presume the question can be rephrased like this: Why did Paul start his second missionary journey in a city so dangerous that he almost got himself killed? That is the question we must divine."

"With only a map?" Watson retorted. "Harder than pulling teeth."

"When you're my age, pulling teeth isn't so difficult," the landlady said under her breath, and grumbling, left the room.

"Macedonia is a large province. Why didn't Paul start preaching in a safe place—in Larissa, in Berea, in Pella? Watson, your entire back is a crisscrossed mess—can you contribute?"

Watson stood painfully. Circled the table. Tapped the map. "Well, I have read the whole of Acts chapter 16. We can trace Paul's entire journey. In Troas, here, on the Aegean Sea's east coast, Paul has a vision of a man crying, 'Come over to Macedonia and help us!' He sets out for Philippi with Silas, Timothy, and Luke. By God's command, really."

"You're just moving the difficulty back one stage. Why did God call Paul to begin his missionary journey in Philippi?"

Watson rumbled on, half to himself. "Once in Philippi, they begin preaching and make acquaintance with Lydia, a prominent woman dealing in purple cloth. One day on their way to prayer, a fortune-teller girl begins following them, announcing, '*These men are the servants of the Most High God, who proclaim to us the way of salvation.*'³ Paul becomes so troubled, he casts the evil spirit out of her. Her ability to tell the future vanishes: her owners are livid and begin a search for Paul and Silas. They lay hands on us instead, drag us before the authorities (have me whipped twice until they realized their error), beat Paul and Silas, and throw them into jail, where we found them singing."

"Be so good as to answer the question, Watson. Philippi was a principal city in Macedonia, but wouldn't Thessalonica have been a far better starting point? Or Athens? Corinth? See here—sailing a straight line west across the Aegean Sea would land them well south of Berea."

Holmes idly picked up a test tube and held it up to the light, eyeing the dried crustiness within, and said: "Romans. People think Romans coexisted in relative peace within the Empire while the legions warred on the frontiers. But this is not so."

Holmes placed an open, important-looking book on the table and tapped it with his pipe stem. "Perhaps history can tell us what maps cannot."

Watson shrugged.

"In 42 BC," announced Holmes, "Octavian and Antony combined forces to crush the armies of Brutus and Cassius, assassins of Julius Caesar. Where? At Philippi in Macedonia. In celebration, it was made a Roman colony—*Colonia Iulia*. This entitled the Philippians to the rights granted those who lived in the cities of Italy."

Watson returned to the divan, content to watch him march back and forth. Suddenly Holmes stopped, looked off into the far corner of the room, and stated: "Romans. People think they were all of a type—a homogenous horde sharing the same privileged customs, language, and homeland. But this is not so. Eleven years later, Octavian (later Augustus) defeated Antony and Cleopatra. Ah!—Philippi would receive a settlement of Italian nobility from the mainland who, as a consequence of favoring Antony, had been forced to hand over their land as a reward to Octavian's loyal soldiers."

Holmes finally packed and lit his pipe, tired of its use as only a prop.

"Romans. People believe Romans were ruthless in putting

down rebellions, swift as Imperial eagles to smash any opposition from disparate groups. But this is not so—or not generally so. Octavian didn't slaughter rebellious Roman soldiers as traitors.[4] Fundamental in his thinking was image: his and Rome's. And a strong army. His 'Italic right' grant (*ius Italicum*) was most valuable to the Philippian colonists, who enjoyed the same privileges as if their land were Italian soil. Some Philippians, therefore, were former Italian royalty (which explains Lydia's dealing in purple cloth) as well as the sons of former legionnaires. The Roman magistrates living there were attended by a body of lictors, so-called, carrying rods and axes, symbols of the magistrate's capital powers. These lectors were Philippi's police force. So, Philippi was first and foremost a military city, a garrison, a purely Roman city amongst Greeks. Their civic pride permeates the passage in Acts 16."

"So, a legion was garrisoned there?"

Holmes shook his head. "Under Claudius, the nearest legions were stationed far to the north, in Moesia on the Danube. This is the point I am anxious to make: Paul (or God) intentionally chose to begin his second missionary journey in the most dangerous place possible. You saw how badly he and Silas were scourged— nearly beaten to death. And we barely got away ourselves."

Watson sniffed, thinking about the little pony and the diminutive cart. "I've read surgeons' accounts of those flogged before the mast in the Royal Navy days of Hawke and Nelson," he muttered. He placed a towel over his back. "Remember Mrs. Hudson's uncle: the shock, the trauma, the loss of blood."

"My point exactly: Paul and Silas were lucky to escape with their lives."

"They escaped with much more," Watson said proudly, vindictively. It was as if the beating were fresh in his mind. "When the city magistrates learned they'd beaten Roman citizens without so much as a trial (very bad business), they became alarmed, remember? With utmost contrition, they *requested* Paul and his companions leave, virtually apologizing to them. Paul and Silas are vindicated! You see? The Lord will never give you more than we can bear."

"The Lord gave me Mrs. Hudson," retorted Holmes. He walked about the table, listening, as if the map would speak. "Next, Paul and his companions travel fifty kilometers west to Amphipolis along the great Roman road, the Via Egnatia (the Egnatia Way), which leads eventually to Rome itself. Amphipolis is well situated on a terraced hill, highly visible from land and sea. Question: Why didn't Paul start his journey there? It was a prosperous city prized by the Athenians and Macedonians as the key to the gold, silver, and timber trade of nearby Mount Pangaeus, and controlled the Dardanelles. Under Roman rule it became a free town, the capital of this Macedonian district. In fact, the Lion of Amphipolis monument commemorating a military victory still stands there."

Watson remained silent, thumping his fingers on the tabletop.

"Next, Paul travels along the Via Egnatia to Thessalonica," continued Holmes.

"To more trouble," said Watson.

"Not the same kind of trouble," pointed out the detective. "Thessalonica is the queen city of Macedonia. A principal metropolis. A shining Greek city under Roman rule, but a free city, meaning she elects her own politarchs, or rulers. The proconsul (the governor) sits at Thessalonica, along with the senior board of magistrates, whereas the assembly of Greek states meets at Berea. But Thessalonica controls the region under Roman supervision, and it is the first city, incidentally, where Paul's preaching results in numerous converts, some of them socially prominent."

"But he escapes before things deteriorate too badly," said Watson, tracing with his finger, "to Berea, a welcome break for Paul and Luke, a vacation of sorts amongst some regal fellows . . . until the Jews from Thessalonica show up—"

"And spoil the party." Holmes nodded, still deep in meditative thought. "Berea: a prosperous center with a Jewish colony, but notice how quickly communications moved between these cities. The Via Egnatia, a marvelously built and maintained Roman road, linked them; amazingly convenient and effective! Also, have you noticed the diminishing influence of Imperial Rome as they travel to the interior of the Empire?"

Watson agreed. "And it disappears entirely as Paul arrives in the greatest Greek city of all, the City of Legend. But in Athens, not much happened in the way of converts."

"Typical of an affluent society," mused Holmes, "having no needs, either temporal or spiritual."

"And finally, to Corinth," said Watson, and rested his forefinger on the west coast of Greece, "where Paul and Luke are reunited with Timothy and Silas."

Holmes sighed. "The Great Apostle settles down and preaches the gospel for a good, long while—a year and a half!—with just the barest glimmer of violence."

"Corinth became an important city for the gospel, Holmes! A pagan, cosmopolitan society of many gods, and with many ethnic backgrounds. Two of Paul's lengthiest letters are addressed to the Corinthian church. Difficult letters for him to write, and for the Corinthians to read."

"I have not bothered," Holmes said, and cleared his throat. "Let's stay to the business on hand."

"But Holmes, so much of what Christians know about living righteously in a pagan world springs from 1 and 2 Corinthians. What a dearth of knowledge we would have without them!"

THE PLAYERS

Watson, walking in the sunlight alongside London's greatest sleuth, said, "I am lost."

"We approach the Crystal Palace," Holmes stated as they paused by a gazebo. He pointed with his black walking stick to the aging glass-and-iron edifice at Sydenham Hill in the distance.

"I meant as to answering the mystery," indicated the doctor, "of why Paul began in Philippi. A sweet little problem. No clues yet?"

"I notice how Paul's journey grew progressively more sedate. First, the grueling test in Philippi; fleeing Thessalonica at night but in tact; noble Berea becomes a little troublesome; Athens is congenial if not lukewarm; finally, the long rest in Corinth. But these are general qualities—nothing specific. A nagging sensation tells me I've waded in wrong foot foremost. I'm missing the obvious."

"Yes. An itch we can't—"

"Scratch." The detective tapped the side of his top hat lightly with his stick. They walked past the boating lake and along the Grand Centre Walk to the expansive circular fountain. "Ah! Paxton's[5] ingenious creations!"

Watson whistled, ever-awed at the sparkling plate glass structure. It was an engineering marvel, utilizing a method of plate glass manufacturing developed in 1848 which produced immense expanses of cheap but strong glass. The Crystal Palace had opened in Hyde Park for the Great Exhibition of 1851, with 14,000 exhibitors inhabiting 990,000 sq. feet, and had subsequently been rebuilt in enlarged form here on Penge Common next to Synenham Hill. Great fountains to the left and right spewed towering geysers of water against the sky. Beyond, the Lower Terrace and Italian Terrace beckoned, where they came upon a pair of men playing chess on a park bench. Just as Holmes began studying the board, one of them abruptly stood and departed, grinning broadly.

"The victor, no doubt," Holmes muttered.

The remaining man, hand to forehead, scrutinized, analyzed, hypothesized. He said, "I'm getting better. Much. But he always bests me. A fortnight ago in the West End tournament, he placed just behind the winner. Me, twelfth place."

"Excuse me, might you try a rare opening?" suggested Holmes, twirling his walking stick about, trying to appear casual. "Something irregular? Catch him off guard with the Slav, the Fianchetto Del Rey? Something other than the predictable Ruy or Giuoco Piano? The King's Gambit, perhaps?"

The man began repositioning the black pieces and the white, alternately, methodically. Holmes leaned in. "Explain, please?"

"When I lose, I reverse the moves all the way back to the start of the game to ascertain where I went wrong. It answers for me."

"Of course," said Holmes. He looked up at one of the pumping towers. Took a deep breath. Watson awakened out of his doldrums, for he knew what that look portended. Something had jogged the detective's brain.

"Your solution will answer for me as well," said Holmes, and smiled up at the glittering fountains of water.

Pimm's

Dr. Watson huddled within a leather booth large enough to house a rhinoceros. Across from him, Holmes eagerly rubbed his palms together.

"In all charity, I must say this is not the best place to celebrate," said Watson. "Simpson's would have been fine; Anderton's, ideal. Why must it always be Pimm's?"

"This is why!" proclaimed Holmes. A dark pewter pint-pot was unceremoniously plopped in front of him by a flat-footed waiter with greasy hair and a greasy apron. "How many times must we tend our manners, Watson? With lords and ladies, dukes and princes—with the prime minister himself—must we sip ever so daintily and with obnoxious care? Here, I might celebrate unguardedly. To our success!"

He lifted the tankard. Pimm's No. 1 gin sling leaked out the cup's sides and down the detective's chin like a glistening mustachio, spilling down over his lapels in dazzling droplets.

"You are revolting, Holmes." But then Watson picked up his tankard and did much the same—libation in its purest form. He wiped his mouth with his sleeve. Burped aloud. "We'm might've ate, rather, of smoked rarebit over Ludgate way, eh?"

"I hate it when you speak base, Watson. The river-rat vernacular comes to you far too naturally. Besides, rarebit is served here, though it has not smoked luxuriously since the morn."

The detective's eyes shone gray over the rim of his mug as he drank again. At length he said, "You have not inquired as to the mystery's solution, Watson."

"I have no objection to hearing it, indeed, if you have none to imparting it."

"The chess player. He reversed the course of events to see how his failure came about: it is a clear example of analytical thought, the same process used by the police—with varying success—for criminal investigations. Facts are tabulated, starting with the most recent and continuing back to the beginning, to arrive at a compelling explanation—or even the perpetrator. The biblical narrative lays out Paul's successes neatly, start to finish. Perhaps we should start Paul in Corinth and track him backward, from finish to start as it were, using our chess friend's reverse methodology. Perhaps then we may discern why Paul started in Philippi."

Watson looked out onto Budge Row, the carriages, the passersby. "I felt sorry for our friend in the park—but twelfth place isn't so bad, surely?"

"Judas Iscariot came in twelfth. Look where it got him," Holmes jibed. "Now, I began by tracing Paul's steps, but in reverse. I started out in Corinth instead of Philippi to see what the outcome would be. In Corinth, remember, Paul stayed a lengthy time partly because his long, trying journey was at an end. But would he have stayed there a year and a half if Corinth had been his starting point? Perhaps not. Probably not. And so Paul might have missed meeting Priscilla and Aquila, and they, Apollos. Athens: nothing would have changed. Berea might have turned out slightly better—"

"Because no interference would have been coming from the Jews at Thessalonica," interjected Watson, "because Paul wouldn't have been there yet."

"Precisely. And it is at Thessalonica where the reverse-steps model bears some fruit. Paul would begin to preach there as before, three weeks or so, when trouble breaks out. Now what happens?"

"Now, I eat."

"You consume. There is a difference."

Watson's arms encompassed a hot platter placed before him, heaped with chops and a side dab of wonderful Pimm's cream cheese with applesauce.

"Thessalonica is the key. What did actually happen there? (Pay attention now, Watson. I am now leaving my speculations. I am concentrating on what did actually occur.) I'm reading between the lines here, but during Paul's preaching in Thessalonica, news would have reached the city authorities of what had happened in Philippi to Paul and Silas, the flogging—most assuredly the earthquake, the public apology."

"It would be remarkable if it had not," said Watson, with a smacking of lips.

Holmes took a deep drink, sniffed. "The facts: Thessalonica governs Macedonia but Philippi is the keeper of peace. The police. How do I know besides our personal experience? In Acts, the Greek word *kolŏnia* is used of Philippi. This term refers to a military colony for the resettlement of disbanded soldiers, established by the *imperator* who appointed a legate to exercise his authority. Philippi, formed on the model of Rome itself, was the watchtower of the Roman State in Macedonia. It would house a prison and a garrison of troops—which it did. Not coincidentally, this was the first time Paul used his credentials as a Roman citizen.

"Thessalonica's governor knew Philippi would refuse his call for assistance in regard to the apostle's 'disruptive' ministry. Why? The Philippian magistrates, the *proetores*, wanted nothing more to do with the apostle, a Roman citizen they'd unjustly flogged. Fear had paralyzed Philippi—fear of Rome's intervention. Their dealings with Paul were at an end, and with it, any danger of offending Rome."

Watson nodded. "Of course. The Romans of Philippi had backed the wrong man eighty years before—Marc Antony. Why stick their neck out again?"

"The Thessalonians resorted to mob action, their only alternative—a relatively safe alternative with Philippi out of the equation and likely to escape Rome's scrutiny. I believe this was the behind-the-scenes political situation of the biblical narrative."

Holmes readjusted himself in his seat—a lion ready to pounce.

"But now, let us rejoin my conjecture model. I will apply my reverse-sequence-of-events model we learned from the chess player: Paul arrives at Thessalonica, but from the south, *from Berea*. As soon as he begins his troublesome preaching and stepping on toes, the Jews complain. The governor detains Paul. He sends to Philippi. Roman law is being violated—treason, no less. This character Paul is proclaiming allegiance to a king other than Caesar. The Philippian magistrates, to keep the peace, send a contingent of soldiers—you saw how fast they set on us in the middle of the night!"

"I do miss my little pony and cart," Watson said, chewing, commiserating, then wiping his mouth—with a napkin this time. "In your conjecture model, only a diminutive church would have survived at Thessalonica, and none at all in Philippi."

"Yes. Paul would have been discredited in Thessalonica. The fledgling church might not have survived. Paul would have been conducted to Philippi under arrest. He doesn't meet Lydia. He doesn't pray with the women by the river. He doesn't cast out the demon from the fortune-telling girl. After he is flogged—if the magistrates still don't know by then he is a Roman citizen— he is summarily imprisoned. The earthquake might still occur, and the jailer and his family would be saved, but Paul does not return to Thessalonica. He must make his way to the sea by way of Neapolis."

"Starting at Philippi was the key," said Watson. "A brilliant master move."

"The opening move on the board for the winning of the Greek peninsula. Philippi, the police state for the area, was disabled in the first days of Paul's journey—in a chess match, tantamount to capturing the hostile queen. And Philippi was the location of the first Christian church on European soil. The whole Greek peninsula lay open to Paul. To the gospel. Paul got out of Thessalonica without a scratch after establishing a church there. Berea next. Corinth last of all, he bearing all those fresh scars on his back and stories of hardship in Philippi."

"This mystery started out so obscurely. So hopelessly."

Holmes' eyes flashed. He took his fork and stole a piece of pork from Watson's plate. "Any puzzle becomes simple once you look at the pieces entire, and in a meaningful sequence. But this was a difficult case for me, Watson, from a curiosity standpoint. It wasn't until I understood the consequences of *not* starting in Philippi that my interest and admiration were aroused.

"And I discovered another interesting jewel in the crown of time-travel. Notice that it is by reasoning backward, analytically, that we achieve our results. Does this not remind you of something?"

"You must pull back on the reins, now and then, and let others catch up, Holmes." Watson laid his head back against the cushioned leather. "You are saying the mental world has an exact correlation with the physical?"

"Precisely."

"Let me think. With the Needle's Eye, accelerating forward was the easiest concept to grasp, but would lead us nowhere.

Slowing down and traveling in reverse was the key to a phenomenal discovery, to time-travel—"

"Yes!" Holmes clenched his fists exuberantly. "And by inference, reasoning backward on the chessboard unlocked the key to this mystery of Philippi."

Holmes fell silent, preoccupied with making more connections.

"My admiration for Paul increased," stated Watson evenly, "when I read his second letter to the Corinthians, where he states he was given *thirty-nine lashes five times*. Three times he was beaten with rods. Stoned almost to death on one occasion. Two lashes were well enough for me to see white and to send my heart into my throat. What a resilient, tough soldier for the Lord was Paul."[6]

Holmes had recovered enough from his mental gymnastics to comment, "And a good shepherd. He shielded Timothy and Luke from harm. And don't forget, he had a penchant for genius."

"Paul, a genius?" Watson raised an eyebrow. "It is the Lord who started him in Philippi."

"I meant in his choice of traveling companions: Luke, for instance."

"He was a Greek."

"More specifically?"

"A physician."

"It is a brilliant man who proposes having, as his closest traveler, a doctor."

Watson swallowed hard. He cleared his throat. "Thank you for saying so, Holmes. Sincerely. Thank you very much."

YOU MISS, YOU DIE

"Hiding would be most expeditious, don't you think, Holmes?" Watson peeked round a stone pillar inscribed with filthy runes, images of sacrifice. Columns lay scattered over the ground, pieces of an arch; a stone head, overgrown with trailing moss and flowers, lay with its ear to the ground as if listening. Beyond, a wide glade glowed green in the sunlight. "Must you stand out in the open? An impervious dread has settled over me."

Holmes seemed not to hear. He scanned either ridge of the Valley of Elah, where the two opposing armies faced each another.

A large warrior came and stood atop a distant swell of grass. He was grim-faced, his long, braided beard thrust into his belt. Both his helmet and tunic of bronze mail shone in the dazzling light. A heavy shield was strapped to his back, and he held a long, two-pointed sword to the front, a forked gisarme like a dragon's tongue. He looked directly at Watson, and his nostrils flared, like a bull's. He bellowed out with a primordial yell, deep-sounding, like a bull's.

"He sees us!" the doctor whispered. "I know we are wearing our fashionable London garb, but still, I think he sees us."

"He may sense us, as we in our world dimly perceive the flutterings of spirits about us," commented Holmes in a removed tone. "But he cannot see us, Watson."

"But Holmes, what if the charm fails of a sudden? What if, by Fate's cruel choice or by sinister design, we become visible? Now would be the worst time to be discovered."

With an almost imperceptible nod of his head, Sherlock Holmes directed Watson's attention over to a stream. A boy with curly chestnut hair and freckles knelt at the water.

Watson asked, "What in heaven's name is he doing?"

"Gathering stones. Five, to be exact. In heaven's name."

"Doesn't he realize the danger?"

"The boy or the warrior?" Holmes shaded his eyes.

It was then that the warrior stood aside, for someone larger was coming up behind him: his master, black-bearded, standing nearly ten feet tall.

"Zanzummim. Spawn of the Rephaim," whispered Holmes, not for fear of being overheard, but in awe. "Here stands the champion of Gath: Goliath so named."

His bronze cap was spiked with horns; bronze, his coat of scale armor, weighing nearly five thousand shekels; bronze, too, the engraved greaves upon his shins; and bronze the javelin slung upon his back. His spear shaft was as long as a weaver's beam, its iron point weighing six hundred shekels. From his belt protruded the hilt of a massive iron blade, the sword of a giant.

"The shepherd boy is—" began Watson.

"None other than David, youngest son of Jesse of Bethlehem."

The giant yelled, a great booming sound. He laughed, pulled

forth his spear, and pointed its sharp head at his shield, which bore the mask of Dagon, father of Baal.

"He curses the boy in the name of his deities," Holmes said.

"David isn't impressed. I shouldn't be surprised, knowing how this famous story must play out. Yet Goliath is a colossal man, and David so young."

But the giant's laughter fell short. The shepherd boy dropped his staff and broke into a run directly for him. A mixture of shock, incredulity, and amusement played across Goliath's face. His armor bearer heaved about the massive shield to the front and advanced before his master, who brought up his spear. David reached into his pouch at a dead run. He fitted a stone into his sling.

"Holmes, look!"

Unexpectedly, the boy switched the sling to his left hand. Watson could hear the sling whirring, faster, faster. The gap between them closed. David leaned back before catapulting forward, whipping his arm down. It was the last thing on this green-clad earth, of trailing moss and flowers, that the Philistine champion would ever see.[1]

Moments later Watson heard a voice. "Old boy. Are you all right?"

The doctor had lowered to one knee and retched on the ground. He felt the cool leather of Holmes' gloved hand against the back of his neck, heard the detective repeat his concern. But how did Holmes expect him to react after witnessing a giant, however evil, driven through with his own sword and summarily beheaded? And David carrying the grizzly trophy by the hair, its eyes rolled back and looking upward into oblivion as if to summon back its soul?

Holmes' soothing voice floated over him again. "What's gotten you so out of sorts? Did you not witness bloodshed in Afghanistan? We've, both of us, seen paintings galore about David beheading Goliath—"

The word "galore" sounded too much like "gore," and Watson retched all over again.

"Did you see it, Watson?"

The doctor looked up, bleary-eyed, and wiped his mouth. "Do you mean Goliath's forehead shattering from the stone, and embedding itself therein? David drawing forth the giant's heavy sword? Driving it downward into Goliath's chest? Hacking off the ponderous head from the torso, with the bloody tendrils running crimson tracks along the ground? Did I see it? Why, I'm sick to my stomach! The violence! The bloodshed! Even a seasoned doctor like myself—"

"Ah, the severed neck. The muscles. The tendons and windpipe . . ."

The doctor winced at the recitation, gasping again. "Holmes, you worry me at times. You are entirely too removed."

Holmes' expression softened. He patted the doctor on the shoulder. "It's back to London with us now, ol' boy. A nip of Vichy, I think, will do you wonders."

In a Pit on a Snowy Day

When Watson's world rematerialized, the first thing he felt was the sting of snowflakes against his hand. The gray sky swirled, what little he could see of it, for he and Holmes seemed to be in a wide pit, certainly not on board the spacious aft cabin of the *Viceroy of India*. Very little could the doctor ascertain from their surroundings—where they might be, or more important, *when*. One fact was for certain: they were not back in London.

The pit was large, with overarching walls forming a smaller circle of sky. Snowflakes swirled dreamlike, covering the ground exposed to the heavens, while he and Holmes stood back in the shadows.

Watson felt an uneasiness, not of the natural kind of being in a strange place or time, nor the residual trauma from having witnessed the brutal confrontation between giant and boy (no matter how fortuitous the outcome). Rather, his restlessness was familiar and yet fleeting. He dug back through his memories in an attempt to unearth the source, but the more earth his mental spade displaced, the greater his disquiet loomed.

"I feel it too," said the hushed voice of Holmes, the pronouncement ending in a puff of frost from his lips. They stood shoulder to shoulder, did the detective and the doctor, instinctively so; for had they been cornered on the battlefield, in the jungle, in a Dorset Street alley,[2] they would stand thus, back to back.

"Something is in the pit with us." Watson nodded toward the darkness across the way. "I sense it. As if something is—"

"Watching us," Holmes said, never taking his eyes away from the exact point on which the doctor, too, focused his attention. "Waiting."

Just then, Watson heard a gurgling growl, like the remnant of water passing down an iron pipe. He remembered now where he had heard that sound before: deep in the jungle of the Indian Empire. In Bengal. In Calcutta. The sound of a big cat on the prowl.

From the darkness two eyes appeared, yellow, with black vertical slits. A bearded mouth came into the light, then the tawny, elongated nose, now the bushy mane, shadowing eyes which looked nowhere but straight back at them. One, two more steps it took, the powerful shoulder muscles flexing as the lion came out from the darkness into the dancing snow, like a child's fanciful dream disturbed by a nightmare. The lion was larger than any Watson had ever seen, paws as large as dinner plates, steel hooks for claws, one swipe of which would rip out a man's throat, his stomach, his intestines.

"He sees us."

"Yes." Holmes breathed deeply and squatted, ever so slowly, to grasp a short wooden pole, sharpened on the end. "Or he only senses us, as with Goliath's armor bearer. Perhaps it is characteristic of this time, that the inhabitants are more tuned—"

The lion grumbled again, staring at them, its growl softly percolating. It advanced another step, sniffed at the air and then the ground, apparently seeking to verify with its nose what its eyes and ears refused to collaborate. It shook its head dully and snapped its teeth with a crazed, derelict look in its almost-human eyes.

Watson realized there must be something particularly unnatural or evil about this creature. Its left shoulder was striped with clotted blood, which looked black in the dimness. On the pit's far side, he noticed a motionless form lying there, of nearly the same size and hue as the predator standing before them.

Another lion. Dead.

This explained the creature's extraordinary behavior. After surviving a challenge from a rival, its senses would be pitched to the highest sensitivity, enough to detect the ever-so-delicate movements in the unseen world. Another step forward, and now it sniffed toward them.

"Watson," Holmes uttered his name so softly that Watson could barely hear it. "Why don't you retrieve your own stick in the event—"

Suddenly, the lion snapped at the air. It wheeled sideways, lowering its body. In a cascade of snowflakes, something landed inside the pit and stood upright: a man. He was tall, graceful, with a form like a maiden's. He was stripped from the waist up, all sinew and thin muscle, his black beard close-cropped, and tiny tattooed emblems encircled each shoulder. He leveled his eyes at the lion. In an unnerving display of calmness, he smiled.

The lion came up from its crouch. Advanced slowly. Its head began to roll from side to side as the man twirled his sword one-handed in a glittering circle. In his other hand he held a thin dagger, steady, lethal. He spoke something—Hebrew, Watson thought. The doctor wanted to call out, to warn him—but to what end? Would he ever hear Watson's warning? And hadn't the man intentionally entered the beast's lair for this confrontation?

The lion lowered its head. The snowflakes swirled. Its shoulders and hindquarters quivered with anticipation. Still, the man smiled and called up to someone laughing overhead. Just then, with the man's attention thus distracted—the lion sprang! Into the air it launched itself, razor-claws reaching for him. A guttural groan sounded from the creature, like desire mixed with disappointment, as the man rolled on the ground beneath its groping claws. The lion landed on its heavy paws and turned, bracing itself to charge again.

"Look, Holmes!" hissed Watson.

The creature lowered onto the snow, panting deeply, apparently content to rest. Perhaps its earlier battle had tired it. The warrior paced slowly back and forth, once turning his back completely on the beast, which seemed marvelously tame, not interested in resuming the fight, or in only lashing out harmlessly with a paw. It growled menacingly as the man approached it to within a few feet.

"What does he mean to do—?" started Watson.

The man took out his sword, a thin blade by ancient standards, and quite inexplicably, laid it flat on the lion's head. Other than uttering a plaintive growl, the creature hardly reacted, as if under some kind of curious spell. Its breathing became more audible, more labored, a gasping tinged with a low moaning. It closed its eyes and settled its great head on its front paws and rolled over on its side.

Watson took in a sharp breath. The entire length of the beast's underbelly was slit open, the red-white entrails peeking out from the folds of blood. Still the chest heaved; still the creature's death rattle echoed within the enclosure until its last breath issued forth, a horrible shuddering moan. All within the pit became motionless: the beast; the Londoners; the warrior over his prey; all like statues frozen in place—all except for the snow, the white flakes swarming hectically, like victorious angels.

Faith and Conviction

"Emim?" muttered Watson, putting down his glass and snuggling deeper into his blanket. The trip back from the *Viceroy of India* had been damp and bone-chilling. He was glad for the coals within the fireplace that crackled and purred.

Holmes had muttered the term between thrusts with his

fencing sword, rehearsing the *tirer au mur*, or stroke at the wall, an elementary technique he learned as a child at the salon of Maître Alphonse Bencin of Pau.

"Goliath, undoubtedly, is a descendant of that ancient line, the name given giants by the ancient Moabites. Zuzim by the Amorites. A mighty people as formidable in stature as the Anakim, so say the Scriptures. They were called Rephaim in Abraham's day." He inverted his sword backward and placed his fist on his hip. "The Septuagint renders them as *gigas*, or giant, or *Titanes*. In any case, they were very, very large two-legged, carbon-based consuming dictatorial units. Ha!"

Holmes thrust again, holding the full-lunge position to test the tempered strength of his thighs and legs, and then he lay the weapon aside.

"What are we to make of all the carnage we witnessed?" asked the doctor. "The slain giant, the lion—"

"Oh, Watson, how you exasperate me! The details of violence in the field are not at all what we must dwell on. Did you not see, rather, what happened at the stream? The stones? The stones David gathered and put in his pouch?"

Watson peered at him over his blanket, bleary-eyed.

"I presumed that you, a medical man and marvelously proficient with numbers, would have caught it straightaway. Here's the question: *Why did David choose five stones?* Don't ask to see a little calling card. None was furnished to us—the mystery is obvious."

His companion was far too tired to entertain the question's veracity, or Holmes' subtle insult. Instead, he shivered. "What age was Goliath, do you think?"

"Finally, a perceptive contribution. The Philistine champion, report the Scriptures, was versed in war from his youth.

He was probably the eldest—and the largest—to be chosen as their representative. But how might we guess his actual years? I see a subtle but persistent thread, Watson, running through the ancient resources at my disposal—perhaps Dr. Clarkson, friend of the London Museum, would speak to it more thoroughly than I: giants were prone to a longer life span than mere men. Something to keep in mind." Holmes looked down at his sword as if contemplating resuming his exercise. "But the strange duel we witnessed, the warrior and the lion . . . How does such a scene *outside the Bible* lend help to understanding why David chose five stones?"

"So, you already know why David chose five stones? Are you mocking me?"

"No," he replied. "On both counts."

"I have a simple theory, Holmes: David's first throw might have flown awry—or his second throw. And with Goliath's armor bearer present, it's odds of two against one. Therefore, the boy grabbed a handful of stones. The number five is arbitrary."

"Not so. In a confrontation with a giant, if you miss, you die."

Holmes walked to his immense Bible, already opened to 1 Samuel 17.

"Scripture is very precise, as if David's action were intentional. Why not state offhandedly, as you so glibly suggest, *he grabbed a handful of stones*? No, rather, the account explicitly states he gathered *five smooth stones*. The number is specific. He deliberately counted them out."

"What I saw of Goliath," said Watson, "I would have pocketed fifty such stones."

"Not I," said Holmes. "I would have stayed atop the cliff and rolled down one very large stone upon him—ha!" Holmes took a deep breath and settled down in a cushioned chair across from Watson, who sipped from his glass tentatively. "How is the fizzy lemonade? Is it just what the doctor ordered? Do you now worship at my nickel-plated gasogene?[3] How you mocked me, Watson, when I brought it over from Montague Street."

He was up again, pacing, muttering. "No, no, no. This present line of patchwork guessing will not suffice. David, even as a youngster, was supremely confident: as he spoke to King Saul in his tent before the confrontation with Goliath, I doubt whether the king had ever heard such self-assuredness, much less from a boy—'*Let no man's heart fail because of him; your servant will go and fight with this Philistine. . . . Your servant has killed both lion and bear; and this uncircumcised Philistine will be like one of them.*'[4]

"David was jealous for his God. Offended at Goliath's blasphemy," said Watson.

"More than that. Young David seems to know how the whole scenario will play out. There is no room for doubt in his bearing, none whatsoever. He already knows how he will attack. How he will kill, which is why he shed Saul's proffered armor so quickly. He knows he'll do it with his sling, with a single stone."

"He certainly wasn't cowered by his older brother's jealousy," answered Watson, smiling. "Can you imagine Eliab's anger at overhearing his little brother saying amongst the soldiers, '*For who is this uncircumcised Philistine, that he should defy the armies of the living God?*'[5] David was brassy, wasn't he? A kind of righteous swagger? It's difficult not to like him."

"Yes. But more importantly, he took an incredibly aggressive stance against a fierce foe which all the soldiers of Israel feared. David actually stood taller than Goliath! Listen to the challenge he makes to Goliath's face: '*You come to me with a sword, with a spear, and with a javelin. But I come to you in the name of the* LORD *of hosts, the God of the armies of Israel, whom you have defied. This day the* LORD *will deliver you into my hand, and I will strike you and take your head from you.*'"[6]

"And he ran quickly at Goliath," chuckled Watson. "All too eager!"

"That is why your position is untenable," remarked Sherlock Holmes. "He didn't take five stones in the event he missed: the Davids of this world don't miss."

Watson stretched out his hands toward the fire. "I'm beginning to see your logic. David knew exactly what the Lord could do through those he chose to empower, and through the insignificant sling in his hand."

"Regal in rage and righteous in indignation. As a boy, he makes King Saul look unnecessary, even annoying. After all, David hasn't cowered in his royal tent for forty days, unable to decide a course of action.

"Think about it, Watson. Goliath's stipulation is this: the warrior who prevails in this contest, his nation will rule the other. The pressure on David is immense as he steps down into the Valley of Death. This shepherd boy isn't just facing a primordial giant. He carries Israel's doom or prosperity—the hopes and future of his brothers and father hang in the balance, of Bethlehem, of his nation!"

"But David's not concerned in the least," said Watson. "Almost nonchalant."

"Again, that is precisely why your former position is unsustainable. While watching his father's flocks day after day, he's practiced with his sling—a piece of leather that has become part of him. Right-handed. Left-handed."

"Why do you think he switched to his left hand?" asked Watson. "More cockiness?"

"Not at all. Goliath, if you remember, was right-handed. His unoccupied left hand would be better able to deflect a sling stone. David threw with his left hand to bring the stone meteor-like over the giant's right side, where Goliath grasped his spear."

"Of course! Oh, Holmes: I can only be ashamed of my faith's shallowness in comparison to his. I'm afraid I more resemble King Saul!"

"*Afraid* is a good word to use in reference to Saul," said Holmes. "In the days before the judges, the Lord commanded Joshua: '*Be strong and of good courage; do not be afraid, nor be dismayed, for the* LORD *your God is with you wherever you go.*'[7] Interesting how the same Hebrew words for *afraid* and *dismayed* used there are exactly those used to describe King Saul's reaction to Goliath's words.[8] But, of course, King Saul is no Joshua!"

"He's no King David either." Watson yawned. Sleep was not far off.

Holmes picked up his fencing sword again. One hand placed on his hip in proper decorum, he extended the blade again, held the position in a prolonged stretch, brought it back. He repeated the exercise.

"David reminds me of you, Holmes: self-assured, confident, active. And yet he relied wholly upon God—which does not remind me of you."

"Everyone knew the young Bethlehemite was as good as dead," Holmes said, ignoring him. "Veteran against youngster; big against small; sword against sling. But David knew better. It was Goliath who never had a chance."

"God was with him," declared Watson. "A small point. And

the same held true in his latter years. As the new king of Israel, he was enabled by God to strike down the Philistines at Baal Perazim,[9] and again in the Valley of Rephaim."[10]

Holmes shrugged. "So, dear friend, we've come full circle: Why did David choose five stones?"

"I'm just a doctor," replied Watson, closing his eyes. "You're the world's first consulting detective."

TERRIBLY REMISS

The bullet-black locomotive pounded into the station, its rhythmic stomping all the more ominous beneath the iron archways as it came to rest at platform 4 at Paddington Station. Holmes, dressed in his finest walking attire, black suit, top hat, leather shoes, and matching black ebony cane, flared his nostrils. Watson knew by practice that their stroll, beginning at Baker Street and continuing along Oxford Street and the northern fringe of Hyde Park to Westbourne Terrace, must inevitably end here.

Holmes loved the feel of raw, locomotive power, while the acrid smoke exhilarated his mental processes, and where better to experience it than Paddington Station? He considered it preeminent in architecture among all the others—Liverpool Street Station, Waterloo, Victoria, Charing Cross—as he also considered Hammersmith Bridge against all other bridges.

"Wonderful machine—what drive and power! What aggression!" The detective shouted to be heard over the sudden hissing of the compound Atlantic locomotive. "Marvelous engineering, French built, I believe—two high-pressure cylinders exhausted into a third, larger low-pressure one—oh, marvelous!" Holmes' eyes settled on the diminutive engine-driver climbing down, his shoes *ting-ting*ing on metal stairs. "And these hot, raging tons of iron are handled expertly by whom?—a family man! Ha! He with his handles, pedals and gauges. From whence do you think our grimy little fellow hails? Penge? Queen's Park? How may mere man have such control and mastery over such a large beast?"

"This has to do with the warrior and the lion, doesn't it?" Watson barely heard himself voicing the question, holding a handkerchief over his nose and mouth, not being a connoisseur of coal smoke in all of its varying bouquets and aromas.

"I love it when you see through my technique—though unintentional this time. And as touching the larger question of David, I must admit to a serious oversight. I assumed, wrongly, that the scene of the snowy pit was not biblical."

"Do you mean to say—?"

"Yes, Watson. I have committed the grievous error of not looking at the larger context, of not reading far enough into the biblical narrative." Holmes waved a small Bible in front of him, and then began thumbing through the pages. "The story is, indeed, part of David's life, but takes place at a much later time: '*Benaiah was the son of Jehoiada, the son of a valiant man from Kabzeel, who had done many deeds. He had killed two lion-like heroes of Moab. He also had gone down and killed a lion in the midst of a pit on a snowy day.*'"[11]

"Isn't this Benaiah one of David's mighty men?"

Holmes nodded. He turned and began to walk back the way they had come, along the platform and around the baggage carts. "And for good reason—like the lightning strike of a snake, he rolled beneath the lion, cutting upward with his dagger, and so felled the beast!"

"And not just any lion, Holmes, but the kind of beast worthy of the ancient Babylonian or Assyrian reliefs, worthy of adorning the Ishtar Gate or Ashurbanipal's palace walls."

"The twin tattoos on Benaiah's shoulders represented a tribute to the Kerethites and Pelethites, whom he commanded. Hardly surprising."

"It's puzzling how this story can aid us in answering the fundamental question about David and the number of stones he took."

"I cannot begin to hazard a guess."

Both men glanced back at Paddington Station, Mr. Isambard Kingdom Brunnel's[12] marvel of utilitarian design. But now it merely reflected their inner turmoil, presenting only a confusing matrix of iron beams, bustling crowds, and obscuring smoke.

LADY LUCK SMILES

"Are you up for the Oxford tonight, Holmes? Or Buffalo's Head? I hear Simpson's on the Strand has a freshened menu—oh, excuse me, *bill of fare*." Watson directed these inquiries to the stoic, morose figure staring out of the window onto Baker Street.

Holmes turned smartly, tucked away his pipe, and waved his suggestions away. "Forgive me. This tobacco has me put off— Gluckstein, I believe."

He hollered loudly for Mrs. Hudson. The elderly lady appeared, dressed in an exquisitely fine amber-lace dress and a cameo, her silver hair pulled back with pins. She brought in tea and a small platter of bubble and squeak,[13] and humming busily, set about arranging the silverware around the plates. Her sprightly and cheerful demeanor discomforted Holmes, who fairly hissed at her.

"The orange juice is for you, Dr. Watson—stirred forty-four times!"

"You are unusually jovial this evening," Watson commented.

"Luck at whist last night, Dr. John Hamish Watson," she chirped. "The cards fell favorably to me and Bernice—though she does chatter on a bit—treble-double for both rubbers."

"Champion!" exclaimed Watson.

Holmes fretted. He took out his pipe again, stared at the bowl's contents, and rapped it irritatingly against the fireplace grate.

"Oh, but I feel so giddy!" she said. "How often we ran trumps—with *four* honors, to boot!" She slapped her hands together. "Four!"

"Yes, well done," the doctor added enthusiastically. "Holmes, won't you at least—"

Sherlock Holmes stiffened. Watson noticed his demeanor change immediately. The detective fell into a silence bordering on brooding. When he revived, at last, he found he had stared Mrs. Hudson completely out of composure.

"I don't care for your grim humors, Mr. Holmes," she muttered. "Dark moods for dark doings, I say."

"Quiet yourself, Mrs. Hudson," he replied. A furtive smile played upon his lips. He snapped his fingers merrily, his mood pendulum having swung back to the other extreme. "On the contrary, I've decided to give you a week off from your duties to me. With pay."

"I would not take it, sir, and return to this cocked-up place. And as much as I dislike your foul moods, your generosity is more untrustworthy still—"

The detective bounded over the stepstool to his Bible, awaiting him on the pedestal. He flipped a few pages and pounded the holy book with his fist.

"You have solved my case, dear lady!" Holmes put back his head and let out a hysterical laugh. "And if you do not leave this instant, I shall be forced to give you a son's kiss—smack on the cheek!"

"Oh!"

"All this talk about forty-four stirs with the orange juice spoon—and four honors! *Four!*" he called to her fleeing form. He guffawed as the door slammed shut behind her.

"Holmes, are you unwell?"

The Sleuth of Baker Street, too busy reading at first to reply, finally looked up.

"Here's proof of why we witnessed Benaiah slaying the lion. The passage was incongruous, except that it was meant to pull me further ahead into David's life, to when he was an old man. I would never have dreamed to look for the answer so deep in the text. Furthermore, the key to our puzzle involves members of the Thirty—David's mighty men."

The detective turned and walked to the far corner of his apartment.

"I was on the wrong track," he said to a gaping Watson. "The mystery is not why David took five stones, but why he needed the extra four—what a daft mule I am! I allowed the number five to be so indelibly etched on my brain that I missed the obvious."

He returned to the Bible, turning the cumbersome pages like an orchestra conductor in slow motion.

"But I was on the right track too. David was a far more confident young man than either of us gave him credit for."

Watson got up, peered over the detective's shoulder. "What are you looking for?"

"A passage I had forgotten, one that concerns David's later life,

but which now blazes in the forefront of my mind like a comet—
Ah! Yes, yes, yes, yes, yes. Here it is! Read it for yourself."

He pointed at the beginning verse of the passage, and Watson
began to read, silently.

When the Philistines were at war again with Israel, David
and his servants with him went down and fought against the
Philistines; and David grew faint. Then Ishbi-Benob, who was
one of the sons of the giant, the weight of whose bronze spear
was three hundred shekels, who was bearing a new sword,
thought he could kill David. But Abishai the son of Zeruiah
came to his aid, and struck the Philistine and killed him. Then
the men of David swore to him, saying, "You shall go out no
more with us to battle, lest you quench the lamp of Israel."

Now it happened afterward that there was again a battle
with the Philistines at Gob. Then Sibbechai the Hushathite
killed Saph, who was one of the sons of the giant. Again there
was war at Gob with the Philistines, where Elhanan the son of
Jaare-Oregim the Bethlehemite killed the brother of Goliath
the Gittite, the shaft of whose spear was like a weaver's beam.

Yet again there was war at Gath, where there was a man of
great stature, who had six fingers on each hand and six toes on
each foot, twenty-four in number; and he also was born to the
giant. So when he defied Israel, Jonathan the son of Shimeah,
David's brother, killed him.

These four were born to the giant in Gath, and fell by the
hand of David and by the hand of his servants.[14]

Watson whistled. "So, four other giants stood in the Philistine
ranks the day David slew Goliath!"

"Assuredly. David gathered five stones at the stream. Why? *Because Goliath had four brothers!*"

"They were younger, surely, on Goliath's death day," went on Holmes, "and less experienced in war. All four apparently survived for years until these fatal encounters with the mighty men of Israel."

Watson collapsed in his chair and clapped his hands together. "Tremendous! David didn't gather four extra stones because he felt unsure. He gathered them because his faith was so strong—a faith of razor-sharp steel! He was more than willing—I will use the word *eager* again—to confront all five giants at once!"

Holmes turned forward a few pages. "This third giant killed, Goliath by name, is confusing, but cleared up in 1 Chronicles 20:5—'*Lahmi the brother of Goliath.*'"

The detective wandered over to the fireplace and lit his pipe.

"I have an insight worthy of your praise," commented Watson. "Goliath blasphemed the Lord, did he not? And do you know the penalty for blasphemy? It is stoning!"[15]

Sherlock, standing at the mantel, let out a puff of smoke. "Well done, Watson."

"There is something else noteworthy about King David. He never forgot his battle with Goliath, even in his last days. In a song he attributes all his victories to the Lord."[16]

Holmes sat down, the clock tick-tocking in the silence between them.

"Have you not noticed how deliciously evil the giant's name is, Watson? *Goliath.* Phonetically guttural, it booms up from your depths and rolls off your tongue, as do other delectably evil names: Og of Bashan and Genghis Khan; Gog and Magog; Jezebel . . . and Mrs. Hudson."

"Shame, now, Holmes." Watson studied the solemn detective, who smoldered like his pipe. "What's the matter, now? You should be grinning from ear to ear!"

"I smile once in the morning and get it over with."

"What has happened to your joviality?"

"We have successfully navigated through over half the mysteries. And yet—yet I feel as if I am groping; searching."

"But you have discovered so much. And solved so much. Certainly your soul rejoices—"

"I am foremost a student of all matters a fortiori, academic, cognitive, deductive—you know this, Watson. My need is predominantly pragmatic, not personal, certainly not emotional, emphatically not spiritual."

"So, these mysteries have only strengthened your investigatory prowess? Your soul has not been uplifted? Where is your higher self, Holmes, which looks past the horizon?"

"Ah, where religion dwells?"

"According to you, religion is man's weakness."

"I wouldn't say *weakness*, exactly." Holmes got up, walked over to the massive Bible, and draped back the pages by happenstance at 2 Corinthians 2. "But the spiritual mind does tend to obscure real facts with fanciful angels and devils—pray, don't assault me with the salubrious charge that it exalts faith. My scrutiny is far more elaborate. The facts—"

"The facts, the facts, the facts!" Watson grumbled. "Tell me. What were the facts about the shepherd boy against Goliath? David slew the giant. The adulteress against the entire Sanhedrin? And yet she leaves exonerated in power!" He awaited the inevitable rejoinder, for Holmes delighted in the exercise of every form of syllogistic disputation.

"These stories—"

"They are more than stories, Holmes." Watson held his breath. Indignation moved him to interrupt the great man. "You and I aren't confined to the written page, to hymns and homilies, as are churchgoers. We were there during Christ's temptation! We *saw* angels!"

"Have we actually gone back in time these six journeys? Really, Watson? Perhaps what we saw were plays dramatically preformed as laid out in the Bible. Reenactments. Perhaps we saw what our minds wanted us to see. But not the events as they really happened—"

"Bah! Who would pay thousands of pounds to play so elaborate a hoax?"

The fly in the ointment smiled.

"Well, shall we not celebrate anyway?" asked Watson. "Perhaps the Oxford Theatre is in order after all. Or back to the Leicester Lounge to match your dingy mood—certainly not the Café Royal? What say you?"

The pendulum had swung back again. Holmes looked off, petulantly. "How mean I feel for libations of any kind. How base a creature I have become. How miserably low!"

"What is really the matter, Holmes?"

"Oh, how I preen myself. Puffing myself up with self-aggrandizing and immodest compliments of intellectual prowess, when all the while I must needs, in the end, rely upon my land-lady's offhand remark to solve the case."

"Mrs. Hudson, you mean?"

Sherlock Holmes looked off into space. "Oh, Watson, how very low I feel."

SEVEN

DEAD MAN WALKING

"HOLMES—I AM BLIND! WHERE ARE YOU IN ALL THIS PITCH blackness?" Watson's muffled plea was spoken through a handkerchief. "What awful smell—?"

He heard a rustling, followed by a rasp, a snap, and a flash of light. Sherlock Holmes held a flaming match, revealing a low-ceilinged, rock-hewn chamber. The lanky detective stooped over because of his top hat.

"See here," Holmes said, holding the flickering match over a body lying on a rock shelf and dressed in a linen gown. Dimly, Watson could make out cloth strips binding the feet and hands, a linen shroud wrapped about the head. He coughed into his handkerchief.

"Watson, why so discomfited at the smell of rotting flesh? Oh, eternal perturbations—and you a doctor!"

"Holmes, a decomposing body casts certain nauseatingly sweet odors which, when combined with perfumed oils and aromatic bandages, do no good service to my stomach. Adding to my excuse, only last night did we not stuff ourselves upon a four-course dinner at Simpson's? Oh, these wretched aromas! D'ye hear the crying and pipe playing of wailers outside? Or feel the chill of this fearful tomb?"

Holmes lit another match, snapped out his magnifying glass, and studied the corpse. "Tell me, in your expert opinion, Doctor: What do you make of him?"

Watson waved away the glass. "He is dead."

"Ah, I shall rename you Dr. Obvious."

"My observations, pathognomonic and otherwise, are hindered with all this linen. With no skin accessible, the body unable to be turned (and given that rigor mortis and all deathly body humors have set in), I cannot hazard a guess to the cause of death. The chin is bound, the mandible pressed to the maxilla by way of a linen sling. Both the carpus's proximal bones, together with the radius's and ulna's lower parts, are wrapped across the stomach to join their twins; identically, the tarsus, including the talus, and the tibia's and fibula's bottom portions are bound together."

"You mean his hands and feet are bound," said Holmes peevishly.

"Quite. And the lower jaw drawn up tightly, punctiliously, for diminution of movement."

"To keep it from gaping open, I presume?"

"Also, wonderful perspicacity, Holmes, in using the gender tag of 'his,' and 'him.' For given the stature and general form, I would be surprised indeed were our corpse other than a son of Eve."

"I hate it when you speak thusly, Watson, in mimicry of me, a sort of laudanum of pompous anachronisms to be imbibed as a sort of vengeful erudition to mock me—ah!"

The match puffed out in an acrid puff smelling like burned gunpowder, but not before burning Holmes' fingers. Darkness pounced upon them.

Suddenly, inexplicably, something stirred close to the doctor, a closeness without touching, and he felt the hair on his arms raise. There came a deep rumble akin to an anchor dragged across a marble floor, the heavy grating of stone on stone. A brilliant crescent appeared on the far wall, a waxing moon of light growing larger, widening. Watson shielded his eyes.

Not Euripides

"Take that, Lucius!" the actor exclaimed, and thrust out with his sword.

"Oh, fair Silva, thou hast cut me to the soul, and hast delivered me unto Death's thin door. Oh! oh . . ."

Silva pulled his sword free. Lucius, having spoken his last, fell forward stone dead.

"Superbly atrocious!" Holmes chuckled evilly and puffed his pipe in the sunshine. He and Watson sat alone on limestone benches, uncomfortably so, high up on an amphitheatre's outer rim, which curved about them on either side. Holmes varied his gaze slightly to take in a figure scurrying onto the stage, waving his arms about. The slain man rose to his feet, and even from this distance, the Londoners could hear him (the director, no doubt) pleading, "Oh, Eurchius Janius"—(the man playing Lucius, no doubt)—"listen to yourself! You are a dying man! You have been thrust through with the sword. Your life's blood is pumping out—no, oozing out—and your bowels with it. Where is your passion? Your—"

"Where do you think we are?" Through half-opened eyes Holmes peered at the distant city, the hazy mountain range in the distance. "Corinth or Athens—no, not Athens. Ephesus, perhaps, but . . ." The sunlight glinted purple off of his top hat and suit coat, the frost upon which had beaded into dewdrops. As in the tomb, he and Watson sat unobserved, as invisible as spirits or as dreams rippling in shadow. "And this play—what d'ye think? Certainly not Euripides, which has to do with birds, does it not? Or Aristophanes. And what is the year? 100 AD? Watson, come now—what has you so unwound?"

Watson knew their time was short, here in the empty theater. Even now he could feel the beginnings of time-travel rise up within himself, the bubbling effervescence not altogether unpleasant. He thought back to the tomb, to the corpse fully bound and yet standing erect, facing the open doorway. Stains had dotted its back due to the settling of burial oils and spices.

"Lazarus, come forth!"

The command had been loud. Authoritative. Even now the doctor felt the wings of his own spirit expand, as if to flutter out through his chest. He remembered the chafing sound of bandages on stone as the body shuffled out of the darkness to come fully into the light. The bound man. The man once dead, but now alive.[1]

THE GROWLERS

"Splendid!" Holmes announced happily, closing the carriage door and placing his best top hat next to him. The four wheeler smelled of old leather. "Carte[2] has done it again, I daresay, with his light opera."

"Too melodramatic"—Watson stared out the four-wheeler

carriage window onto the rainy London night—"by far. Electric light hurts my eyes. I prefer the old Gaiety."[3]

"Or opera with the de Reszke brothers at the Garden? I sing exactly like Jean with a bar of soap in my hand—la, la, la! But what of finishing off this delightful evening with a nightcap at Divan's? Not to your liking either?"

"A warm coverlet suits me."

"How frumpy you are, Watson. So it is, on a rainy night I am beset by two growlers.[4] What irks you so?"

The doctor merely took off his gloves and laid them on the seat.

"Mm. This Lazarus affair, no doubt? Christ doesn't fare so well, does he? He delays coming to Bethany for a couple of days, knowing that his friend Lazarus has already suffered and died. Christ did so intentionally, just so his disciples might believe, did he not? Watson, you wouldn't have treated a comrade in such a scurvy fashion, I'm sure."

"Jesus knew he'd resurrect Lazarus. Even a skeptic like you must believe in him."

"But Christ had already raised Jairus's dead daughter.[5] And the widow of Nain's son being carried on a bier, dead as a black chestnut—he brought him back to life.[6] What's to be proved by yet another miraculous resuscitation?"

"Please, Holmes. You're not helping—"

"Our client is getting inventive—witness what I found tucked in the cushion of my reserved seat at the opera." Holmes displayed a cream-colored card. "Here's edre's the question: *Why did Jesus delay in coming to Lazarus?*"

"For the glory of God, surely. Scripture plainly says so."

"This passage cannot be as manifest as you suppose."

"Why must you always admire complexity? I understand that other mysteries have needed more involved explanations. But why seek out controversy over the simple truth? Why stirrest thou the cauldron, unless thou a warlock be?"

"Double, double, toil and trouble . . . ," muttered Holmes sinisterly.

"You look like a warlock in that frock coat." Watson felt the carriage lurch slightly as they rounded a corner. "Lazarus has been preached from time immemorial. The theme is constant: resurrection. Why, Sunday last, the visiting archbishop—"

"His Grace not withstanding," commented Holmes, coming out of his remonstrations of Macbeth, "still I am compelled to muddy clear waters with inquiry. First, ponder what we witnessed in the tomb; then evaluate; then test. What details are we over-looking—stumbling over?"

"Perhaps our client erred," Watson said, half to himself, rapping his knuckle on the rain-streaked glass as if it might spell out the secret in raindrops. "If ever a story existed without mystery, Lazarus's is it."

"Then why were we afterwards transported to a Greek amphi-theater merely to watch a rehearsal? And for so short a time? Not that I wanted to see the conclusion of that awful play—it was dreadful, wasn't it? Why, the hero's sword belt was tugging down his pants!" Holmes sighed and pulled out a smallish book from his suit pocket, entitled *Cowboys, Indians and the Great Frontier.* "I brought this along should tonight's play turn out more dismal than the weather."

"It has a rather garish red cover," observed the doctor.

"Mrs. Hudson inadvertently left it behind after dusting. Can you imagine reading such tripe?" He thumbed through the pages.

"It describes bull riding, to my mind a rather violent if not compensatory form of self-gratification—What think you, Watson? Self-abasement is more like it, not to mention tiresome . . ."

"Not as tiresome as us, Holmes—"

"As if being our landlady isn't excitement enough. Wrapping one's legs about a snorting, sweating, malevolent beast and flailing about the arena, arms all akimbo." The detective turned the book sideways to view the illustration. "See here!—a woman straddling a horse, like a man and shooting pistols from both hands. Who can condone this, given circumspect and civilized norms?"

"A dusty pastime, too, I should think," Watson contributed.

"Our landlady may not be the woman we thought." Holmes made a clicking noise with his tongue. "In truth, Watson, I cannot imagine a bull which could throw Mrs. Hudson."

He pocketed the book.

"Our Mysterious Client," he announced quietly, looking out his window as if to catch sight of the mysterious card-giver, "revels in leading us by the nose in not too subtle a manner; I have learned that much. The trouble comes when I look too deeply into our time-travel scenarios, when I read too much into events. We just attended an opera, where the client knew we would be; the scene in ancient Greece was a play. And since the story of Lazarus is recorded only in the gospel John, I may be able to satisfy you on why we were sent there."

"Indeed?"

"It is simply this: the Gospel of John is a play—well, at least this part of it is. Christ plainly states that he only says what he hears the Father saying. He only does what he sees God the Father doing. In chapter 5, verses 20 and 21, Jesus says: *For the Father loves the Son, and shows Him all things that He Himself does; and He* will show Him greater works than these, that you may marvel. For as the Father raises the dead and gives life to them, even so the Son gives life to whom He will.'

"Christ, to my mind, is actually acting out what he sees the Father performing on the celestial stage. He says something very odd in John 12:49: that the Father commands him not only what to say, but *how* to say it."[7]

"Like the director of a play."

Holmes nodded. "I might be tempted to regard this insight—the Gospel of John as a play—as a trivial one. But it may turn out to be the vital key to understanding the Lazarus story—ah! We have arrived at the house." He pounded his stick against the carriage ceiling. "I trust Mrs. Hudson has tea ready. And for you, of course, your warm blanket." He fiddled with his change purse. "Don't forget your gloves, Watson."

THE UNDERTOW

The detective plucked up his Stradivarius and drew a circle in the air with his bow. "I am reminded of a tragedy when I was a lad in Munich—or Heidelberg?—of a girl drowned. Caused by a river's undertow. So it is with this story: a deeper current runs here."

Watson, with legs crossed, wagged one foot toward the warm coals in the fireplace. Holmes struck up in the middle of a Paganini scherzo and then stopped short.

"After considerable study, I have found yet another fascinating feature of John's Gospel, the emerging of two levels of belief: belief based solely on Christ's words, and belief buttressed by Christ's miracles. Faith has a higher quality—no, that is not precise enough—Jesus places a nobler regard for those who believe in him because of his testimony rather than those who respond to his miracles. *'Believe Me that I am in the Father and the Father in Me, or else believe Me for the sake of the works themselves.*[8] That is why Thomas's doubt is showcased in this gospel and nowhere else, because it so clearly contrasts those willing to believe based solely on words, and not on sight. Christ, finally appearing to Thomas, says to him: *'Because you have seen Me, you have believed. Blessed are those who have not seen and yet have believed.*[9] Do you twig it? As with a river, two levels exist: the tranquil surface characterized by the miracles, and the deeper current of belief characterized by taking the Lord at his word."

"What does this have to do with Lazarus?"

"Just this: there must be a deeper understanding of John 11 than what is plainly evident, more than just resurrection—impressive as that is—more than what the miracle so dramatically portrays."

"But what can be more meaningful than a man raised to life? I must protest! The theme of John 11 must be resurrection!"

"At its simplest and most easily understood level, most assuredly. The miracle level will always be the most obvious, as with the river's surface. But what deeper truths lie beneath? What of an undertow? How might Christ's words point us to a deeper understanding, not only of Lazarus, but of a completely different and profound truth?"

"*'I am the resurrection and the life'*[10] certainly seems profound enough. Straightforward and yet wrought with mystery."

Holmes mused, "Christ also said, *'I am the door.' 'I am the good shepherd.' 'I am the way, the truth, and the life.' 'I am the vine.'*"[11]

"But he didn't say it in *this* passage."

"Oh, Watson, you're more conventional than Lestrade![12] If you aren't willing to help me, then get out of my way."

The doctor snuggled deeper into his chair and applied himself to enjoying his evening tea. No use in speaking to a fencepost, in reasoning with a stone wall.

Holmes laid his instrument aside, rubbed his hands briskly together. "*I am the resurrection and the life*'—verse 25—is the key verse of John 11, on the miracle level, at least. In that we agree, heart and soul. But what of another key verse for the word level, for the deeper level? The verse might appear inconsequential—I would wager on it—and so we read over it."

Watson sipped, watching over the rim of his cup as Holmes walked to the fireplace and stared into the large mirror over the mantel.

"It's almost as if—" he turned around, "as if the passage was meant to be fully understood at a later time, much like Christ's image of rivers of living water. Only later did believers understand he meant the Holy Spirit."[13]

"But there's no indication he's doing so in John 11."

"I disagree. For instance, Christ's weighty statement about being 'the resurrection'[14] is addressed to Martha—no theologian by any stretch—and a seemingly contradictory statement pregnant with paradox. Only by deep study have theologians plumbed its depths. Volumes have been written on it, dissecting its profound claims, its meaning. Yet he relates it to a daft woman more inclined to dusting sideboards than sitting at his feet.[15] Oh! I need an open door, Watson, a window left open. I must escape outside chapter 11 to find the clue within. The illuminating statement lies without—I feel it—something Christ might have done or said—"

Watson broke his posture to try one more time: "But then

you are outside the passage's context. You would be violating a long-established methodological rule: do not read out of context. Unless you can find a link."

"Then it is I who must get out. I shall take a turn along the river." Holmes grabbed his coat from the rack. "Down Bond toward Fleet Street—you know the route. Sunday morn may find me kneeling before Cleopatra's Needle, ha, ha!"

"Take a stroll at this hour?" Watson's questions pursued him out the door and down the stairs. "What of the weather? A single-stick[16] is in order, I should say!"

From the apartment window he watched Holmes dart across Baker Street, only to be devoured by the night mist. Watson went to the pedestal and opened the detective's ponderous Bible to John 11, sipped his tea, and read. He looked for the link to enlarge the context beyond the bounds of chapter 11, an exit point leading outside the Lazarus story, but with a doorway back in.

"He'll never find such a verse"—the soothing, pungent tea tickled Watson's mustache hairs before wafting up into his nostrils, clouding his thoughts—"because it's not there."

BOXTYS AND BURNT CREAM

"Holmes, come down from there instantly!" Watson shaded his eyes against the sun and shouted to the top of an immense black carriage which sat off the curb of Trafalgar Square. Nelson's column towered 145 feet above them. "The police most surely are on their way!"

"Yes, do come down, sir!" said a rotund waiter at his elbow, and then whispered to the doctor, "Truth be told, sir, the police were here. And departed. Dining atop a carriage is peculiar behavior, to be sure, but no chargeable offense. The driver—you see him there nodding asleep—has been duly compensated by Mr. Holmes."

Watson huffed. "This is uncharacteristic behavior, even for Holmes, you know. He is a fellow who does things others wouldn't unless they had to, or unless they were under duress or under the influence of stimulants, narcotics, or an irresistible intoxicant. He is quite harmless, otherwise."

"But I fear, however," whined the waiter, "that running back and forth across this avenue to the Grand[17] will incur the displeasure of my superiors—the breaking of platters and dishes—not to mention the danger to me in skuttering across the street, back and forth—"

"Oh peace, Jenkins!" said Holmes, laughing merrily. His face appeared over the drag's edge.[18] "Come up, Doctor, come up! Join me in an early morning repast. Jenkins, I might do with more coffee."

Watson snapped an embarrassed look over his shoulder, grunting as he ascended to the roof and seated himself cross-legged at the white tablecloth spread over the carriage's roof. China plates and crystal glasses twinkled with the silverware.

"Holmes, you must know this is highly irregular. Who ever heard of such a thing—breakfast on a carriage's top? And in Trafalgar Square? See how the people stare!" A bird flapped overhead, circled, and flew off in the direction of the National Gallery. "Even the pigeons think you're mad."

"I am in celebratory bliss!" He grinned in the sunlight. "Help yourself. Last of the coffee? The boxty[19] and rum butter are excellent together; the large ramekin next to the tea cakes holds the most scrumptious burnt cream, excellent accompaniment with your coffee; cream crowdie[20] started me off, and haddock pie (but it's really Billingsgate cod) lies under the silver cover—"

"Fish with oatmeal." Watson winced. "Holmes, you are disgusting."

"How I love it here atop the bustle of London, seeing life onstage." The detective stretched out his arms, his fingers grasping greedily as if for unseen fruit. He relaxed and smiled sleepily. His eyes fell to gazing at a cup before him. Several minutes passed.

"What now, Holmes? Have I remarked how pathological your behavior is? Clinical, even. Numerous of my colleagues come to mind who might help with your current mental malaise."

Holmes gestured. "Tell me about this exquisite teacup, Watson, the first thing which comes to your mind."

"I wish it were mine."

"About the cup, Watson, the cup. Observe it. Study it."

Watson screwed up one eye. "It is a cup."

"Mm."

"Its surface is therefore hard—oh, really, Holmes. This isn't enjoyable."

"Observe on."

"It is white and gold."

"Undoubtedly."

"And small."

"Bravo!"

Watson scratched his chin and huffed. "It is empty."

"Ah. It is empty. Emptiness is an attribute of a different quality, isn't it? We have hit upon a concept, I believe, an opinion, which transports this item into another realm—a realm of purpose."

"You are in your own realm, Holmes. But still, the cup is empty."

"But it is certainly filled with air, is it not?"

"Come, Holmes. It is meant for something substantial, surely.

"Ah, the purpose! This is what makes *empty* a different attribute: it is conjecture on the observer's part. The cup is everything else you stated, and a person alien to our world—from a world where refreshment is unnecessary—would agree with you as to the cup's texture, its material composition, its appearance. Those are facts beyond denying. But there's nothing intrinsic in the cup's form which suggests emptiness, or that it should be sitting rim upward or turned down, for that matter. What is it in a walking stick that suggests it must perform the function as an inanimate companion in the park—?"

"Or a carriage top as a breakfast table—"

"And when we assert *emptiness*, we have crossed over from the actual to the potential—the presupposition of what this cup, indeed all cups, is intended for. This ceramic item has a predetermined role to play, as to its deeper significance for others. The craftsman designed it in this way."

"Your point?"

"Watson, why must you be so dull? For instance, the man two chapters before Lazarus, in John 9, is blind. The disciples see him like observers cut off from heaven, aliens looking at an article without discernment of its deeper purpose and significance. But Christ informs them he is not blind as other blind men: his blindness is predetermined. The Craftsman molded him this way from birth for a purpose. But we are citizens from a dark world and do not see it, for we are blind to the deeper level's richness. Now, take Lazarus. He is dead. And cold. And he stinketh, just as other men who die. But this dead man is not dead like other dead men, any more than the blind man was blind like other blind men. Truly, Lazarus's death has a grand purpose far beyond our limited understanding, a finale to be enacted at the final curtain. And so, for Christ, blindness is seeing, and death is living."

"I am in a fog," mumbled Watson, munching. "The tea cakes are excellent, though."

Holmes fell into another deep meditation. "Wait. I think I have it!"

"You cannot have found any other reason why Christ delayed in coming to Lazarus—or you *are* a warlock. I studied the passage myself."

"I see you brought your Bible as I requested—that large lump in your coat pocket? Give it here. Yes—ah! The blind man. The blind man in John 9." Holmes thumbed through the little Bible. "Here it is, a verse *outside* of chapter 11—John 10:37. It states something most peculiarly: *'Do not believe Me!'* Now, I always thought Christ admonished everyone to believe him. But here he says, *'Do not* believe me, if I do not do the works of my Father,' in other words, "Don't believe me unless you see me do what my Father does." This is an echo of an earlier verse, *'Most assuredly, I say to you, the Son can do nothing of Himself, but what He sees the Father do; for whatever He does, the Son also does in like manner.'*[21] Remember, in John 5:21 Jesus says: *'For as the Father raises the dead and gives life to them, even so the Son gives life to whom He will.'*"

"But how do you link the *'Do not believe Me'* verse in chapter 10 to chapter 11?"

Holmes seemed preoccupied with the concavature of a spoon, or perhaps with its high state of polished luster.

"I'm heartened by your insistence of staying true to proper

textual criticism, Watson. To whom is Christ saying, *'Do not believe Me'* in chapter 10, but to the Jews who have followed him from chapter 9, when he bestowed sight to the blind man?"

"But you've only succeeded in moving the problem back a step," pointed out Watson, "as you are famous for saying to me countless times. How do you link chapter 9 to the Lazarus story? And why would you do so?"

"Because chapter 10 is obviously linked to 9. If I can link chapter 9 to 11, then chapter 10 is linked to 11 as well, at which time the 'unbelief' verse is in play—most powerfully, I might add, for I must have John 10:37!"

The waiter arrived just then, and with his hands heavily bundled, handed up a pot of steaming coffee.

Holmes continued: "It is chapter 9, the passage about the blind man—thank you, Jenkins!—which points me to the key verse in chapter 11, the deeper verse which unlocks the mystery of why Christ really delayed in coming to Lazarus. It is verse 37 of chapter 11: *'Could not this Man, who opened the eyes of the blind, also have kept this man [Lazarus] from dying?'* Don't you see? Because the Jews from chapters 9 and 10 were present at the raising of Lazarus in chapter 11, anything Christ might have said to them in these previous encounters is applicable—nay, might be fulfilled in chapter 11!"

Watson gave him an uncomprehending look.

Holmes breathed out impatiently. "Christ basically states, 'Do not believe in me unless you see me do what my father does,' and shortly thereafter the story of Lazarus unfolds."

"I'm not understanding at all, Holmes. What unfolds?"

"What happens in chapter 11? Not at the detail level, but overall? Not at the street level where we must always trudge along, but from the carriage-top level where we might see things freshly and in their entirety?"

Watson popped a scone into his mouth.

"I ask again, what happens in chapter 11? Listen closely, Watson; this is the key: Christ delays while someone he loves suffers and dies, so that in a few days he can approach his tomb, have the stone rolled away, and raise him from the dead."

The doctor stopped chewing.

"In the story of Lazarus, Christ was reenacting exactly what his Father would do in a few days—for him. *If I am not doing the works of my Father, then do not believe me.*[22] You see, in less than a week the Father himself would delay while his beloved Son died, so that in a few days he could approach the tomb, have the stone rolled away, and raise him from the dead."

Watson swallowed. "I think you have it, Holmes. It is wonderful!" He wiped his mouth with his sleeve in absence of a napkin. Then he grinned and snapped his fingers. "I understand now why Jesus didn't roll the stone away himself—a detail that always puzzled me. A person who could raise the dead should need no help in that regard. But he was imitating his Father down to the finest detail!"

Holmes nodded. "Even so," he said, "this story of Lazarus was but a rehearsal for everyone to see what the Father must do for his own Son. In short, chapter 11 is a rehearsal for the big play to come—the tragedy, rather, with Christ playing the part of his Father."

Watson nodded and looked off. Tears welled up in his eyes. "So, when Christ wept at Lazarus's tomb—"

"It means this: when Christ Jesus died on the cross, his Father wept for him. Heaven wept. So, Watson, is John 11 about the resurrection?" Holmes wolfed down a tea cake before answering the question himself. "It is. But on a deeper level it is about Christ as the complete Mediator—experiencing the sin of mankind on the one hand, and the abject sorrow of heaven on the other."

"I can hardly fathom how Christ could bear the world's sins," Watson said, "but that he felt so keenly the terrible separation of the Father, compounds his sorrow, does it not? As he hung on the cross, he felt the anguished heart of his Father, for he had already experienced it with his beloved friend Lazarus." The doctor dabbed his eyes with his handkerchief. "What a wonderful Savior we have."

221b Baker St., London

It was Watson who stared out on the gloomy night, and Sherlock Holmes who watched him from heavy-lidded eyes. The snap of a match, the spark of fire, the lighting of the cigar, and still the great detective did not look away. The pungent yet pleasant aroma of Indian tobacco filled the sitting room as well as the bedroom beyond before Holmes cleared his throat and spoke.

"Now maybe you'll tell me, my dearest friend: What has been bothering you? You've not been yourself of late."

Watson turned to him briefly and then faced the window again. "I need to confess a great sin: when first we stood in the tomb, when the stench of putrefaction reached my nostrils, my faith faltered. I thought the body was Christ's—the cadaver which lay beneath the bandages—even though the Scriptures profess Jesus never suffered decay. And so I doubted."

"And once you discovered Lazarus was the man?"

"I did not celebrate. I begrudged Jesus, as you did, but secretly. How could he delay while a most beloved friend suffered and died just so he might bask in the limelight? I tried to deflate my anger, to deny my resentment, but it persisted. I pictured Lazarus lying on his sickbed, becoming weaker, his vision growing dimmer, listening for the faintest call or excited shout that the Lord had arrived on the outskirts of Bethany. To save him."

"And now?" Holmes had still not looked away, but watched his dejected friend sit at his writing desk by the window.

"I see matters more clearly. I see the event, as you had admonished atop that silly carriage, through heaven's eyes. God never tests us with anything he is unwilling to endure himself. Lazarus could not have known he was enacting, however unwittingly, a drama being played out in heaven. Much like Job. Certainly there are Christ figures in the Bible—Old Testament Joseph comes to mind. But how glorious to be picked to actually play the part of Christ down to the last detail—and in real life! I am humiliated for what the Lazarus story wrought in me: a lack of faith . . . and a pettiness."

"Why do yourself such injustice? Surely your despondency is natural and just."

Watson raised an eyebrow. "The man breakfasting atop a carriage in the center of London professes to know what is natural?"

"Think of Mary's reaction as the Lord arrived in Bethany, the same Mary who sat mesmerized at Christ's feet, the same Mary who literally worshipped him. Notice, she stayed inside the house, leaving her sister, Martha, to greet him. Mary did come to him, finally, when summoned by the Lord himself. Don't you think she was despondent? What state do you think her faith was in? As well as being woefully hurt by the Lord's inattention? A little aggrieved at Jesus?"

Watson nodded. "But Holmes, back on the miracle level: What was it that made Jesus weep? He knew Lazarus was already dead when he got word from the messengers to come immediately to heal him. Lazarus had been dead four days before he finally arrived in Bethany. What made him so sorrowful to weep?"

"What could it be, Watson, but the sorrow of those outside the grave, the gathered weeping eyes? Of hearing Martha's apparent confession of faith and yet witnessing her lack of faith in hopeless grief. This same faithlessness grieves the Lord, still!

The doctor swallowed hard. "How is it, Holmes, a skeptic such as yourself can have a larger faith than mine?"

"Watson, must you also be a blockhead like Lestrade?" His eyes twinkled as sat forward, drawing Watson's attention. He paused, looked fully at his friend, and said, "Faith has nothing to do with it, old boy. I'm just a better reader than you are."

EIGHT

WHO'S YOUR MAMA?

Watson knew better than to ask where the Needle's Eye had transported them. Both he and Holmes, standing in their best tweed suits, used the rapt silence to ponder the location of their new surroundings. They stood upon a large balcony of a country dwelling, looking out over misty hills creased darkly by a river. In the distance a line of camels plodded along the trade route, resigned to the journey ahead, beneath ponderous loads of spices.

The white curtains behind them were parted by lovely hands and arms. A dark-haired maiden in a white robe joined them, oblivious to their presence, her dark eyes taking in the same scene as they. Why had the Needle's Eye transported them here? Who was this girl? Wealthy? A mere servant girl? And why did her eyes, her whole expression, convey a captivated expectancy?

Holmes narrowed his eyes, inhaled sharply, and looked to the east. The sun, glorious lamp of day, suddenly burst forth from its stronghold and frowning with a hectic halo as it ascended, thirstily licked up the mist.

The maiden quit the balcony, standing for a moment in the wide doorway leading into her bedchamber, the chimes within *ching-ching*ling musically in the strengthening breeze. She traced her cinnamon-colored hand along the long curtains that billowed like sails with diamonds of dew glimmering and shimmering down the floating creases, running before the wind like sparkling schooners beneath a sky bluer than the Darnley Sapphire.[1]

Something was happening. The white curtains began to flow wildly, erratically, in a wraithlike dance. Holmes pointed to the horizon, where the clouds boiled as if in a cauldron. He and Watson left the balcony without a word, following the maiden into her room, and stood at the back wall to see what they would see. Watson, for his part, had never trembled so, a feeling that began as a tremor of wariness and flowered into abject terror as he looked toward the open doorway.

Something ponderous had landed on the balcony.

Intense light flooded the room. The maiden turned away, crying out and overturning a stool as she groped along the floor. She tucked into a corner and stopped her hands tightly against her ears, for with the light came a roaring wind.

Watson felt his heart laboring. His knees trembled violently. He felt a palpable constriction around his throat. He could only groan feebly; he dared not steal a glance to see how Holmes fared, for all his thoughts, his consciousness, were consumed with unfathomable dread.

In cascading falls of color, a creature of tremendous stature crouched down and fished its white face through the curtains. Its long jawbones jutted out, wolflike, with sharp teeth bared. Its hair, if hair it could be called, stood tufted at the crest like snow crystals be-jeweled with diamonds. In the shrieking wind the head turned from side to side. The eyes fastened on the maiden. She bowed her head and pulled her knees to her chest.

The wind stopped. The maiden's eyes appeared above her arms as there came a tinkling sound, like tiny bits of musical metal falling upon a marble floor. Sharp wings at either side of the creature's head tore gashes in the ceiling as it advanced toward her, horrible in firm resolution. It appeared in all manner of stature, from the amazing thickness of its neck to the great size of its hands, similar to a god, magnificent in countenance.

Its white armor glowed with a bluish hue, wonderfully engraved with etchings. Its feet flanked with long spiked wings were so brightly polished that it appeared to be walking on lightning. Upon its breastplate glittered a constellation of rubies and diamonds—the much-prized Medallion Pleiades and the Fighting Brograsse, the greatest honors bestowed in Deep Heaven. A long sword it bore at its side, encrusted with gems. At its other side it bore a long trumpet, fearful and wonderful in its fashioning, able to blast a world into disharmonious ruin.

The creature opened its vasty jaws and spoke. The sound of rushing waters filled the room. And the maiden trembled.

"Lift up your heads, O you gates," it pronounced, looking down with blazing eyes on her tiny form. *"And be lifted up, you everlasting doors! And the King of Glory shall come in."*[2]

The maiden returned its glance and marveled that the thing had grown silent. Could it really see her with those horrible eyes? But then the maiden guessed correctly—it was waiting for her to answer. She summoned her courage and to her amazement heard herself utter the correct response: *"Who is this King of Glory?"*[3]

"The LORD *strong and mighty, the* LORD *mighty in battle."*[4]

The floor rumbled as the being stepped closer, and the sound was like a thundering doom. The maiden pressed back more firmly into the corner. The creature lowered its face to hers. The teeth opened and closed, grinding together, so that her knees shook, but not from fear. Rather, she felt the crushing weight of Glory, of one who stands in the audience of God.

"Be unafraid, Mary," it pronounced, pondering her frail form. Blue flames licked about its shoulders, fire from the very Throne. Its voice became more subdued, but only as the thundering surf is softer than a crushing gale. It explained how the power of the Highest would come upon her, the name of the child she would bear, Jesus, and that the throne of his father David would be given him.

The creature's eyes flashed, reflecting other worlds, perhaps a twinkle of inquisitive humor in those fierce lamps. It fell silent. Waiting. The maiden summoned her courage and heard herself respond: *"Behold the maidservant of the Lord! Let it be to me according to your word."*[5]

THE WICKED WITCH OF THE NORTH

The woman was old now, looking into the polished bronze mirror and perhaps thinking of her younger days. Her neck had grown loose and grainy, like a chicken's. With an ivory comb she brushed her hair, supplemented nicely with black dyes, and blackened her eyebrows with mineral pastes. She tilted her head again. Not bad for an old queen mother.

She lifted a small lid from a petite-handled pottery vessel, and the air became filled with the pungent perfume-essence of myrrh. Whenever she felt lonely and abandoned—which was often of late—she craved the fragrance, as it reminded her of her homeland near the Great Sea.

She scrutinized her face again, the lines around her eyes, her nose, her full lips. So much besides her looks had changed since she came to Israel from Sidon—oh, grand, beautiful Sidon! But she could still put on a grand show. From an ivory ointment-flask she applied a special lotion of spikenard for her hands, for her neck, crooning softly in the warm extravagance of gingergrass. Other queens employed special servant girls for such tasks—the application of cosmetics and the combing of the hair—but no, no, no: she trusted no one so close to her exposed neck.

Using a tiny ivory spoon, exquisitely decorated with storks and ostriches, she extracted cosmetics from a small box inlaid with ebony and lapis lazuli. Her skin spots vanished under her brisk application. Next she extracted a miniature bronze spatula, dipped it in a pool of luxuriously bright paint, and coated her eyelids in purple—the same hue as the Mediterranean in the evening. She blinked. Ah!—an excellent effect, and it would match her robe. She attached her flashing yellow earrings of topaz from Mari; her sardius necklace in the likeness of the goddess Isis, a gift from Egypt's King Osorkon, flashed red and gold from her chest.

She rose from the little table and donned her rich ceremonial dress and fastened around her waist a girdle decorated with gold falcons with piercing cornelian eyes. She twirled once, took one last look at herself, and smiled to see the flash of blue dart from her glance, just as in the days of old.

She would show him, charm him.

Something startled her—movement out of the corner of her eye. Two cloaked and hooded men stood in the back of her chamber. Two of her priests, no doubt, but naughty priests who must be taught a lesson in over-familiarity. She instantly rang for the guards as she felt for the gold dagger she kept as a companion in her robe, and approached them.

"Who are you?" she crooned seductively. "Do you not know it is the death sentence to venture unbidden into my chambers?"

"We are here as observers only, Your Majesty," said the taller man, and laid back his hood. He was no priest, but was clean-shaven, and his short-cropped black hair was combed straight back and gleamed brighter than a raven's wing. But it was his eyes, so gray and pitiless, that arrested her attention. "Your guards will be delayed, Your Majesty, occupied as they are at holding the gate."

"You are not from Israel?" she heard herself ask. "Assassins, perhaps, from Assyria, from the land of the Hittites? I have never heard your strange accent, and yet I am a woman accustomed to the world's wide stage."

"We are from a place you will never see."

"What are your names?" Now she had the presence of mind to observe the black-haired man's smaller companion with deep-set eyes.

"Names are unimportant, madam—"

"But I require it. And if you knew who stands before you in regal splendor—who *demands* your name—you would give it with a faint head and trembling heart."

"I do know you, madam." Pitiless gray eyes met remorseless blue eyes. "I picked a wilted orchid once, and out crept a spider."

"Do you mean that as a picture for me?" She felt her hand tighten on the dagger's handle. "Yes, I have lived out my youthful days, I suppose, and yet I can still sting. Again: Who are you?"

"I and my companion are from the future. Unbelievably, we

live many thousands of years hence, and we tremble for a loftier monarch, a kinder queen.[6] Undoubtedly, we are allowed to converse with you, O Queen, because it will have no accounting in history. And know this, too, madam: we do know your name. Unregrettably, we are here to witness your death."

The Queen mother backed away to the table, undaunted, and laughingly walked her delicate fingers across its surface to a small statue, which she lifted, caressed. And kissed.

"He will not let me die," she breathed hoarsely, and kissed the gold statue of Baal again. "From Great Sidon I brought him, introduced him to this parched and severe land whose people worship a parched and severe god."

The sound of heavy footfalls echoed through the hallway. "And now we shall see," she rejoined, "who shall witness whose death."

The door opened, and three large men entered the chamber.

"Seize these trespassers!" she shrieked, and pointed her dagger at them.

"Your Majesty," said the foremost guard urgently, "Jehu has entered the courtyard—"

She turned with a rustle of her dress—it sounded like the rushing of the surf—and ran to the window. Holmes and Watson followed quickly, looking down from an adjacent window in the tower's top.

An armored man stood below in his chariot which was fashioned of iron and drawn by four horses. A decapitated head with the shoulder and arm attached was impaled on a spike fastened to the side of his chariot. A gold signet ring shone from its bloody hand, which seemed to beckon for mercy that never came.

She swallowed hard, taking in what remained of her son,

King Joram of Israel. Holmes could hear it, a slight trembling in her question as she called down, smiling through her sneer. "Is it peace, Zimri, murderer of your master?"

The warrior pointed up to the window and called, "Who is on my side? Who? Throw her down!"

The queen wheeled on Holmes and Watson, snarling and brandishing her weapon, the dagger flashing with emerald and ruby light. But her features contorted, fury replaced with surprise as she was grabbed from behind by two of her men. She stabbed at Holmes as she was lifted, her shocked glance meeting his as her dagger passed harmlessly through his sparkling midsection. High in the air they lifted her, threw her outward, and then she was gone.

She saw Mt. Tabor jerk sideways in the distance as she twirled. Halfway down the tower wall she hit a cornice which shattered her shoulder. She landed heavily on the ground, snapping her leg in two, leaving her in a dazed, detached consciousness. As if in a nightmare, she observed the red blotches spattered on the wall and on Jehu's horses—her own life's blood—and sensed, dully, the heavy horses' hooves pounding into her chest and stomach, her warm blood flowing from her mouth and over her remarkable necklace, fashioned in Thebes. And the dogs . . . the dogs, grinning.

BART'S

From the archway of St. Bartholomew's Hospital, two figures walked slowly to the street, accompanied by attendants. The taller of the pair attempted to bear himself regally, with his top hat, overcoat, walking stick. And yet his unhurriedness betrayed unaccustomed frailty, not one of practiced old age but of a younger man having endured a recent catastrophe. He and his companion were painstakingly helped into a large carriage with the aid of an elderly woman dressed in fine, black lace, setting off her marvelously sculptured white hair.

"Thank you, Mrs. Hudson," breathed Dr. John Watson, after she had patted a blanket over his knees. Across from him, the greatest detective London would ever know settled in. But he neither regarded his assistants nor expressed appreciation when the selfsame service was applied to him. Holmes' vacant eyes turned toward the window as the carriage lurched forward and rumbled along Holborn Street, changing to High Holborn, and then to Oxford Street.

"Mightn't you tell me what happened," she asked of Watson, "which has hospitalized you and Mr. Holmes these six days, sir? Which has frosted your mustache to white?"

"A terrible holiness," replied Watson quietly, for Holmes exhibited a precarious, even fragile equanimity, "a glorious presence of such weight that we were nearly crushed, and an interview with the wickedest woman who ever lived."

Sherlock Holmes seemed not to hear them and stared distantly out the window.

At 221b Baker Street, they exited the carriage. But at the front door an act most defining astounded Watson: Holmes, with a seraphic smile accompanied, oddly, by tears, lifted his silver-headed walking stick horizontally. He braced his arms downward, his knuckles going white as the stick trembled under his immense strength, and with a loud snap, cracked it in two with the strength of a longshoreman.

THE INTRUDER

"Is there not a single match in this infernal dwelling?" growled Sherlock feebly. Dressed loosely in his robe and his hair all a-tussle, he resembled his unlit cigarette: pale, thin, and lacking fire. His question, the first words he had uttered in days, so overjoyed Mrs. Hudson that she overlooked his vituperate vehemence.

"You may smoke all the Guinea Golds you wish once you've partaken of your soup." She wagged her finger at the bowl touching his elbow. "Doctor's orders, sir: eat your soup."

"You are the very devil, Mrs. Hudson."

"She's a saint," Watson declared, sitting opposite him at the fireplace.

"Not unless carping triviality and dullness are virtues," Holmes muttered. He went to stretch, but the motion seemed to bring him pain. Watson smiled at the departing Mrs. Hudson.

"At least now I know why angels say, 'Fear not,'" Watson said, touching his mustache delicately, as if the white hairs were painful. "I was impressed with Mary's fortitude in the presence of the heavenly messenger."

"Jezebel cut a strikingly ominous figure as well, but not a heavenly one. As thoroughly evil as Gabriel was holy." The detective fell silent, tired. "Watson, our current faculties are weak—mine, at any rate—but we must engage the mystery at hand. 'Mothers' seems to be the theme, given our last two forays into the past as the Needle's Eye's guests. We have witnessed the best and the worst of mothers."

"Mary, surely, as the mother of the Lord," remarked Watson, and then shrugged, "but Jezebel, a mother—?"

"You saw the head impaled on Jehu's chariot—her own son,

King Joram, Ahab's heir? And her actions in usurping her husband's power and in introducing Baal led to the slaughter of seventy more sons of Ahab, as well as Ahaziah, her daughter's son, king of Judah. Her daughter, too, nearly brought about the downfall of Judah. Yes, her maternal instincts were thorough and profound!"

Wincing, Holmes reached across a tan-colored card in response to Watson's questioning look. Holmes didn't bother explaining the surprising location where it had appeared. It read: *Why is Jehoiachin[7] included in Jesus' genealogical record?*

Watson frowned. "Who is Jehoiachin?"

"Have you read Christ's genealogy?"

"I hear it drolly recited in church every other Christmas."

"The list of names is shocking, really. I suppose allowance must be made for the odd embezzler here and murderer there, not to mention Gentiles and evil kings, but when an outright intruder lurks on the list, a name which does not belong . . ." Holmes gestured, "Please, Doctor, would you be so kind as to read from my Bible which I've located near the window—Matthew's genealogy of Christ? It is opened to the page."[8]

Holmes spied a stray match beneath the ashtray. With Mrs. Hudson safely out of the room, he lit up as Watson read.

"Do you see it?" asked the detective.

"Yes, Jehoiachin is there. But his name is of the needle-in-the-haystack variety and blends in with the others. What makes him an outcast?"

"Read Jeremiah in the Old Testament, and you will see clearly enough:

""*As I live," says the* LORD, *"though [Jehoiachin] the son of Jehoiakim, king of Judah, were the signet on My right hand, yet*

167

I would pluck you off; and I will give you into the hand of those who seek your life, and into the hand of those whose face you fear— the hand of Nebuchadnezzar king of Babylon and the hand of the Chaldeans. So I will cast you out, and your mother who bore you, into another country where you were not born; and there you shall die. But to the land to which they desire to return, there they shall not return. Is this man [Jehoiachin] a despised, broken idol—a vessel in which is no pleasure? Why are they cast out, he and his descendants, and cast into a land which they do not know? O earth, earth, earth, hear the word of the LORD! *Thus says the* LORD: *'Write this man down as childless, a man who shall not prosper in his days; for none of his descendants shall prosper, sitting on the throne of David, and ruling anymore in Judah.'"*[9]

"Fascinating, Holmes. And disturbing. The Lord is often portrayed as having limitless pity and forgiveness. Apparently not. What a beastly king Jehoiachin must have been!"

Holmes blew out a pleasurable cloud of purplish smoke. "His father, Jehoiakim, was an unjust man, wicked by nature. He shed much innocent blood in Jerusalem, including murdering the prophet Uriah." Holmes looked off, perhaps remembering the cold queen, whose last act was to try and kill him. "Makes one ponder if there are people born without souls, destined only for destruction."

"But Jehoiachin only reigned three months."

"The Lord had seen enough from Jehoiakim, his father—the apple falling not far from the tree. The Lord desires no prayers on Judah's behalf.[10] They have crossed the line, thumbed their noses for the last time at his unalterable law. He will have no pity upon them.[11] He commands the young king (as wicked in disposition as his father) and his iniquitous mother, Nehushta, to step down.[12] To be so prominently mentioned in the text, Nehushta was probably the real power behind the throne, as was Jezebel for the morose and temperamental Ahab."

"So, Jehoiachin and his mother were banished—"

"Jehoiachin in Hebrew," interrupted Holmes for an observation, "means 'Yahweh will establish.' There is delicious irony for you. Imagine the young king and his mother in irons, being led ignobly away from Jerusalem by the conquering Babylonians. To the land of Nebuchadnezzar. Never to return. There, to die in Babylon with this promise: *None of Jehoiachin's offspring will ever sit upon the throne of David.*"

"Maybe, in the time between Jehoiachin's banishment and Christ's birth, the throne became an outdated concept."

Holmes shook his head. "No, the angel specifically told Mary that the Lord God would give him (Jesus) the throne of his father David. Remember?"

Watson frowned. He turned the royal cream card lightly in his fingers. "And yet Jehoiachin's name is listed in Christ's genealogy . . ."

"You are not upset by this contradiction?"

"*Seeming* contradiction."

Holmes snorted. "God told Jeremiah specifically that none of Jehoiachin's heirs will sit upon the throne of David—"

"I've learned my lesson, Holmes, from the Zechariah son of Berechiah affair.[13] What begins as unexplained will bear out. I have faith in the Scriptures."

"You have faith in *me*," said Sherlock with a smile. He tapped his cigarette ash into the soup.

The Barbarians

Holmes, a few days later, wore a comfortable (if not fashionable) suit which made pacing appear like a dance. He had exchanged cigarette for pipe, with its aromatic plume.

"I am struck by the varieties of genealogical allowance," he stated to an attentive Watson, sitting in his favorite fireside chair. "You don't have to wade more than ankle deep into this matter to ascertain that genealogies are seldom concerned with strict accuracy, but are created for a specific purpose in mind."

"You have already resorted to excuse-making?" asked Watson.

"Indeed not. It is a tacit fact: some biblical genealogies frequently ferret out unimportant or embarrassing family members—such as Moses' lineage. The list of Aaron's descendants in Ezra 7 omits six names which are given in his genealogy in 1 Chronicles 6. And Ezra's genealogy lists only five generations between Zadok and the time Ezra returned to the Holy City. Some genealogies were meant for military purposes, others for taxation. The Levitical priesthood's, on the other hand, kept precise records to maintain Judaism's purity. If your name was not listed in the priestly genealogy, you were out.[14] The same standard held for the royal genealogies as well, tracing accurately the list of kings from David down to the present."

"But Jehoiachin's name is clearly written," persisted Watson.

"Matthew's account is abbreviated, demonstratively so, in his three units of fourteen names each. It is not incorrect, but strict detail is not its concern. We, in this modern age and in modern London, must take care in imposing our strict requirements on an ancient culture so wholly unconcerned with our biased opinions."

Holmes clamped his teeth on his pipe and crossed his arms. "Interesting: Zerubbabel, an important fellow in the restoration of Jerusalem, is listed as the grandson of Jehoiachin by way of his son, Pedaiah.[15] But in Ezra, Zerubbabel is the son of Jehoiachin's son Shealtiel.[16] So, then, words such as *son* or *daughter, father,* or *mother* were widely used and held wider meanings. A *father* could be a grandfather, or not necessarily a family member at all, but simply a man influential to the family. The same with mothers. Brothers could be such because they were joined by treaty."

"All of this is so confusing," lamented Watson.

"This is my finding: just because names were left out didn't render the genealogy inaccurate. So, Matthew's account is legitimate, if abbreviated."

The doctor rubbed the back of his neck. "But Matthew's genealogy lists Jehoiachin as a legitimate descendant of Christ—"

"Yes, yes, yes—"

"And Jeremiah prophesied this would never be the case. But Holmes, think! Since our theme centers on the mother, what do we know of King Jehoiachin's?"

"In 2 Kings 24:8 we find out more about her: Jehoiachin's mother—the queen mother—is called 'Nehushta,' which means 'serpent' and remarkably resembles 'Nehushtan,' the name given to Moses' bronze serpent, which the Israelites worshipped.[17] Think of the control and influence she must have had on the eighteen-year-old Jehoiachin! Nehushta must have been vile indeed—on the order of a Jezebel—to have been so contently married to a king on the order of a Jehoiakim, Jehoiachin's father." Holmes gestured hopelessly. "But what else may we learn of her? What more can we safely conjecture about Jehoiachin's mother? Who was Nehushta's mother? Was she wicked?" He shook his head. "I am like a blind man in a dark room, looking for a black cat that isn't there."

Holmes took a deep breath. He rubbed his temples as if a headache, having spent but a few moments in its infancy, had begun to mature into adulthood, made no less inevitable by a knock and the door opening.

Mrs. Hudson, bearing her lunch tray, began setting the table. She went about her labor silently, apparently having internalized Holmes' insulting remark as to her viability for canonization as a saint. Holmes, trying to make up, said cheerily, "So, Mrs. Hudson, what is for lunch? I feel uncommonly wolfish. How 'bout you, Doctor?"

She announced, "Cold beef, sliced, is here. Bread. And soup, same as before, which you must eat." She looked in the bowl at his elbow and shot him a cold look. To have her loving visits to them in the hospital, her loving care, so cruelly repaid by ashes flicked in her soup!

"She means to poison us, Watson, d'ye see?" laughed Holmes over jauntily. "Again, I point to her Scotch ancestry as adept in eviscerating the civilized man, in putting the commoner to the knife. I mean to watch my step with such a landlady!"

"As well you should, sir. Robert d'Bruce, King of Scots, is my ancestor on my father's side. He'd done for the English in his time. But be warned, Mr. Holmes, my mother's forebears swallowed up the Roman Ninth Legion north of the wall.[18] Nor would *they* have any compunctions in poisoning the soup of any Englishman. With ashes or otherwise."

She gathered up the befouled soup, placed the desecrated bowl on the tray, and left.

"Ah, the barbarians! Marvelously murderous. Delectably bloodcurdling!"

Watson, sitting at the table and almost done with his lunch, asked, "What is it, Holmes?" This, in regard to a solemn mood which had descended on the detective. "This food is very tasty, even if poisoned."

"I contemplate the bewitching effect one aged landlady has upon my psyche. Mrs. Hudson has done it again, Watson, has opened the door—no, the window—to let the light flood in."

He sprang to his feet and made his way over to where his massive Bible lay. He grappled a great many pages in one hand and, like folding over a mattress, turned forward into the New Testament.

"Oh, I am such a daft mule! What first vision did we witness at the beginning of this mystery?"

"Why, Mary's meeting with the angel—"

"Yes, yes, yes! It is not Nehushta, the *mother of Jehoiachin*, which matters here. It is Mary, the *mother of Jesus*! It is the mother's relatives that are essential, just as Mrs. Hudson admonished. I recall somewhere in the back of my mind a separate genealogy of Christ which calls out for our examining. Does it really exist, though?" Holmes kept turning the pages through the Gospels. "Matthew's list of Christ's descendants, the one we have been harping on, is *Joseph's* line, not Mary's!"

"What? Jesus has two genealogies?"

"Yes, as does Mrs. Hudson—as do all of us." Holmes tapped himself on the forehead with his thumb extended from his fist, like a smoking pipe. "Mary's line is recorded in . . ." he snapped his fingers ". . . in Luke!"[19]

Holmes stopped turning the pages and let his finger glide down the page. As he read to himself, he chuckled, he nodded, and he chuckled again, and then he hummed with a low, reverberating buzzing reminiscent of a saw being rasped back and forth across a piece of hollow wood. "You see it?"

"What matters is what I do not see," nodded Watson, wiping his mouth with a napkin and looking over his shoulder. "Jehoiachin's name is absent. This is Mary's lineage, you say?"

"Indeed. A royal line in its own way, traced from King David through his son Nathan, not Solomon. Matthew's genealogy is directed to Jews needing proof of Jesus' credentials, to establish Christ's *legal* father, the official line by which Jesus rightfully inherited the throne. Joseph adopted Jesus as his son. Luke, in contrast, begins his genealogy by saying, '*Now Jesus . . . , being (as was supposed) the son of Joseph . . .*' A curious way of handling the Son of God's genealogy, wouldn't you say? Luke's list is not through Joseph—he flatly says so. After all, Matthew had already traced Joseph's side. Mary is Christ's *actual* mother—his only blood parent. Furthermore, Luke's Greek audience would understand Christ being presented as the Perfect Man, the focus of Greek philosophy and thought."

"So,"—Watson traced his fingers over the page of names—"this is also why Luke traces Christ all the way back to the first man, Adam."

"Oh, Watson, your ingenuity astounds me! How often you reaffirm my choice in you as my principal friend and confidant! Yes indeed. And keep in mind, Luke has been termed 'the Gospel of Women.' As a physician he would have a sensitivity to mothers and childbirth. It's not surprising Mary's Song is recorded in his gospel."

"A little surprising, then, that no women are listed in his genealogy of Christ."

"I commend you once again, my good doctor. But many names in Luke's list are obscure, unrecognizable, untraceable. Perhaps they are Greek versions of Jewish names—which would make sense. Luke will impose no Jewish stumbling blocks for Gentiles who wanted to embrace Christianity, especially in a climate where Claudius has expelled all Jews from Rome. On the other hand, he lists some strikingly Levitical names—Levi twice—which validates Luke's testimony stating Mary was related to Elizabeth, John the Baptist's mother, whose lineage was of Aaron's line."

"Well done, Holmes. So it seems that Christ is of royal descent on both sides! Once again, my faith in the Bible is vindicated—oh, and in you as well."

"That's not all, my dear Watson. In Zechariah 12:12, I came across this interesting lament having to do with the Christ, the one they have pierced: *'And the land shall mourn, every family by itself: the family of the house of David by itself, and their wives by themselves; the family of the house of Nathan by itself, and their wives by themselves.'*"

The doctor sat back and took a deep breath.

An hour later, Watson sat watching the great detective read from a book as he paced and smoked—a talent Watson was inwardly confessing he did not possess when Holmes stopped abruptly, put his head back, and let out a shrill-like cackle. The doctor nearly jumped into the fireplace.

"Could you do with a laugh, Watson?" said Holmes, holding up his history book. "Here is a ludicrous incident in reference to Luke's genealogy which happened in the fourteenth century. Are you attending? Listen: A particularly negligent scribe was copying the Gospel of Luke. The genealogy from which he was transcribing must have listed Jesus' descendants in two columns of twenty-eight lines each." Holmes' smile broadened so widely that he could hardly draw on his pipe. "Instead of copying each column downward, as was proper, the scribe copied across the two columns, line by line."

Sherlock Holmes dropped his pipe in a spasm of frivolity, collapsing in the chair across from Watson in a heap of howling laughter.

"You'll have to do better than that, Holmes," Watson said, rubbing his eyes.

"Oh, Watson, don't you see?" Holmes found his place on the page again. "Here, it comes out: The result of the scribe's error was that each person in the list had the wrong father, and because the names must not have filled the last column of the exemplar, God himself is cited *within* the list instead of at its close, and then as the son of Aram! Ha, ha, ha! The father and creator of the human race ended up being, not the Almighty, but rather a fellow named Phares! Ha, ha, ha!"[20]

Watson had to join in the laughter, partly from the story, but more so because Holmes was so clearly delighted. After the dark days following their hospital stay, Watson wondered if Holmes had reverted to the same desperate state of mind as he had found him aboard the *Viceroy of India*, and had worried whether Holmes would ever recover his lighter side. And so it was good to see, even as he recollected thusly, Holmes letting out a fresh torrent of hilarious laughter.

Watson's humor suddenly dissipated. Holmes had scooped up a ball of ash from the carpet where his pipe had fallen and stood at the table with his hand suspended over his soup bowl.

"Not funny, Holmes."

"I should be shackled and exiled forever by my landlady"— the detective grinned.

"I wouldn't give a fig for your life if you do it."

"—shamed, forgotten. Cast into the Abyss. Never to return. Left to languish and die in a foreign prison."

The smile on Holmes' face vanished, replaced by a horror outweighed by any fright ever affected by angelic beings. He snapped a glance over to the door. It was cracked open to the barest sliver.

Mrs. Hudson was watching.

NINE

RUN FOR YOUR LIFE

BETHLEHEM LAY SLUMBERING IN SILVER SHADOW BENEATH THE moon. The night air flapped Holmes' traveling cloak, whisking away his pipe smoke. Dr. Watson shivered, readjusted his derby hat, and peered into the gloom.

"Someone is heading this way, Holmes."

Customarily, Sherlock did not smoke a pipe out of doors, for inevitably, duty called unexpectedly, and he must tap out a half-smoked bowl. He grumbled, blaming himself and circumstance, when soft hoofbeats interrupted him. Travelers hurried along the road leading from the sleepy town. A cloaked and hooded woman sat atop a donkey with a small boy, led by a tall man. They passed by the invisible Londoners hurriedly and were lost in the distant wilderness.

"Heading south-southeast," whispered Holmes, half to himself. "Egypt. And just in time!" He sniffed the air and, with his walking stick, pointed toward Bethlehem. With a sudden burst of speed, he sprinted toward the town below. Watson chugged along behind.

"I sense a deeper chill!" called Holmes as he ran. He stopped at

179

the edge of town and glanced down the narrow street. "Its course runs deep, deliberate, cold metal upon hot flesh—the advent of anachronous murder."

A cow mooed from a stable nearby to the brittle backdrop of crickets. Watson came up and leaned against the corner of a nearby house, breathing heavily.

"Holmes! Will you not hazard a guess as to who the travelers might be fleeing upon the road? She and the child upon the donkey? He who led the way?"

The doctor's inquiry died amid the rumbling of thundering hoofs—a company of approaching cavalry, silent, resolute. They dismounted at the town's edge, drew their swords, and stormed down the central street, their silver blades reflecting the stars.

The sharp report of a door being flung open broke the stillness. A shrieking woman, a bundle pressed to her chest, ran from out of the glowing yellow doorway, pursued by three soldiers. As they passed by, Holmes struck out viciously with his walking stick at the men, and Watson dove at their legs, but the soldiers passed through them as if they were but ripples in a dream. The trio of soldiers were on the woman in seconds, tearing the bundle out of her arms and throwing it to the ground. The shocked cry of an infant pierced the night; little hands waved from the cloth bundle. Two soldiers raised their weapons, laughing, the woman wilting in the grasp of the third as they hacked downward with their swords.

The crickets fell mute; the moon passed behind a cloud. Other distant screams broke night's tranquility, sharp shrieks, heartrending wails which pierced their hearts.

"Nature hides her face from black blood in the night, from howled murder," Holmes said. His voice trembled in the saying of it, and Watson tore at his hair to watch the woman crawl, whining pitifully, to the motionless bundle. "And so shall we."

A Formidable Escort

Holmes, dressed in his traditional black robe and having dismounted his horse, studied a waist-high monument which was really no monument at all, but a road marker. Watson, still atop his horse and dressed in his biblical, tan robe, trained his telescope westward over a countryside of rough scrub and swamps.

"I can just make out a lake, I think, Holmes."

The detective, deep in thought, pulled back his hood and looked north and south along the road.

"We are ten kilometers south east of Caesarea, according to this marker—see these Roman characters?" He traced his finger in the granite's chiseled writing. "Antipatris lies another thirty-two kilometers southeast from us. Your body of water is terribly vast for a lake, Watson. I'm afraid it is the Mediterranean Sea."

"Which means this remarkably fine road is the Way of the Sea, is it not?"

Sherlock Holmes thumbed through his pocket history book, which must have contained maps, because he turned it sideways. "No, this is not the *Via Maris*, though it could pass for it, as nicely paved as it is. The Way of the Sea comes up from Egypt and passes through Gaza and Ashkelon, but at Joppa it turns northwest, away from the sea, because of coastal swamplands, and continues on through Antipatris and inland over the Plain of Sharon to Megiddo. You and I stand upon a military road that cuts across northwest from Antipatris to Caesarea."

"Antipatris?"

"Herod the Great built the city in honor of his father, Antipater," remarked Holmes, glancing up at Watson, but looking through him. "My question is, why have we been brought here?"

Watson sniffed the brisk west wind. Yes, he could smell it: salt. Holmes stooped down and picked up a small roll of parchment, shaking off the dust and opening it. He handed it up to the doctor, whose momentary reflection on the writing was cut short by a faint sound, like a multitude of kettledrums.

"Do you hear that, Holmes?"

Holmes had already mounted and taken his horse's reins firmly in hand.

"It cannot be thunder on a clear day, Watson, unless New Testament weather is remarkably unlike our own. We must vacate the road—immediately!"

They nudged their horses away to a small copse of trees. Holmes took the telescope and peered southward. A company of horsemen appeared on the road—more than a company—a contingent. They moved swiftly, small shields strapped to their arms, bows slung at their backs and small swords at their belts.

Romans.

"Light cavalry," said Holmes in a detached voice, focusing the glass on them. "Armed for speed. They might be a sort of *sagittarii*, or mounted archers, but I doubt it. They must have left Antipatris very early this morning to be this far along the road to Caesarea. I assume that is their destination." Holmes brought down the glass, cleaned the lens with a handkerchief, and reapplied his attention. "Interesting: their flag bears an infantry insignia as well. This cavalry unit is a sort of *cohortes equitatae*[1]—I studied Roman military heraldry after our Philippi affair." Holmes snapped the glass down. "So, where are the ground troops?"

The clink of harness could be heard now, two scouts riding well in advance of the main column. As they passed in the distance, the scouts looked their way.

"Do they see us?"

Holmes didn't answer, but pointed the telescope toward the host. "A red-caped soldier rides at the head of the column, their leader, no doubt, the *praefectus equitum*. I make their number to be a little over two *turmae*,[2] about seventy or eighty soldiers—wait!" Ever so delicately, Holmes rotated the front lens of the telescope. "An older man rides in their midst, a civilian, by the looks of him." Holmes chuckled and handed the telescope over. "What do you make of him?"

Watson had trouble with the glass at first. Peering at the expansive sea was one thing, but focusing on jostling horsemen was another, but then he reminded himself to keep both eyes open when peering through the telescope. He focused on the helmets and flashes of color, the banners, the sun glinting off the amulets on the horses' bridles. A shock shivered down Watson's spine.

"It is our old friend—the apostle Paul!" Watson said, turning from the eyepiece. "I recognize him from the prison in Philippi. Is this scene even in the Bible, Holmes?"

The question fell unanswered as the column rumbled by and disappeared northward toward Caesarea.

The Londoners nudged their horses forward without a word. They had traveled enough together to know each other's thoughts. They hit the road and galloped northward to follow the Roman cavalry and keep a sharp eye out for clues, no matter how slight or seemingly insignificant.

"What brings Paul here, I wonder?" asked Holmes over the clip-clop of the hooves.

"What brings *us* here?"

The road was amazingly smooth, well maintained even by modern standards. They passed another stone mile marker—and would, explained Holmes—every sixteen hundred yards or so, equivalent to one Roman mile. Couriers passed this way, he went on to say, conveying messages on horseback. Much like the American West's pony express, with resting stations every twenty-five miles, riders could replace their tired mounts with fresh horses.

Holmes waxed eloquent on the relatively small size of ancient horses (and people). They had just rounded a sharp bend in the road when—

"Ho!" Watson shouted and jerked back on his reins. He pulled his horse sharply around and galloped wildly in the opposite direction. Sherlock Holmes followed suit, right on his heels. Indeed, the scouts *had* seen the pair of time-travelers, had fallen back with the scouts of the vanguard, and had waited to hear the hoof falls of any pursers before spurring after them at full gallop.

Without a proper saddle, with no stirrups, with nothing but his own knees pressed inward to keep him upright on the beast's back, Watson rode as best he could along the road back the way they had come. The pounding hoofbeats of Holmes' horse drew near as he pulled even with Watson, the two horses, side by side, flying like the wind.

But the Romans were gaining. Watson spurred his horse again and felt the sweaty surge of the beast in a fresh burst of speed. Still, the Romans drew nearer. Watson saw a hand holding a whip rise against the sky and then descend as the scouts drove their beasts mercilessly. Watson leaned forward, his cheek brushing his horse's mane, smelling his sweat, his terror. He let up with his knees and fell into a rhythm with his charge, feeling the beast's ebb and flow as it reached out and pulled the ground beneath them faster, faster.

The Romans were no longer gaining and looked as if they might stall. But no ordinary soldier led the chase that day. Marcus Chrestus Junius,[3] born a slave and named after an ambitious soldier and equestrian, had risen through the army ranks, first as a lancer, ultimately as an archer. It was said that none in the eastern Roman theatre could match his skill with the bow, nor equal his marks of excellence from galloping horseback. He turned sideways in the saddle, extended his bow with his left arm, and drew back the arrow. At this range, he could not miss.

But just as the arrow sang away from the string on its lethally straight line, the two horses ahead of them slowed down and wandered off the road. And in the short moment it took the scouts to overtake them, the two riders, inexplicably, had disappeared.

BIRTH AND DEATH

The hansom carriage rambled spiritedly eastward toward the Surrey side of London, onto the stately, seven-arched structure of iron and granite stretching over the River Thames, known as Westminster Bridge. The Houses of Parliament loomed up on the right, dominated by Victoria Tower.

Holmes tapped the carriage's ceiling with his walking stick and jerked open his front panel. He exited the cab as the horses were just slowing, and cantered out onto the sidewalk as Watson paid the fare. The detective slanted his watch, then began snapping his fingers in time. He shaded his eyes and looked up at the Clock Tower.[4] Big Ben, the largest bell in the land, sounded out: thirteen tons of bronze declaring to all of London it was nine o'clock in the morning.

"Nine seconds slow!" Holmes snapped shut the solid gold timepiece and displayed it to Watson. "Gift from the king of Prussia, d'ye remember?"

"Doesn't ring a bell."

"Ha, ha, Watson. Well, it loses nine seconds a fortnight! How might a country produce a chess master like Mr. Zuckertort[5] and yet fail to fashion a working pocket watch?"

They crossed busy Westminster Road, dodging carriages and couriers, to the bridge's other side and stared out over the tranquil waters of the Thames. To the north Scotland Yard rose above the trees, while farther down the river, Charing Cross Rail and Foot Bridge partially obscured Waterloo Bridge angling away to Somerset House.

"I am meditating," Holmes reflected, "on the particular consequences of time, of a few seconds lost or gained. Fantastic comparisons come to mind of what nine seconds might have had upon history's course. For instance, the bullet fired from the French ship which struck down Admiral Lord Nelson at Trafalgar. Consider the consequences of nine seconds with the variances of wind or the sun; the slight roll or vibration of the deck; or the interposing of a sail."

"To what end, Holmes? Such speculations must end in frustration."

"You and I witnessed Mary, Joseph, and the Blessed Child escape from Bethlehem. *Just in time.* Why? Because an angel warned Joseph in a dream to flee for Egypt. *Just in time.*"

"What are you getting at—?"

"Fine gennelmen, have ye an extra shilling for a down-on-yer-luck lady, such as myself?" A grimy-faced woman in tattered clothes spoke the greeting. Behind her crowded a litter of filthy children, clinging to her skirt. Holmes flared his nostrils and gripped his brown cane in a sign of extreme annoyance, until she held out a cream-colored card.

"A gennelman yonder give me this card, as is proper, for I am a messenger." She turned around and pointed with a long-nailed finger. "Oh, but he is gone now."

Holmes took the card, looked it over, and then peered sharply behind her, along the bridge's sidewalk. She held out a filthy claw.

"The man who sent you—who gave you this card—he already tipped you for your services, did he not? And handsomely so?" Holmes' severe tone and stare caused her to visibly wilt.

"Truly he done it, zur, as you said."

But then Holmes' features softened. He deposited a few silver coins in her hungry hand, and she fled in a fluttering of rags.

Holmes handed Watson the obligatory calling card—which read: *"What made the timing of Christ's birth the right time?"*

"I was on the right track, anyway." Holmes patted his vest and breathed deeply. "The Bible clearly states Christ was born at just the right time, that when the time had fully come, God sent his Son, born of a woman, to redeem us. I believe it is in Galatians where Paul declares, *'But when the fullness of the time had come, God sent forth His Son, born of a woman, born under the law.'*⁶

"Romans 5:6, on the other hand, declares Christ *died* at the right time." Holmes drew an imaginary circle with his toe on the sidewalk. "Yet for the two-year-old boys left behind in Bethlehem, sleeping innocently in their mother's arms, time had run out.⁷

Herod's henchmen sent to kill Jesus saw to that. So much for God's timing."

"What in heaven's name are you doing?" Watson exclaimed.

As light-footed as a dancer, Holmes sprang up onto the bridge's banister, balancing on his toes, high above the water. He stretched out his arms and faced the river, and with one hand grappled one of the bridge's beautiful three-tiered lamps—decorated in green iron with gold leaf—situated atop the separating column between the arches.

"What will you accomplish up there? Do you not know your danger?"

The tall sleuth stood statuesquely against the crisp blue sky. "It is coincidence, is it not, that you and I were not one of those ill-fated boys murdered by Herod? Why should I cheat time further? I have already done so, magnificently, with the Needle's Eye!"

Watson pulled down the rim of his hat over his eyebrows. "Begrudge God all you wish over who lives and who dies, Holmes, but don't present such a poor showing of it."

"Why am I allowed to be here? By what right do I live, move, have my being?"

"We are here all the same," replied Watson.

"But this is not my primary line of inquiry, Watson." He smiled down at the doctor. "Rather, it is to question what the Lord deems as the *right time* for the birth of his Son. The right time—it makes no sense. And yes, I do still harbor some animosity toward him—allowing the deaths of the innocents."

"But we read of these sort of happenings every day. It is an awful truth behind our most frightening fairy tales, Holmes, and Scripture fairly rings with it. Sometimes evil kings have their way. Sometimes children don't come back."

"I cannot dismiss the haunting cries from my memory! Did you not hear the woman's panicked screams? The whooping of Herod's murderous soldiers?"

"Holmes, do you think after my years of service in Afghanistan that this dilemma would be lost on me? For a devil of a choice it is: live under God's curse in a cursed world, or curse God and die." Watson breathed deeply, looked off, and scenes from his old years came rushing in. "Remember Cawnpore[8] as a start. As I said before, I'm heartily ashamed to see such a lowly exhibition by you. Good day to you, sir!"

Watson turned on his heel and strode off in a huff. He decided, yes, to indulge himself, to reflect solemnly on the problem during a comfortable ride to Baker Street. He blew once upon his cab-whistle.[9]

The Right Time

Sherlock Holmes grinned from his chair at the fireplace, smoothed back his hair. "When I jumped down from the bridge—land side, of course—a half dozen of London's finest surrounded me, a sort of police amphitheater, with Lestrade among them. Ha!"

Watson watched in an ill humor. He took a drink, then a deep breath.

"Oh, may we not clap hands and be friends again, Doctor? If the Metropolitan Police can forgive me, how can you be so out of spirits? I have marshaled the facts of Christ's birth and am ready to lay them before you. Surely my reputation and your confidence in me encourage you to listen?"

Holmes tapped the ash from his pipe, and went to retrieve

some tobacco but thought better of it. Pipe smoking carried with it an assumed domestic tranquillity, or at least an openness for what might be discussed. Watson, however, exhibited neither inclination.

Holmes sighed. "I am amused and vexed; do you care to know the reason? I amused how the Needle's Eye, or rather, this K2L2 chap, is so pleasant with us. In our last mystery—you are correct—the scene of Jezebel had little to do with its solving. So I am vexed to contemplate that our being chased and shot at by the Roman scouts along the picturesque Mediterranean was a complete waste of time, and meant only to enchant or to mislead us. Or perhaps it is the strongest scene to bring this mystery to an end."

Still, Watson sulked, even as Mrs. Hudson knocked on the door and presented a calling card. Holmes knew the visitor's identity, knew he must resurrect Watson from his doldrums for fear this visitor might—in all probability would—make matters infinitely worse.

Professor Norberton heaved himself up the stairs, over the landing, and filled the doorway. He shook Holmes' hand limply and smiled at glum-faced Watson. Of course the doctor would remember him from Nevill's bathhouse.

"I apologize for my appearance," said he, indicating his fine tuxedo, "but I am on my way to Albert Hall and then dinner—hey, hey! I thought to give you my whole evening, but kind Fate has designed otherwise."

"I sense a woman in the mix." Holmes said it with a hint of encouragement, relieved that the professor, sitting down noticeably on the front edge of the divan, would not be smothering their entire evening. "Sherry? Port?"

"Many thanks, but I must be on my way. What is it—?"

Norberton's glance fell on the side table. His eyebrows shot up. His hand passed over a gold dagger with inlaid precious stones, and picked up a squat arrow. He whistled to himself, eying its straightness from the feather end of the shaft, and pressed the point between his thumb and forefinger. "Remarkable. Roman, isn't it? Or Syrian. And new. Where—?"

"That is not the specimen which interests us," said Sherlock Holmes, grinning to remember what near a thing it had been, Watson returning to the present with the arrow sticking out of his robe, "but rather, this parchment."

Norberton reluctantly gave up the arrow and accepted a sheet of paper and said, "Well, this is not parchment, technically. That particular term we reserve for vellum, which is a writing surface derived from animal skins—"

"Yes, quite." Holmes' interruption was sharp as a knife.

"Rather, this is papyrus—" His own words had a sudden and alarming effect on himself, like a sleepwalker suddenly shaken awake. His breath caught in his throat, and his face turned so red that Dr. Watson thought he might have to perform an altogether unpleasant but obligatory resuscitation on the patient, on the same order of kissing his aunt's hairy cheek.

"The construction is remarkable, the texture unmatched!" He studied the writing after accepting a magnifying glass from Holmes. "The text is written in a practiced hand. Three paragraphs; the first is in Latin; the second, Greek; the third in Aramaic, which seems to have been written more recently, for the ink is smeared."

"What does it say?" asked Holmes, excitement brimming around his eyes.

"Quite an elaborate hoax, this one is—he, he!" the professor chuckled, gesturing with his thick fingers. "This sample has been made by the ancient method, pressing two sheets of papyrus together crossways until they become bonded: the front, or recto side—the best side for writing with horizontal fibers—and the back, or verso side, with fibers running at right angles to the front layer. I'd be willing to consider this specimen as genuine—its appearance, its construction, its texture (as I mentioned before) and overall dimensions—"

"But what does it say?" Holmes was vainly attempting to mask his impatience.

"—but for its condition. It is not aged at all, not brittle, not yellowed. A glaring oversight in a counterfeit—hey! Nor crimped or crumpled on the edges." Norberton held it up and made a clicking noise with his tongue. "See here: the surface of the paper has been scored by a scribe with a blunt instrument as guide lines for his writing. And two vertical lines on either side to mark the margins. Why would someone go to the trouble of this marvelous counterfeiting sleight of hand, to fool us, but leave off the aging—"

"How accurately is the text phrased?" asked the detective, trying a new approach.

"Genuine as the summer sun is long!" he said, laughing, by now the only person present in a humorous mood. "At a glance, I would say that all three paragraphs say the exact same thing but in different languages. You see, these top two sections would be written in Latin and Greek by a scribe in Rome. The third section would be written later in the language of the region to which this proclamation was to be couriered—in this case, Judea, because of the Aramaic. That is why it's smudged (being newly written). It must have been subjected to the elements, such as rain—"

Holmes glared at him. The professor smacked his lips as if he could do with a dram of sherry. But Holmes was in no accommodating mood.

"As to the proclamation itself . . ." Norberton took a deep breath and studied the document. "I stay with the Latin, for that is really what I—"

"Yes," said Holmes tersely.

"'Tiberius Claudius Caesar Augustus Germanicus, Imperator, Pontifex Maximus,'" Norberton read in a loud, oratory voice. He pointed a pudgy finger at the papyrus. "You see, this is from the emperor Claudius—it goes on: 'Holder of the Tribunician Power, Consul Designate, to all the territories and Roman protectorates, greeting . . .'" He read on, grumbling and grunting. "So, the genuine article, of which this is a fantastic copy, would have been sent by ship to Alexandria, where lived a large Jewish population, and probably by way of Caesarea—"

"Oh! The theater!" prompted Holmes. "You've almost forgotten your pressing engagement, professor, and dinner afterwards?"

But Norberton was in his own scholarly world and would not be budged. "Amazing. This is a call for the dissolution of an entire people. This is an edict commanding all Jews residing in Rome to leave. Really amazing—"

"Why is that?" spoke up Watson. "Is the language accurate? The content in agreement—"

"That's the point, precisely. We don't have the original document." Norberton looked dubiously at them. "The Imperial edict casting out the Jews was enforced in 41 BC, but this document of yours cannot be but a few decades—"

"Well! Look at the time!" announced Holmes, gesturing to the mantel clock.

Norberton seemed in a daze as Holmes slapped him on the back, got him to his feet, shook his hand, and summarily dismissed him from the flat.

The detective fell back into his chair, exhausted.

"I would appreciate being elsewhere on the next occasion you invite him over for a chat," said Watson.

Holmes looked off, his mind otherwise engaged. He began to giggle, almost insanely, no doubt remembering Norberton's befuddled countenance, but then he grew serious. "In all aspects circumstantial, political, religious, sociological, it was a disastrous time for Christ to be born, much less a better climate when he died some thirty-odd years later."

"And yet, Christianity flourished," said Watson, stubbornly.

"By chance, surely. Retrospect is all rose-colored." *Wrong tack*, Holmes decided, as Watson fell into a strict meditation.

"I shall set the scene, Watson, though my head is filled with so many Herods, Antipaters, Agrippas, and Aristobuluses, that I scarce know where to start. Think on the Advent and the political situation at the time: Herod the Great rules in Jerusalem as king of the Jews as an act of favor from Rome; first, by permission of Antony and then Octavian. Even though Herod embarks on an ambitious building project—such as the great temple—he is unable to endear himself to the Jews. (He is an Edomite, the Jew's traditional enemy.) He mistrusts the Hasmonaean family, the rightful heirs to the Jewish throne, and even though he marries into it, he ends up murdering his wife and other leading Hasmonaeans. He is vicious, cruel, and worse, maniacally suspicious. His poisoned anxiety leads him to kill three of his sons."[10]

Watson's eyes brightened with interest. Holmes packed his bowl full and lit his pipe while his companion digested the information, and added, "We clearly see Herod's conniving and suspicious nature illustrated in the visit from the Magi—"

"And his murderous nature, slaughtering the little boys in Bethlehem."

Holmes nodded, his glance shining as brilliantly as Watson's. "Remember, too, the angel's warning to Joseph on their return from Egypt. Herod the Great was dead, but his eldest son, Archelaus (Herod the Ethnarch), worst of the brood, reigned in Judea. And so Joseph settled in Galilee, and Christ grew up in Nazareth."

"Archelaus: He is the Herod which Christ called a fox, correct? The Herod who beheaded John the Baptist?"

"No, you speak of his brother, Antipas, who ruled after Archelaus's banishment."[11]

"The one who ordered James killed? Struck down by an angel and eaten by worms?"

"No," replied the detective patiently. "Herod the King, called Agrippa, committed that awful deed. He was Herod the Great's grandson."[12]

"Ah! The Herod who reviled Paul for attempting to make a Christian of him?"

"No, that was a different Agrippa, the son of Herod Agrippa.[13] Confused?"

"I can only marvel at the multitude of Herods. Thank God their reign eventually came to an end."

"There may have been many Herods," quipped the detective, "but there is only one Sherlock Holmes."

"Again, we must thank God."

Holmes leaned forward. "The religious climate was beastly. The Pharisees, pro-Hasmonaean, were looking for a ruler in the mold of Judas or Simon Maccabees, a king to score significant and bloody victories against another heathen power, Rome, and to expand Israel's borders to their glory days under King David. Certainly not a Messiah preaching forgiveness and turning the other cheek." Holmes sat back and puffed his pipe rigorously. "The right time for Christ to be born? In my opinion, it is well nigh the worst."

"To our minds, perhaps." The doctor looked off. "It is the Lord's way, is it not, to confound conventional wisdom? Remember, the Lord works in mysterious ways."

"I have found him to be rather direct," stated Holmes.

He walked to the large Bible and opened it to Acts, the twenty-third chapter, and began reading at verse 19: "'Then the [Roman] commander took him [Paul's nephew] by the hand, went inside and asked him privately, "What is it that you have to tell me?" And he said, "The Jews have agreed to ask you to bring Paul down to the council tomorrow, as though they were going to inquire more fully about him. But do not yield to them, for more than forty of them lie in wait for him. Men who have bound themselves by an oath that they will neither eat nor drink till they have killed him; and now they are ready, waiting for the promise from you."'"

Stopping momentarily at verse 21, he scanned downward, skipping the next verse, and began reading again at verse 23: "'And he [the commander] called for two centurions, saying, "Prepare two hundred soldiers, seventy horsemen, and two hundred spearmen to go to Caesarea at the third hour of the night. . . ." Then the soldiers—'" he stopped again and scanned his way down to verse 31, "'as they were commanded, took Paul and brought him by night to Antipatris. The next day they left the horsemen to go on with him, and returned to the barracks. When they came to Caesarea and had delivered the letter to the governor, they also presented Paul to him.'"

"Well, at least we know what happened to the infantry," said Watson. "Once the escort made Antipatris, they no longer feared an ambush, and the cavalry proceeded on with all speed to Caesarea."

"Quite plausible," said Holmes. "Even in Pilate's day he had an army of occupation, of 120 cavalrymen and 5,000 infantry stationed at Caesarea, a detachment of which was housed in the Antonia Fortress in Jerusalem. These are undoubtedly the soldiers we saw."

Holmes crossed his arms and then brought a hand up, pressing his finger against his forehead.

"All of the events are against us in this mystery, Watson. Everything points, in a contrary way, to being the absolutely *wrong* time for Christ's coming. The Lord couldn't have timed it worse for his Son's birth, for his death. The emperor Claudius has expelled all Jews from Rome—even the Christians. Paul is summarily arrested and is conducted to Caesarea and on to Rome, where he will ultimately be beheaded by Nero—the same Nero who will proclaim wholesale slaughter against all Christians in Rome."

"But we as civilized planners cannot fathom God the Father's plan," Watson asserted. "Mary and Joseph were dirt-poor. They were far from home. The timing of Mary's delivery was such that the Savior of the world was birthed in a stable! Somehow, though, God sees through these difficulties. Perhaps it is a paradox we must learn: God works best in impossible situations. As much as it pains me to point it out, the slaughter of the Bethlehem boys was prophesied.[14] So, too, the reason for Christ coming in the first place—to be the sacrificial lamb, to die on the cross for our sins. He *chose* Iscariot as one of his disciples. You might smoke that along with your tobacco."

"The point I am anxious to make, Watson, is simply this: Christ could have been born at any time and been in a hostile enough environment to be killed. His message caused the world to hate him. What made this particular time so special? So *right*? And if the Lord's plan was for his Son to be sacrificed, should the time or method matter? Certainly, God could find a different time, virgin, place of birth, wise men, and so on."

"This is getting ludicrous, Holmes. Really it is. You are not the first person to try and solve God's timetable. The Old Testament prophets searched with the greatest care, trying to find out the time and circumstances of Christ's sufferings and glory.[15] God chose this specific time for a reason. Or, I imagine if more than one time were available, this one was the most suitable. This mystery of 'the right time' must remain unsolved."

"Oh, that again. Give up. Run away. Watson, as an army man, you should know that if you bury your head in the sand too many times, sooner or later you will be shot in the—"

"Oh, Holmes! How can we fathom the wisdom of God?" Watson opened his hands. "Timing is scattered all through Scripture: *'that in the dispensation of the fullness of the times He might gather together . . . that he may be revealed in his own time . . . but has in due time manifested His word through preaching . . .'*"[16]

Holmes leapt out of his chair, absent his pipe, and began to pace. He picked up his Stradivarius, plucked at the strings, and laid it down.

Watson studied him intently, his working jaw bones, his muttering half to himself. His frozen pose at the fireplace mantel stirred when steps on the landing were heard, followed by a soft knock at the door. Mrs. Hudson appeared and approached him courteously. Sherlock Holmes snatched the note from her little silver tray and, reading it, cried out, "Quickly, Watson! We must away! There is no time to lose!"

THE FUGITIVES

A small brougham carriage rumbled along, heading northwest out of London. Holmes craned his neck and looked out the window the way they had come.

Watson slouched in the other corner. "The police will never search for us in the Heath, Holmes, especially aboard a brougham. Who is the chief constable hereabouts?"

"It matters little, Watson." Holmes tapped the window. "We shall soon be in and out of Middlesex—"

"And danger."

"Danger? Ha! The police need time to cool their tempers, that is all, or their hurt reputation. The whole affair at Westminster Bridge ruffled the feathers of some higher-up. I'm not well liked at Scotland Yard. (A friend in the department sent the warning note—there's Tobias vying with Lestrade again.) Oh, this is so annoying. But it will be safe to return to Baker Street soon enough. For now—ah! What desolate country is Hampstead! Such shabby undergrowth and pools, similar to the Broads in some respect."

"But the road is good—how the carriage flies! Wonderful!"

"The horses are mismatched, Watson; surely you noticed. And the one with a hitch in his gait pulls the carriage to the left."

"But oh, how exciting to be the culprits for a change!" chuckled Watson. "To be pursued by the police! If only it were for a more serious crime. Great joy! I have cake and biscuits Mrs. Hudson wrapped for us."

"Excellent, for we cannot stop—eyes, ears all about. We shall huddle here aboard our getaway and eat like conspirators."

He sat back, his mood turning sullen as he thumbed through a pocket-sized New Testament. "It peeves me how the answer to our riddle eludes me, Watson. What is the common theme here? The thread which winds through the two scenes to which we were transported back in time to witness?—Mary and Joseph fleeing Bethlehem with the Christ child, and our friend Paul, being conducted to Caesarea?"

Watson waited patiently for the rejoinder. It would not be long in coming.

"*The right time*," Holmes growled. "The answer is right beneath my nose—I feel it!"

The carriage bumped. Lurched. Sagged to a stop. Holmes jumped out, Watson stumbling up behind him while jamming on his hat. The cabman apologized profusely: the road would get progressively worse from here, he explained, might break an axle, probably would, but a crossroads lay ahead, where higher ground and a better road could be got.

The detective looked dazed. He took a few aimless steps away from the carriage, the gravel crunching beneath his shoes, and Watson feared he might veer off the road like a drunken man. He stopped and looked about the countryside as if dreaming or sleepwalking. What had gotten into Holmes? He turned his head slowly back and forth, thinking perhaps.

Holmes snatched out his Bible from his suit pocket and came striding back. "That's it!" he cried, thumbing frantically through the small pages. He cackled and slapped the astonished cabman on the back. "Watson, I've got it!"

"That I might be arrested?" asked Watson. "For aiding and abetting?"

"Watson, oh, Watson!" Holmes walked down the road again but did not tarry, but came quickly back. "I concentrated solely on the tiny region of where Christ was born and where he conducted his ministry. I needed to look at the bigger picture."

"You'll not dine atop another carriage, will you, Holmes? Lunch, this time?"

"Very good, Watson. But I suspected it might be the right time for Christ to come, partially, because it was a time of relative peace. Christ gathered his disciples, trained them, and began his public ministry. This could not have been accomplished, let's say, during the Hellenistic period—too much strife, and with the Maccabees' nationalistic movement, Jesus might have been killed outright before he could accomplish the barest miracle."

"That's your answer?" Watson asked, incredulously. "There have been other times of peace."

"I said *partially*." The gleam remained in Sherlock's eyes. "Our cabman, here—our bright cabman, our illustrious cabman—pointed out the essential point. Here: I will read some excerpts from Acts:

"At that time a great persecution arose against the church which was at Jerusalem; and they were all scattered through-out the regions of Judea and Samaria, except the apostles. . . . Therefore those who were scattered went everywhere preach-ing the word. . . . And [Paul] spoke boldly in the name of the Lord Jesus and disputed against the Hellenists, but they attempted to kill him. When the brethren found out, they brought him down to Caesarea and sent him out to Tarsus. . . . So, being sent on their way by the church, they passed through Phoenicia and Samaria, describing the conversion of the Gentiles. . . . So when they were sent off, they came to Antioch; and when they had gathered the multitude together, they delivered the letter. . . . Then after some days Paul said to Barnabas, 'Let us now go back and visit our brethren in every city where we have preached the word of the Lord, and see how they are doing.' . . . Now when they had passed through Amphipolis and Apollonia, they came to Thessalonica."[17]

Holmes cackled again. "Come to think of it, what is the book of Acts, essentially? It is a travelogue—people traveling from one region to another swiftly and with ease. Why? Because they were able to. Yes! That's it! It has to be! When persecution broke out in Jerusalem after Stephen's stoning, Christians fled quickly, efficiently. In fact, Saul's planned retributive trip from Jerusalem to Damascus was known before he ever got there.[18] My dear Watson, answer this question: Rome was known for what?"

"For law, for statesmanship, for government, for ingenious approaches to citizenship, for maintaining peace. For pillaging and burning, sexual immorality, hedonism—"

"Something more basic, more utilitarian. Christ was born at a time when something existed for the first time in history." Holmes tapped the ground with his walking stick. "Why are you and I in fear of being overtaken by the police?"

Watson looked at him dubiously.

"Let me ask it another way. Why is our cabman afraid to venture any farther?"

"Because, zur," the cabman interjected, scratching his head beneath his billycock hat, "due to the deplor—deplorable state of the roads."

"Correct, good sir. The answer to our mystery is this: the roads!"

"The what?" The doctor folded his arms, frowning. "These roads are awful."

"Not these roads, Watson. Roman roads! Remember from our adventure in Philippi? The Roman Empire established a system of roads never dreamed of before—the Appian Way, the Via Egnatia, the Via Maris, to name a few—wide, paved, well marked, and safe. Imperial couriers stopped for fresh horses at established points every twenty-five miles. The roads were marvels of engineering, with four layers of construction and drainage ditches. It is the common theme of where the Needle's Eye took us: the roads!"

At the remark about Philippi, the driver's eyes had widened. Now, he was downright baffled.

"Mary and Joseph needed only the slightest head start. Once they were safely away from Bethlehem and made the Roman highway, they were gone. And Watson, what was it that enabled us, inexperienced horsemen, to keep our distance from the Roman archers? Think of the persecuted Christians from Jerusalem: once they reached the outer perimeter of Palestine, the Empire's outer reaches were theirs. Look how quickly the gospel spread after Pentecost. Antioch, where followers of Christ were first called Christians, was along well-established roads leading from Palestine to Asia. Paul regularly arrived and departed from Antioch—no wonder it is the home of Christian foreign missions!

And think of how quickly and easily Paul made his way across Palestine, Asia, and Greece during his three missionary journeys. Why? Because of good, safe roads. The titles of his epistles read like an imperial atlas: Romans, Corinthians, Philippians, Colossians, Galatians, Ephesians, Thessalonians—all because of the roads! The *roads*, Watson!"

"I'm beginning to see it." The doctor nodded emphatically. "Christ's ministry, his death, his resurrection, the thousands of believers who came to faith at Pentecost—all would have been for nothing if, when persecution arose, they were all cornered in Jerusalem or within the Judean borders and summarily slaughtered. The gospel's light would have never made it out to illuminate a dark world. That is what we were meant to experience in fleeing from the Roman cavalry!"

Holmes tapped him on the shoulder. "Here is my other error: I concentrated on the political and religious tension centered in Jerusalem. But that is really part of the plan, as it forced the Christians to flee their comfortable abodes for safety. Once they left Judea, they found, in the Empire, an environment relatively open to new gods, new religions—remember Paul arguing openly at the Areopagus in Athens amongst the Epicureans and stoics? Paul's trouble normally arose from Jews, their jealousy and religious zeal alarmingly noticeable in the surrounding peaceful and accepting culture."

"Interesting irony, Holmes, how Christianity turns Christ's parable on its head: the lone stalk of wheat growing up amongst the tares for protection!"

"Yes. Rome's relative indifference to indigenous religions allowed Christianity to thrive," added Holmes, "even though a few emperors—Nero, Marcus Aurelius, Diocletian—got out of hand. Incidentally, if the roads failed seasonally, an extensive sea network lay at their disposal. In short: Christ was born and died at the right time, in the fullness of times, in spite of the turbulence and relative poverty of his nation. Rather, it was the right time because of the wonderful escape routes into a vast, indifferent society where Christianity could—and did—flourish!"

"The answer was literally right below our noses!" said Watson. "Good show!"

"Thanks to you. Two things you said stuck in my muddled brain. First: Christianity flourished—a necessary element in the equation. Second: God chose the *first available* right time to send his Son. I began, subconsciously, to search for the one answer which would satisfy both assertions."

"Let's not forget the poor boys of Bethlehem," reflected Watson. "Can we regard them as the forerunners of John the Baptist, preparing the way for the Lord? '*The crooked places shall be made straight and the rough ways smooth; and all flesh shall see the salvation of God.*'[19] I hope these little ones were honored by being the first to welcome Prince Jesus back into heaven after his ascension."

The detective snapped his head up, lifted a small telescope, and held it steadily to his eye. "Watson, a carriage approaches from behind us—ah, it is the police! Do you see their bright buttons and badges from here? I fear they got wind of our direction, after all."

"What happened on Westminster Bridge, Holmes? Surely nothing warranting this—"

"Ah!" A black-and-white butterfly flitted onto Holmes' hand. "See here, the wonderful skipper—*Cyclopides*!"

"Holmes!"

"Oh, just a small matter of my jumping down to the sidewalk; of an overexuberant constable; of his Roman helmet getting knocked off and falling into the Thames."

"Knocked off? Into the river? Oh, good heavens! How?"

"With the flat of my hand acting as the vehicle—"

"You assaulted an officer of the law?"

"Not assaulted, not exactly assaulted . . ."

"Then exactly what?"

"And since our carriage cannot answer at present, I thought a nice jaunt across those fields of heather might be in order."

"Holmes—" sputtered Watson. "You scoundrel!"

"Quickly, Doctor! Don't just stand there like a lamp—pay jarvey[20] our fare, and we will be on our way." The detective scanned the countryside. "Ah—see? Let us make for that suitable path yonder. Though unpaved, it is still suitable for our use. Now is the *right time* for our escape! What fun! Ha, ha, ha!"

TEN

HUMPTY DUMPTY

"OH, CONFOUNDED MISERIES!" MUTTERED SHERLOCK HOLMES to himself, for he certainly did not wish to be overheard. He marched in step with an immense army in a long line—if *line* it could be called—curving around in a great arc before and behind, ten troops abreast, the frontmost soldiers on the rear guard's heels as they circled the city.

The humid air teemed with spices. Holmes, trudging steadily along, felt a tiny bead of sweat trickle down his back beneath his robe. Ah!—he veered out of the ranks just as he spied his traveling companion taking a rest within the shade of a tree.

"Oh, confounded miseries!" he said again, evidence that his temper had risen to a remarkably un–Holmes-like stage to have so woefully limited his vocabulary in repeating himself. The Needle's Eye, and whatever hidden agent actually governed its operation, had not furnished his companion with biblical dress but had kept her original wardrobe of choice. In the absence of his brown walking stick, which lay idly on board the *Viceroy of India* (and with which he might have beaten her over the head), Holmes leveled his finger at her.

"What graceless and churlish state of mind coaxed you into such a costume? Or to place such a gaudy, obscene metal object upon your head?"

Mrs. Hudson looked up. "'Tis my mixing bowl, sir, which I donned for a helmet." She pressed it down firmly over her white ringlets. "This bedspread draped about me stands in as a robe. These galoshes beside me—"

Beside her they lay, like dirty, forlorn puppies, she having taken them off to rub her feet. On and on she complained concerning the sad state of her toes, her feet, her ankles, and having been forced to march twice around—

"Did I not inform you, Mrs. Hudson," said Holmes, "that we as time-travelers may not land in benign surroundings? And here you sit, dressed in such a vagabond fashion—if fashion it can be called."

"'Jericho is our destination!' is what you said, sir. And there it stands, I see, bristling like a cat. A resplendent sight!" Through a clearing in a grove of banana and palm trees, they both gazed upon the ancient city of Jericho standing upon a mound, the walls rising more than twenty feet high. The army of Israel continued to march a safe distance from hostile arrows and sling stones. "And you said the Needle Traveler would furnish me with authentic biblical homespuns. A pox on that! My boots are not made for marching, no sir, and with all this tramping about, here I sit to rub my feet and read—"

"Read? What—what is that—?" Holmes, finished neither with pointing nor with inquiring, fastened his eyes on a bright-red volume, Mrs. Hudson's gaudily illuminated book on cowboys, Indians, and bull riding. "I should have burned that book! Have you gone mad? What do you mean by bringing it three thousand years into the past? What if you misplace it?"

"Wild reading for wild times," she snapped back.

Holmes huffed. He imagined archaeologists scraping in the strata of Late Bronze Age Jericho, only to unearth what amounted to a penny dreadful on the American West, alongside a mixing bowl commemorating Queen Victoria's Diamond Jubilee! Holmes began to chuckle insanely, but his humor faded as Mrs. Hudson pulled out a fireplace poker. "And might I not defend myself worthily with this? Ha!"

Holmes wrapped his arms about his head in frustration. If only Dr. Watson were present! That he did not lie unwell in bed in London three thousand years hence. But it was Mrs. Hudson or nothing—the last time he had journeyed off into the past alone, he'd come back completely naked—that could not, would not be borne again! Mrs. Hudson had seemed cogent enough, believing him as he had explained the wild story about the *Viceroy of India*, about time-travel. And she had braved unflinching the trip downriver to the paddle steamer—

Holmes caught him out of the tail of his eye. A commander broke from the ranks and approached them, a large man. The hilt of his sword was carved in the likeness of a snake, undoubtedly, Holmes surmised, of Egyptian influence and craftsmanship.

"Give glory to the God of Israel, and give him praise." The Israelite warrior raised both hands in the air. "Who are you who sit thus by the roadside and do not join your brethren marching?" His glance passed from Holmes to take in Mrs. Hudson's robe. "Perhaps you are wayfarers from Jericho, enemies and sitting thusly because the city is barred to your passage? Answer swiftly."

"I've marched six times around that pile of bricks!" exclaimed Mrs. Hudson, ignoring him. "My feet need a good soaking—"

"Not to mention your head," murmured the detective from London. "Sir, we are keen to obey you. Indeed, we must finally join in following the seven priests carrying their seven trumpets in strict obedience to the Lord's instructions. So come, Mrs. Hudson; let us take the broad walk! See, the ark of the covenant passes by for the seventh time with its armed guard. Forward, Mrs. Hudson! Forward! Do take care not to trip over your . . . robe."

"What fabric of robe is that? What pattern?" questioned the officer. "What is your family? Your clan?"

"Clan of McPherson," replied the fierce Scottish maiden.

"What she means—" Holmes began, but there came a grating sound as the officer drew his sword.

"Are you Levites? Or of Judah?" he questioned. "What is your tribe?"

The detective shot Mrs. Hudson a look. "Don't you dare—"

"Cherokee!" she blurted, patting the pocket where her book lay.

"Oh, eternal perturbations!" exclaimed Holmes again—this time he didn't care who heard him.

"Up to your feet!" ordered the man. "Both of you, follow me."

"And what if, perchance," inquired the detective, "we belong to Rahab's family?"

The man looked down his nose at the detective. "The same woman who hid our spies atop her roof, and so spared their lives? How do you come to know her?"

This explanation would require real embellishment, thought Holmes. He could converse circuitously to win some time, hoping to impress the man with his knowledge of flax (beneath which Rahab hid the two Israelite spies), a one-meter-tall plant with pale-blue flowers and used for making cloth; or with the history of flax, the Egyptians having cultivated it long before the exodus; or with how the flax plant was processed, pulled up, and placed in water so as to separate the fibers from the stems, laid in the sun or on housetops to dry and to be later woven into linen or used for wicks; or with flax's by-products, how from the shiny seeds linseed oil was derived (would the commander know of *that* little tidbit?).

Holmes had always prided himself on being rather quick-witted, but for the life of him he couldn't formulate how to intertwine a story which began with the bravery of Rahab, whose constituent elements consisted of the wonderment of flax, but which must inevitably conclude with the clan McPherson and the Cherokee tribe (that is, if this man—of the baddish, thuggish variety—might be patient enough to wander far from the point of who they were and what they were doing there). Another part of his brain, the brooding, seething, vindictive part, planned on how to repay Mrs. Hudson, when the time came, for this terrible chain of events.

Just then, Chance, with her sisters, Timing and Circumstance, came to the aid of one Mr. Sherlock Holmes. There came a trembling up through the ground, which caused Mrs. Hudson to peer wild-eyed from beneath the rim of her helmet-bowl. Trumpets blared deafeningly. The people shouted with one voice, Holmes' landlady amongst them, thrilling in its exaltation. A deeper rumbling sounded, coming from under the ground, for-midable in its portent.

Mrs. Hudson jumped to her feet, gripped her poker. And screamed.

"Stop!" yelled Holmes.

"Stop!" ordered the commander.

Too late. Neither Holmes nor any such Israelite commander—be he Joshua himself—might clamp down the lid on the Scotswoman's searing temper. And as the Israelite troops stampeded toward Jericho, Mrs. Hudson ran with them. Only then did Holmes realize there no longer remained any discernible structure in the distance—only a tidal wave of smoke and debris advancing toward them.

The great walls had collapsed. Jericho, the City of Palms, was no more.

221B BAKER ST., LONDON

Dr. Watson shuffled into Holmes' sitting room and sat at the breakfast table; *breakfast,* because it was morning, and *breakfast table* because it held a dish whose piping hot contents were concealed beneath a silver dome. He poured himself a steaming cup, huddled deeper in his wool scarf, and shivered.

"Coffee instead of tea, Watson?" Holmes stopped pacing with his newspaper, rolled up like a baton.

"I feel somewhat improved. Slept like a baby."

"Babies don't snore." The detective sniffed and looked off.

The doctor sipped. "Holmes, was the distance to Jericho so great? Could you not see the city's actual destruction?"

"I blame myself." Holmes thrust out his lower jaw, produced his pipe, and ran the black stem along his jaw line. "Due to Mrs. Hudson's idiosyncratic behaviors, I concentrated wholly on her. I witnessed nothing noteworthy of Jericho's demise. Worse, the Needle's Eye transported us to no other location. Whatever information to be gleaned was present in this one circumstance, on this last day when ancient Jericho perished."

"Did you see the two spies enter the city?" asked Watson.

Holmes shook his head despondently. "Nor did we witness Rahab hiding them under the flax on the rooftop, or letting them down the wall, or the scarlet thread, for we did not arrive until day seven as the marching neared its end. Oh, my dear Watson! What a wasted affair! The event has passed into history forever. I am reduced, like you, to reading the account in Scripture."[1]

Holmes slumped down across from him at the table, reached over, and lifted the silver dome. The toast he chose clattered on his plate like a tile. He cracked an egg. The half-cooked white and yolk spilled out onto his plate, and he breathed an oath.

"I have ruined my chance at Jericho," the detective snarled. "And my landlady's culinary abilities are ruined with it."

"The toast and eggs are my doing, Holmes," Watson confessed. "Or rather, I over- and under-cooked them. Mrs. Hudson is still asleep—"

"Indeed, I am not, sir!"

Here she came in her sleeping robe, shuffling through the door with an empty tray. Holmes rolled his eyes and turned sideways in his chair, to the clattering of china plates, the china teapot, and the china cups, as she gathered them up.

"Now, what is this?" She lifted up the hem of the tablecloth and dabbed it with a napkin. "What careless person has overturned the jam bowl? Who? If people had half a brain—"

"Watson has half a brain; why don't you ask him?"

"And you the other half, sir?"

Holmes eyed her and said, at length, "Mrs. Hudson, are you cross with me?"

"Cross with you?" she snapped. "I don't even like you."

"Flint and rock in the same room," chirped Watson. "You've been listening at the door, Mrs. Hudson? Good for you! Mr. Holmes is a rank beast, is he not?"

The detective smiled bleakly. He unrolled his newspaper and applied himself to yesterday's *Evening Standard*.

"Mr. Sherlock Holmes is all courtesy; says he blames himself for missing the fall of Jericho," Mrs. Hudson said, plucking up the last cup, "but not at all. He blames me. I did my best standing in for you, Dr. Watson. Why, I feared for my life!"

The doctor grinned. "Very ungenerous of you, Holmes."

In response he turned the paper down. "Do not believe her, Watson. Wee Mrs. Hudson standing before you, exhibited the fiercest lust for battle on the order of the ancient Picts, with a monomaniacal scream which I owe to her bloodthirsty Scotch ancestry. I called for her to stop, but to no avail—outright disobedience! Intolerable insubordination, I would say, were it not for my absolute abhorrence of alliteration."

"But surely, Holmes, what can we demand from Mrs. Hudson? That the duties of a landlady should be thus expanded!"

"I am not so enfeebled, Dr. John H. Watson," she quipped, "nor so elderly. I can see lightning and hear thunder." She took up the tray and turned to go.

"Mrs. Hudson possesses a penchant for cards, does she not?"[2] Holmes' inquiry stopped her in her tracks. "And therefore, for combinations of numbers? An admirable counterpart to you, Watson, as a military man.[3] How would I solve this mystery without you both?"

"Mystery?" asked the doctor. "Has something piqued your interest, Holmes?"

"A singular aspect of Joshua's battle plan." He stuffed a small ball of shag tobacco in his pipe and applied the flame. "The number seven—its predominate place in the story. *Why were the Israelites instructed to march about Jericho one time for the first six days, but seven times on the last day?* That is the mystery to be solved—the calling card was stuck in that horrible book of Mrs. Hudson's."

"Calling card—?" She frowned.

A plume of aromatic smoke, like a question mark, rose from Holmes' pipe and hovered over them.

"Numbers have significance in Scripture," declared Watson.

"Sometimes," she muttered. Holmes gestured to a chair. She did not sit, but she did set the tray down.

The doctor pontificated. "For instance, forty could stand for trial or destruction: the forty days of rain during Noah's flood; the forty days of wilderness wandering; the forty days of our Lord's temptation; the forty days King Saul deliberated over Goliath.[4] Seven, on the other hand, is the perfect number; seven days of creation; the seven churches of Revelation; the seven priests carrying seven trumpets about Jericho; the seven thousand people in Israel who had not kissed the lips of Baal—"[5]

"Seven thousand is not seven," Mrs. Hudson gibed. "You were taught no arithmetic in that physician's college?"

"Nor how to boil an egg," chortled Holmes. "There is your eye for numbers, Mrs. Hudson."

"And for logic, sir. Remember the evil spirit which returns with seven spirits more wicked than itself?[6] The seven things detestable to the Lord?"[7]

"She has derailed you, Watson! Defamed and debunked you!"

"Why all this pipe smoking and scratching of heads?" asked Mrs. Hudson. "Yes, it rained forty days in Noah's time, to drown all the sinners! But Jesus walked the earth forty days before he ascended to heaven. Trial or destruction, you say?"

Holmes took the pipe from his mouth. "Bravo, Mrs. Hudson. Really."

"What I say is true. And forty years in the wilderness to kill off the Israelites who—"

"So, not every number has significance," Watson said. "Or the same significance. Is this what you're inferring?"

"I'm not inferring anything—I'm coming out and saying it, sir. Point-blank."

"And Watson and I feel the bullet, Mrs. Hudson. Truly."

"But the number seven must have some other meaning . . . or effect," insisted the doctor. He took a drink of coffee and coughed slightly. "For instance, the number three. It cannot be arbitrary that Jonah would spend three days in the fish's belly. Christ cites Jonah's experience as a parallel of what his would be in the heart of the earth, or his tomb.[8] The military man in me demands an explanation of why, in the case of Jericho, the number seven is so prevalent."

"You are correct, I'd wager," replied Holmes, and blew a perfect smoke ring, "and yet the number seven, in the context of being the perfect number, cannot support the weight we have placed upon it."

"What about archaeology?" prompted the doctor.

Holmes waved with his pipe. "Scant digging has been attempted upon the ancient mound of Jericho, revealing hardly a trace of 1400 BC. The first diggings in 1867, by one Captain

Charles Warre of the Royal Engineers, has revealed little of Late Bronze Age Jericho, save that it is the oldest town ever excavated. We will receive no help there." He snuggled the pipe's bowl to his cheek, feeling the warmth. '*Why did the Lord instruct the Israelites to march about Jericho once for six days, and then seven times on the seventh day, the very day of the city's destruction?*' I have a suspicious feeling that no supporting scripture will bear us an answer. It must be an argument from silence. Believe this: the evidence, as always, is right before us, but we must use reason alone. To solve this mystery we will be left to our collective wits, such as they are."

Watson nodded. "Our shared common sense."

Mrs. Hudson snickered. "God help us."

HEAVY PIECES, MINOR PIECES, PAWNS

Mrs. Hudson fairly jumped out of her skin as Holmes barged into the sitting room, stopped before the dining table, and opened his arms. A shower of chess pieces toppled noisily onto the wooden surface. He clustered the smallish pawns in the middle and fenced them in with the taller pieces: kings, queens, knights, bishops, rooks.

"Here stands the city of Jericho," he announced. "Her high walls, with her defending troops (the pawns) bottled up inside."

Mrs. Hudson offered a question. "How thick were the walls, Mr. Holmes? They made a deep rumbling when they fell."

"Yes," he mused, and took a deep breath. "They must have been wide, indeed. After all, Rahab had situated her dwelling within it and her roof was broad enough to hide two men beneath stalks of flax. But how to account for the walls collapsing? An earthquake?"

"There you go again, Holmes," Watson said, shaking his head, "trying to explain a miracle of God through natural means. Who do you think was responsible for Jericho's walls collapsing?"

"If so, a miraculously well-timed earthquake," cackled Mrs. Hudson.

"She's bested me again, Doctor!" smiled Sherlock Holmes. "If Watson could but cook better, I would have you change places, Mrs. Hudson, and furnish you with your own pipe and magnifying glass."

Georgie Porgie, Pudding and Pie

Mrs. Hudson, still in her bathrobe, watched Holmes, his hands grasped behind his back, a frown shading his brooding gray eyes. "So, let us become acquainted with the facts—Mrs. Hudson, do sit down!" He began to pace across the red carpet, now reading from a small history book: "Jericho: City of Palms, eight acres in area and eight hundred feet below sea level; situated eight miles northwest of where the river Jordan dumps into the Dead Sea; climate, tropical; only a few inches of annual rainfall; surrounded by palms, banana trees, balsams, sycamores, and henna."

"What about Rahab, the harlot of Jericho?" asked Watson.

"A manufacturer of dyed linen. As to her being a harlot, the early usage of the Hebrew word *zonah*, from its root word, *zan*, probably referred to one who feeds people, or provides them with victuals. Rahab might have kept an inn for travelers passing through Jericho. Inns are an effective source of gossip, and the two spies would naturally have gone to such a hub of activity to gather their intelligence, listening to the wayfarers and travelers speaking unguardedly with one another. Notice, too, the city's officials approached her with some respect, which they would do with a leading citizen of the city. In any case, her dwelling must have been situated high on the wall, for she let the two spies down by way of a rope through her window."[9]

"A good, long rope, then!" the landlady surmised.

Holmes pressed his fingers against his temples. "I had begun deliberating on Joshua—remarkable fellow. Though this was his first command after Moses' death, he never doubts or wavers. But this line of thought led me nowhere. There is something lurking in my mind, half-baked—like the egg you cooked me, Watson. But it is taking form. Something you said at Jericho, Mrs. Hudson, flashed through my thoughts like feverish lightning burning a hot course through my brain—but it is gone again!"

Watson snapped his fingers and yelped, "Ah!" He jumped up from his chair and left the room and made his way down the stairs, reappearing a short time later, out of breath, with a steaming tray which he proudly placed on the table.

"Oh," Holmes muttered dismally. "I thought you had solved the mystery for us, Doctor."

"While you two traipsed over the countryside of Jericho, I struggled bravely from my convalescent bed and applied myself to culinary cooking—"

"*Culinary cooking*? Is that much like *hair beautician*?" mused Holmes. He put the newspaper aside and inspected what might be a pie lying beside a dubious yellow mound of cake crested with red dollops.

"—or rather, baking." Watson puffed out his chest and

announced: "Mrs. Martha Hudson, Mr. Sherlock Holmes, may I present my apple pie and steamed lemon pudding topped with raspberries!"

"Oh, wonderful!" she exclaimed.

Watson gushed, "It is but a trifle."

"If only it were but a *truffle*." Holmes tapped the ceramic-like pie crust with his pipe.

"It is not quite shoe leather," Watson said.

"I agree," said Holmes. "You can drive nails through shoe leather. Watson, do you remember me saying that there are crimes which are not really crimes—"

"And this—a lemon pudding!" Watson proclaimed, unabashed.

"Oh, formidable!" chortled Mrs. Hudson, clapping lightly.

"They are made this large in the Orient," said Sherlock. "For the dead."

Watson ignored him. He took a large knife in hand and cut into the pudding. It quivered like a giggling fat man being unmercifully tickled, but then it took a sickly bearing and deflated entirely, falling inward on itself.

"Pie for me," said Holmes.

The doctor teetered on the verge of tears.

"Another time you must not overeat the eggs," whispered Mrs. Hudson. "And a cup of sifted flour is not a cup of flour sifted."

Holmes sank his chin deep into his chest. Here came the flame of memory searing though his brain, but this time he reached out and snared it. A scene flickered before his eyes, of Mrs. Hudson sitting down, rubbing her feet, her galoshes, her fireplace poker. Offhandedly she had commented that Jericho was *bristling like a cat. Bristling!*

He snapped out of his deep meditation only to find her staring at him with a twinkle in her eye, like a mother waiting for her lagging child to catch her up.

"Ha!" he cried, and turned about. He grabbed his violin and bow, then rasped upon it in an eccentric, Italian, excitingly staccato-ish manner.

"Whatever are you doing?" asked Watson, bewildered.

"Celebrating, good doctor—are we not, Mrs. Hudson? But not in so grand a style as Sarasate!" cried the detective. He and the landlady laughed together. Danced together across the floor. "We are celebrating your wonderful cake! Your Jericho cake—ha, ha, ha!"

THE CEREMONY

Two men stood on the wide stairs of the Embankment building, the red-brick and granite fortress known as New Scotland Yard. Sherlock Holmes, resplendent in his black overcoat with satin lapels and matching top hat, conversed in subdued tones with police Inspector Lestrade, who discreetly flashed him a badge.

"Found this one. Shiny and new, Mr. Holmes, over at Shadwell.[10] This ceremony is strictly unofficial, you know."

"Excellent. I'm glad of it, Lestrade. Yet I am profoundly uncomfortable standing hereabouts. Scotland Yard and I have always been on somewhat questionable terms."

A fashionable black carriage stopped on Derby Street. Two people issued from that livery, an elderly lady dressed in a burgundy dress, helped along by a man the inspector knew so well from cases past: Dr. Watson.

Holmes smiled. "You look marvelous!" he said, taking Mrs.

Hudson by the hand and helping her solemnly up the stairs. Her hair shone luxuriantly silver: it was clear she had taken great pains with her curling tongs and hairpins.

"My hair's all done up, sir," she said, blushing. "With silver and pearl clasps."

"Fitting for the occasion," Watson said reverently on her other side.

"Yes," Holmes said warmly, with mischief edging his voice. "I know how important pageantry is to you Cherokees."

When they arrived at the staircase's top, Holmes nodded to Lestrade, who announced: "It has come to the Metropolitan Police's attention, and of the presiding powers housed therein, that is, here at New Scotland Yard, that an exemplary standard of detective excellence has been set by one Mrs. Hudson, Landlady of 221b Baker Street. Acting within my authority as representative of said powers, already, I do hereby, forthwith and so on, present you with this honorary badge, endowed with all the rightful duties and privileges as Deputy Inspector of Scotland Yard."

Mrs. Hudson's eyes widened. She received the weighty article in her gloved hands and held it to her chest. "Oh!"

Lestrade smiled, tipped his hat, and departed into the vast building.

"Neither of you has revealed the riddle's answer," stated Watson. "Impolitic of you. Impoliteness of the first order."

"All right, then," said Sherlock Holmes. "Imprimis: you are the king of Jericho, Watson. You are frightened to death. Why? Because of this new foe who has just crossed the Jordan River and invaded your land. They have slain the Amorite king, Og of Bashan in his fortress of Edrei. They have conquered his powerful kingdom of sixty fortified cities on the east side of the Jordan, stretching from Mt. Hermon to the River Jabbok. No wonder Rahab had said that '*the terror of you has fallen on us, and that all the inhabitants of the land are fainthearted because of you.*'[11]

"And now, the Israelite army is on your doorstep.

"What do you do as king of Jericho? What else can you do, but marshal your troops for battle; ready them to rush out, if need be, into the plain to do battle—correct, Mrs. Hudson?"

She still caressed the police badge, hardly noticing him.

"But amazingly, the Israelites make one pass about your city and melt away to their camp. The next day, you hasten your troops to the gate again, only to witness the Israelites march once about your walls and summarily disappear. The next day the same thing happens, and then again, and then again. Complacency sets in. Your troops begin to stand down, to joke, to yawn. The Israelites reappear, march about your city one time, and then retire to their camp."

Watson stroked his mustache. "And then?"

"The seventh day dawns." Holmes tapped his walking stick on the stone stairs. "The troops of Jericho have gathered, as so often before, but then the unexpected happens. After marching once about the walls, the Israelites do not retire: They keep marching. Two, three, four times around, on and on. What do you do? Think of your ill-fated lemon pudding, Watson. Mrs. Hudson saw it right away."

His mouth flopped open. "The raspberries!"

"Precisely. Put yourself in the place of Jericho's troops. You become cautious, alarmed. You clamor up to the top of the walls to witness this new phenomenon, while the rest of your comrades below draw close to the walls and the gate, expecting an attack. What are the Israelites up to? What are they planning? I remembered Mrs. Hudson's comment—that Jericho's walls were *bristling like a cat*. In actuality what she saw—"

"Were the soldiers atop the walls, with their spears," filled in Watson.

"And then, suddenly, the seven trumpets blast out!" Holmes made a wide gesture with his arms. "The Israelite host shouts as one man."

"And the walls crash down," giggled Mrs. Hudson.

Holmes made a sharp gesture and said, "The Israelites rush the city, but they have little fighting left to do—"

"Because most of Jericho's soldiers have perished in the tons of falling stone," concluded Watson. "They fell with the walls or had the stones fall upon them."

"Precisely. The Israelites varied their routine on that last day, marching about the city seven times instead of once, for this very reason. And that is when the Lord brought the walls tumbling down." Holmes took in a deep breath of fresh air. It was a fitting end to the last mystery.

Mrs. Hudson beamed. "'All the king's horses and all the king's men / Couldn't put Humpty together again'!"

Watson looked sideways at Holmes. "Seems to me, Mr. Sherlock Holmes, you've accomplished something you'd never done before."

Holmes imparted his patented quirky smile.

"To my way of thinking," Watson went on, "you have never before solved a case with Mrs. Hudson as your sole aid and confidant. Could you have ever envisioned such a circumstance?"

"Indeed not. And I am still reeling with the reality."

"Still, can't you acknowledge that something extraordinary

has happened, something new under the sun, something magical, or be just a little more thankful, Mr. Holmes?"

"Thankful? Ah, Dr. Watson, the Almighty has put me in a most peculiar and pretty predicament." Holmes peered down upon the elderly lady fondling her police badge, and sighed. "Ah, Mrs. Hudson," he lamented. "There will be no living with you now."

SIX CUPS OF TEA

DARKNESS, BUT FOR THE SPREAD OF STARS LIKE GEM DUST, PRE-
sided over the misty surface of the River Thames. Silence, but
for the last chorus of stars fleeing west away over Tower Bridge,
lent magic to morning's mystery. Stillness, but for the ponderous
moon completing her sleepy course through the heavens, stood
sentinel over me as I huddled in my blanket upon the promenade
deck of the *Viceroy of India*.

I shivered slightly, hugged my blanket closer, listening. Time
seemed an intruder here. Faraway noises sounded near to me: a
cock crowing; the barking of a dog; the grating of a wooden ship
against the ageless wharf of St. Katherine's Docks, which had
witnessed the sailing forth of Drake, of Hawke, and of Admiral
Lord Nelson in his time. Indeed, the air tingled with expectancy, but for the dull, rhythmic murmuring of waves against
the ship's hull.

A sudden rustle of wings startled me. A huge ghostlike form
of a woman arose from the mist. The robed vision stilled itself
above the foggy coverlet, seemingly the very essence of fog, and
yet it appeared too substantial to sustain its airy dominance

without movement. Dewdrops dripped from her pale crown which was flecked with pearls and trailed with straggled ivory. As if performing a rehearsed dance the winged creature turned slowly, peering back over her shoulder at me with dark ruby eyes. Another purposeful thrust downward with her wings, and the mist beneath her churned as if from a cauldron.

I spied an infant nestled against the apparition's shoulder. My heart leapt into my throat, for I thought it dead, so deathly pale it appeared! But the baby yawned, rubbing its cheek in the shadowy tranquility of its mother's protection. The spirit circled slowly again, beating her wings with the whisper of eternity as the white vapors frothed about her. With a slight but definite nod my way, she floated away westward, with the stars.

I don't know how long I stood thusly, rooted in enchantment as the slow, inexorable earth tilted. I watched expectantly even as the horizon behind me began to lighten.

I whispered, "Verily, I have seen her. I have witnessed Night departing with her child."

"Indeed, you have," came a voice from behind me. Sherlock Holmes, dressed in his tweed cloak (and therefore better prepared than I against the nippy morning breeze), came alongside me and drew on his pipe. "Never fear, Watson; you are not losing your good sense. I saw her too."

My faithful friend handed me an unlit bulldog pipe and applied the flame for me, and I felt the growing warmth of the bowl in my hand. We shared a quiet pipe together; the spicy smoke inundated my head, my senses, a pleasant accommodation which did not lessen the pleasure of the fresh breeze that carried the aroma away. I turned, for the fog behind me glowed and flickered yellow as if to mask a burning ship—the rim of the sun blazing up from faraway France, and lighting up the expansive promenade deck.

I followed Holmes across the wood planking and ducked beneath an awning extending out from the brass side railing. We sat comfortably at a wicker table, enjoying the light, airy breeze as the city of London began to awaken. Holmes was no stranger to this scene—he had spent hours meditating here between our magical journeys, for days on end, as well as a considerable time convalescing after our stay at Bart's. Did he enjoy the river? The associated traffic and noises of the river wharf? Only a small portion of his twenty-three thousand pounds would buy a handsome boat, though I could not reconcile him with the sea.

"Perhaps it is because we stood directly over the Needle's Eye," Holmes postulated, gesturing with his pipe. "The reason for the Vision, I mean."

"Time-travel has left a stamp upon us," said I, puffing on my pipe. "Surely ten adventures into the past must affect us, must have its consequences, no matter how pleasant, no matter our location. For instance, in these gusts of wind which ruffle about us, I note an airy call, a chorus of angels—"

"I smell only the putrid signature of the Rotherhithe tanneries. Why, the wind's full east!"

"And fair for the French to land," I commented. Holmes clamped his teeth about his pipe so severely that I couldn't tell if he was smiling or wincing.

"Between you and Mrs. Hudson, I am at a loss," he continued, pressing on with his theme as we rose from the table and descended the side stairs into the dining cabin, to the smell of eggs and sausages; of coffee and toast; and of roasted potatoes and onions. It was an elegantly furnished room, with a heavy table draped in a white tablecloth, rich paneling covering the walls, and a chandelier which tinkled ever so softly when a vibration traveled through the ship.

"Our landlady remains bunked in the old captain's quarters, port side." This he remarked between mouthfuls of scrumptious, steaming breakfast and the slurping of coffee, Mrs. Ferguson's former medieval fare having improved substantially into palatable mid-eighteenth-century victuals.

"Scandalous behavior, normally," I replied, and I couldn't help but smile at his consternation. Between sips of coffee I busied myself with tabulating the cogent facts of the Jericho mystery for which I had been absent. "But surely our maid, Mary, will manage Baker Street as well as she may. Still," I added, staring at Sherlock's heaped plate, "the deposit of thousands of pounds does lead one into a celebratory mood, inclined to excess."

My coffee trembled in my cup as I drank from it. The Vision still enthralled me, and the thought came to me that the closer I moved to God, the more magical I might seem my ordinary surroundings.

But Holmes followed a different tack. He lamented, "Oh, Watson, what is to become of me now?" The sunlight through a stained-glass window cast strange patterns on his face, making him appear to be both smiling and crying. "Life is such a dreary *plod-plod*. Are there no miracles left for me?"

A pattering of feet sounded across the roof from the deck above, and soon, little smudge-faced Billy Button appeared at Holmes' elbow, the bill of his patched hat skewed to one side. He gestured with his filthy hands.

"Hullo, Mr. Holmes, zur, and Mr. Ferguson sends his salu . . . his saluta—"

"Billy, let's play a game called Mind Your Manners"—Holmes

motioned to a chair—"Do sit down and take off your hat—no one here will *bone* it. Yes, and hide your cigarettes in case Mrs. Hudson appears."

Billy Button would not sit down, but whispered in the detective's ear. Holmes replied in a low voice, to which Billy screwed up his monkey face and laid his patchwork satchel down from his shoulder.

"Have a biscuit, Billy," I said, "though it may be tastier if eaten atop a carriage."

Holmes smiled between a mouthful of eggs and sausage to remember his strange dining circumstances in Trafalgar Square. Billy Button grabbed a biscuit and some butter, and I said: "The sender concerns me, Holmes: the hidden fellow who supplied us with our timely mystery cards." I twittered my pencil back and forth like an erratic seesaw between my fingers. "His identity—"

"Little effort was needed to solve that tidbit, meant only to tease us: K2L2—King of kings and Lord of lords. I'm surprised at you, Watson."

"Our sender is Christ himself? What could he learn from our exploits?"

"We are the ones meant to learn—or rather, you, Watson, and those who read your embellished memoirs of our mystery cases. As to whether or not our sender is *actually* the Lord, well . . ."

"You had shown such promise, Holmes. I had thought, seeing all you had seen, you might become a believer."

"A believer, ha!" Holmes checked himself and tilted back in his chair to peer down the vacant hallway. Mrs. Hudson must be allowed to sleep. "I *am* a believer. In man. In the triumph of science. In the rational disciplines."

Billy Button chomped on his biscuit and looked back and forth at us.

"But if there is no God, then man is solely responsible for the evil and mess we witnessed. How will we unmake this tragedy? Through rational thinking? Education? I have seen the greatest evils, the vilest machinations perpetrated by the most civilized of societies!"

"According to the great thinkers, we do not need God for a sense of right and wrong. Man is still honing his morality. By and by, the obstacles will crumble. Man will shine resplendent!"

"So, that is why you did it?"

That question, softly spoken, came from the doorway. Mrs. Hudson had managed to sneak up on us both, but Holmes was quicker than me, rising and holding out a chair for her. She sat down cheerily at the table but gave no indication of explaining her bizarre statement. It was then that an image came crashing into my thoughts, vivid in its stateliness and efficacy. Holmes, too, seemed to understand, and sat back down, ever so slowly.

"Your walking stick," she stated evenly. "Ebony, with the silver duck's head which your brother Mycroft gave you. Mr. Watson and I always wondered why, upon your return from the hospital, you snapped it in two."

The detective composed himself, sitting back and thinking, as if reclining on the divan in his sitting room. "I did enjoy its weighty balance, the silver's silky feel against my palm, the crisp *tap*, *tap*, *tap* it made along the avenue. It was a prized possession, given the giver."

"But?" she pressed.

"But the moment I *needed* the thing, the moment I could not bear up without its support, it became abhorrent to me—an abomination beyond redemption."

"And so you destroyed it," I put in, "the crutch which your pride—"

"I have no misguided pride, Watson. I have honest abilities; talents bereft in others. I give credit to Lestrade in my successes: Scotland Yard glows with my brilliance!"

"Which makes you shine all the more," I commented, "in your humility."

"You are near to insulting me."

Holmes had never used such a severe tone with me, and yet I pursued the matter while Mrs. Hudson was content to nod her thanks to Mrs. Ferguson for pouring her a cup of coffee.

"And yet you insult the Lord, dear friend," I rejoined. "You witnessed his agony on the cross. How he graciously healed our infirmities at St. Bart's—"

"St. Bartholomew's is built upon ancient Roman foundations. Who knows but the mystical genius loci worked their healing upon us?" Holmes wolfed down a mouthful of roasted potatoes, then wiped his mouth with a napkin.

"Look, Holmes, God took a risk in creating this world. It cost him his Son. Christ died agonizingly on the cross because there was no other way to redeem it."

"Even for God? Can he be thus confined?"

"We are in a story. A magic yet tragic adventure—maybe magic because of its tragedy, where he chooses to confine himself. Would you have it any other way?" I leaned forward. Holmes chewed, but his eyes were attentive. "Listen, Holmes: This may not be the best of all possible worlds. But it may be the best means by which to get to the best of all possible worlds. In fact, it may be the *only* way."

"Stated like a chronicler," he replied.

The tension lessened. For once I had held my ground against the Wizard of Baker Street. Mrs. Hudson, strangely quiet, picked at her food. Her eyes twinkled with an almost insatiable vivacity, and yet at the same time, something integral was missing in her, as if her politeness were a detached formality, as if she outwardly enjoyed our fellowship but her inner attentions were elsewhere.

"Mrs. Hudson," said I demurely, "you're out of humor this morning."

The smile again. The nod again and a slight giggle, and I noticed her badge lying by her plate. Mrs. Ferguson placed a fresh plate of beautifully roasted onions and potatoes on the table, with a ladle rather than a spoon, for they were juicy onions. I applied myself to the eggs and biscuits.

"When, Mr. Holmes?" Mrs. Hudson asked at length. "When might we travel off into time once again? Dr. Watson?"

Her voice quivered, and a feeling of profound pity so overwhelmed me that I felt my eyes moisten. Holmes looked at her keenly, too, her nervous anticipation bordering on delight, and it dawned on me—I could sense it in her bearing—that she had never felt so alive as when she had stormed Jericho, or been included in the investigation of the crumbling walls, or been presented with a genuine inspector's badge.

My heart went out to her, our spry landlady, who had cooked us innumerable meals, served us countless teas, for her demeanor displayed all the overt manifestations of addiction. Surely Holmes could sympathize with her on that account. But what comfort could we give her. What assurances?

"Police!" called out Mrs. Ferguson, appearing from the kitchen and gesturing frantically. "Mr. Holmes, a police launch has pulled alongside us! A fine mess we're in, now! What's to happen with ol' Fergy and me? Oh—a fine mess!"

I nearly dropped my coffee cup. Mrs. Hudson snapped fully

awake and Billy Button froze, his hand halfway to grabbing another biscuit. And yet Holmes continued comfortably with his breakfast, laying down his silverware only as the harsh orders of an officer resounded down the hallway. Holmes was far too calm—he had to have known the police were coming, and then it dawned on me that this was the news Billy Button had brought him. And Holmes had reacted most circumspectly. What else could he do with elderly Mrs. Hudson in his care, not to mention all his friends and companions and helpers?

A large sergeant and three constables appeared in the doorway, and Holmes pushed away from the table, threw his napkin on his plate, and in spite of their call to "Hold there!" walked up the stairs to the upper deck, with Billy Button on his heels.

Out in the brilliant sunshine, Holmes lit his pipe, pursued by the barking, bustling police, and finally, by me. He strode to the brass railing at the rear of the ship, where we had seen the Vision at daybreak. I felt a presence against my side and found it to be Billy Button, hugging my coat sleeve, and it brought me such unexpected pleasure and a fierce surge of protective energy.

"Why, Sergeant!" said Holmes turning around, never taking his eye off of Billy and giving the boy a wink. "To what do we owe this auspicious visit? Ah, Constable Robertson, is it not? You helped me quite prodigiously with the Mandarin Court affair!"

"Indeed, sir." One of the officers flushed red. "Some time ago it was, sir, cronowordgically speakin'. I was wondering if you was remembered of it—"

"Familiarities are not in order, sir, not this morning," interrupted the sergeant, his red mustache and sideburns bristling and crackling as if ready to spark and catch fire. He was smartly dressed in his uniform, and filling it out to such a great extent that the bright silver buttons strained to keep him within their bounds. His silver shoulder insignias and his badge, mounted on his roam-style helmet, twinkled in the sunlight. "You can stop with this pleasant show, Mr. Holmes. See here: I have a warrant for you and for any other such fellows involved on your ship—" He stole a glance at the little boy. "Don't think I don't know you, Billy Button. We've a long-standing warrant for you too: stealing apples and tripping a man who walked with a cane—"

"So, now the man walks with two canes," remarked Holmes.

"Come along with you, then, Billy." The sergeant motioned for the boy to follow.

"No, he stays," said Sherlock. "You go."

"You're not appreciating the predicament you're in, Mr. Holmes."

"I might assert the same thing about you, Sergeant. Who authorized your raid upon the *Viceroy of India*? And what do you plan to do with *my* ship—which you have so properly called it— since it houses *my* property?"

"That's all the admission of guilt I need," the sergeant said confidently. "I know your low opinion of the police, sir, that we can't see the forest for the woods. But we're fast onto you. We're unbolting the lot, sir, as we speak—you can hear my men at work below—and carting away the steel frame, the platform, and the engine. By nightfall, naught will remain of your naughtiness." He raised up on his tiptoes and smiled. "You should know, Mr. Holmes, you can't keep a thing like this secret for long—especially with the likes of these river-rat people."

"I prefer them infinitely to your type, Sergeant, who barge onto my ship, hats discourteously un-removed in the presence of ladies, and raid this, my pleasant villa on the Thames, with a warrant."

The sergeant squinted in the sunlight. "More of a summons, to appear and explain—"

"Ah, a *summons* for questioning! For sciscitation! Am I not to be hanged, then, along with apple-stealers and trippers of old men?"

"I, for one, am surprised at your eagerness, Sergeant," I said, indignantly. It pained me greatly to hear the magnificent machine being disassembled—destroyed. "I have catalogued many cases where my friend, Sherlock Holmes, has aided Scotland Yard with peculiar and singularly obstinate cases. Indeed, I have been present for some of them."

"And we've been most heartily appreciative," replied the sergeant, "but with too much a show of gratitude for my taste. Mr. Holmes' shady methods may arrive at the correct solution sooner than us, but we police employ safer and more lawful methods."

At last, Mrs. Hudson appeared on deck, sniffling into her handkerchief, and nodded toward the lawmen. "Took my investigator badge, they did, Mr. Holmes. Confiscated it in a most blackguard fashion—"

The sergeant started, "I don't know how she, a civilian, came to be in possession of a police badge, but it is municipal property—"

"Let me be clear with you, Sergeant." Holmes' vocal current had turned from the frigid to the dangerous. "For you to insult and insinuate against this timid lady over such a stupid and trivial thing as a badge, and to think yourself larger for it—a pathetic and preposterous performance—says something definitive about you, Sergeant, and must call forth my most ardent and vehement rebuke. Yes, I am confirmed. I infinitely prefer the river people to you."

"We'll see how you throw about your insults down at the Yard, Mr. Sherlock Holmes, you with all these secret doings on the river. When the chief inspector hears about this—"

"But he shall hear about it from me," replied Holmes with a flair of his hand, "how the whole lot of you allowed a fugitive to escape."

The sergeant snapped his head around and stared wide-eyed at the vacant place where Billy Button had stood. Indeed, I had hardly felt the lad leave my side. One of the officers unbuttoned his chest pocket and went for the silver chain, but Holmes faced him.

"No good will come of blowing your whistle, Constable. Surely you can see Billy is gone. He can scale a building or drop down a drainpipe—you'll not catch him now. T'would be a raw goose chase, as you would so elegantly put it. Frustrating, isn't it, Sergeant? You hook a prize fish, have him all but reeled in, and—snap!—the line parts!"

He inhaled deeply, considering.

Holmes lowered his voice. "Now, have you no heart's mercy to restore Mrs. Hudson's badge to her, Sergeant? Surely it is a mere bauble, beneath your lofty contemplation? The chief inspector need not learn about such a minor slip-up in the matter of Billy Button's escape, since a characteristic criminal element in the case has not really been established."

The sergeant's blue eyes glazed over as he weighed the two alternatives: his career against a glittery medal of no real consequence. In a split second he motioned, and the constable reached in his pocket and handed the badge back to Mrs. Hudson.

"Whoa!—What's that?—Hold on!"

Those cries rang out from the sergeant and his men as the deck lurched beneath us. At the same instant there came a rumbling, another lurch, and then a loud, rhythmic splashing. We all ran to the starboard railing and peered down. The great ship's paddle was turning! The lines from the wharf had been cast off, and the foaming water rushed backward around the police launch. The bow of the *Viceroy of India* slowly gathered around until she pointed to the middle of the river.

I could hear heavy tools being dropped on the floor of the cabin-saloon below us, the policemen running out onto the lower promenade deck and looking up. Already the sergeant and his men had descended the stairway and were scrambling aboard the police launch. The sergeant looked up and shook his fist at Holmes, yelling and stamping his foot before issuing a profanity-laced diatribe including the barely discernible "arrest," "damages," "warrant," and other such ungentlemanly words.

But Sergeant Gilchrist (as later we learned his name to be) could have no satisfaction from the likes of one Sherlock Holmes, who put back his head and laughed. But that was not all, for it happened that just as the launch pulled away from the ship's side, Sergeant Gilchrist went to board her, and he, falling headlong into the river, was rescued only by the great exertions of his men, grappling, heaving, and hauling him aboard like a tusked walrus, sputtering and cursing like bedlam.

"Who says baptism must not precede salvation?" blurted Holmes, snorting and laughing in uncontrolled mirth, losing all decent composure by staggering against the stern railing and gasping for air. He burst out in a fresh torrent of maniacal laughter to the fainting point, so that I slapped him on the back in lieu of any other remedy. The last we saw of the launch, it was drifting eastward toward Wapping, and I made Holmes turn away, for fear of reawakening his spasms of frivolity.

He did giggle to himself, but his stark solemnity returned in earnest when he discovered he'd dropped his pipe overboard, that, and the timely appearance of Mrs. Ferguson with our morning tea, to the backdrop of Tower Bridge, its twin spires outlined sharply against the deep-blue sky.

"The Needle's Eye is gone from us," Holmes said glumly, "for we must put in at some port eventually. And the authorities will be waiting for us."

Mrs. Hudson, holding her teacup, exclaimed, "Oh! But shall we say, 'Cheers'?"

Mrs. Ferguson poured the gold-rimmed cups full of tea. Mr. Ferguson joined us from below, wiping his hands on his apron, greasy from successfully tinkering on the ship's engine.

"The old lady sails! I thought the engine beyond all repair. Shall we pop over to France for lunch?" Holmes smiled, saluting Mr. Ferguson with his steaming cup, the wind ruffling his hair. Indeed, the ship now was splashing merrily westward up the Thames. "She's an old ship; who would have thought her able?"

"There's your miracle for you, Holmes," I said in a burst of intuition.

"Earlier, I gave you a false impression of myself, Watson," replied Holmes, loud enough for all to hear. "There is a stubborn part of me *not* ruled by science—"

I grinned and said, "The heart part of you, Holmes—"

"I have no heart. Or blood either, Watson; you know that." He reached into his pocket and pulled out a small Bible—Holmes with a Bible! He traced his thumb over it, as a lover might caress his beloved's cheek. "The Bible is the only book that, as I read it, it reads me."

"But surely that is not all, Holmes?" I said. "Have not our mysteries moved you at a deeper level? We have journeyed from Joshua to the apostle Paul and all points in between; we've witnessed the fall of kings and the exalting of common sinners; we've seen giants slain and men raised to life!"

The sun beat down upon us so that even the formidable Sherlock Holmes seemed diminished in its intensity.

"In all our Bible travels," said the great Sleuth of Baker Street, "Jesus is the only person whom I suspected knew that we were present. Did you attend?" He took a lengthy sip from his cup before continuing. "If I were a religious man—which I am not—I would say this: I would rather believe in a false Jesus than a true anything else."

"Oh, Sherlock," whispered Mrs. Hudson, and laid her hand on his arm, "I am so proud of you! Tell us your favorite mystery of all—it will be enough for us and for Dr. Watson."

Holmes flared his nostrils. He grew irritated when people called him familiar or fawned over him (whether deserved or not), and he became downright repulsed when they touched him.

"The Feeding of the Five Thousand," he announced curtly, gently pulling away his arm.

"But we never witnessed that miracle, Holmes," said I.

"True, but it is extraordinary in that it could have never happened without the aid of a very small, insignificant boy." Holmes snapped his fingers and called out, "Billy!"

Billy Button popped up, hopped over the deck railing, and skipped over to us, accepting a cup of freshly poured tea—the sixth cup.

"Billy, you have been a brave lad!" announced Sherlock affectionately. "If I chance to pass Harris's in the Strand, I shall procure you a pair of new shiny boots, for I am certain your large toe winks out at me."

Sherlock Holmes reached in his pocket, pulled out a shiny guinea, and placed it in the youngster's palm. Billy might normally have squealed at such extravagance, but clearly, he was preoccupied. He stared into his cup and scrunched up his face all over again. Holmes and I, along with the Fergusons, laid back our heads and chuckled heartily—we all knew what was coming—except for our landlady.

"'Pon my word, ma'am," said the youngster apologetically to Mrs. Ferguson, "but wouldn't you have nothin' stronger to mix in with this tea?"

"Oh, scandalous!" Mrs. Hudson slapped her hand against her dress, her fussing barely rising above the chorus of laughter. "For shame, Billy Button! Shame on all of you!"

I walked to the railing and looked out over the fair city of London, and do you know who I thought of? I thought of you, dear reader. What do think of me and my journeys over the abyss of time? Have I kindled in you an understanding of the dark misgivings which linger in my nightmares? Have I awakened in you any pity for my anxious tremblings and joys, my mortal fear for my life in these ten adventures, one following after the other in the seeming interminable march of time? Perhaps you have laughed at me, cried with me, or perhaps you feel the slightest seed of faith awakening ever so gently within you. Or have you merely waved your hand to read of my voyages into the past as too wonderful and fantastic to be believed?

INVESTIGATIVE STUDY
QUESTIONS

ONE

THE HANGING MAN

WHY DID AHITHOPHEL HANG HIMSELF?

Please read 2 Samuel 17:1–14, 23. Why do you think Ahithophel hanged himself?

_____

_____

_____

Please read 2 Samuel 16:23. Ahithophel was a trusted counselor to King David. How highly was he regarded?

_____

_____

_____

Please read 2 Samuel 23:34. From this verse, what might we conclude about Ahithophel's family? What might indicate that

Ahithophel's counsel included not only municipal and judicial advice, but military recommendations as well?

_____

_____

_____

Please read 2 Samuel 15:1–12; 16:15. What can we learn of the relationship Absalom must have cultivated with Ahithophel? Does David's former counselor seem at all reluctant to follow Absalom, the young usurper?

_____

_____

_____

Please read 2 Samuel 15:30–37. As David wept, retreating up the Mount of Olives (not the last tears a king of Israel would shed there), whom did he perceive as his main adversary? What trap did David lay? Was that the most important thing he did?

_____

_____

_____

(Note verse 31. David did something crucial: He didn't trust in his craftiness. He didn't rely on the strength of his veteran soldiers. He _prayed_!)

Please read 2 Samuel 23:39. Whose name do you discover? Does this name mean anything to you? In what context?

_____

_____

CONNECTIONS

Have you ever had feelings of revenge? What caused them? Did you feel justified in your feelings? Did you take any action for the wrongs committed against you?

_____

_____

_____

_____

Why do those closest to us hurt us the most? In Psalm 41:9 David wrote, "My friend has lifted up his heel against me" (paraphrased). He could have meant Saul, Absalom, or any number of people who sided against him. Have you ever wanted revenge against a friend or family member?

_____

_____

_____

_____

Envy. Jealousy. Hurt. These lead to revengefulness. Both Absalom and Ahithophel allowed their injuries to smolder until they destroyed *themselves*, not the person they hated. Where do your feelings of revenge arise? At home? In the workplace? At church? In traffic, where you have to get even with the other guy?

_____

_____

_____

_____

What is the connection between anger and revenge? How long, according to the Scriptures, should anger last? (Ephesians 4:26) What connection is there between forgiveness and revenge?

_____

_____

_____

King David, for all his faults, did not harbor resentment against Absalom. Moreover, he named one of his sons "Nathan" after the very prophet who confronted him about Bathsheba. What does this tell you about David's heart?

_____

_____

_____

Remember, David *prayed*. We see it clearly after his sin with Bathsheba. We see it as he fled Jerusalem up the Mount of Olives. Is prayer the key to changing our attitudes (or at least moderating them) before they become destructive and it's too late?

_____

_____

_____

TWO

———————————

DIGNIFIED HARLOTS

IN JOHN 8, WHAT DID CHRIST WRITE ON THE GROUND?

Please read John 8:2–11. Pay careful attention to words or phrases you might easily overlook. What is your overall impression of what happened?

_____

_____

_____

With whom do you identify in this passage?

_____

_____

_____

What curious, unexplained thing did Christ do?

_____

_____

_____

Please read Mark 7:1–13. Who instigated this confrontation?

_____

_____

What was the basis of their complaint (verses 2 and 5)?

_____

_____

What was the basis of Jesus' response: tradition or the law?

_____

_____

Please read Philippians 3:4–6. What insight does this give you into the self-conception of the religious leaders who brought the adulterous woman before Christ?

_____

_____

Please read John 7:45–52. With whom were the Pharisees angry? What was their complaint? When confronted with the requirements of the law, what was their response? More importantly, in regard to the law, what sin did they commit?

_____

_____

CONNECTIONS

What affections have you married, instead of love for God? What heart-idols have you set up to obscure God in your life? (Remember, even good things, like a wife, kids, and your job, will become a hindrance if they take the preeminent place reserved for God!)

After doing this study are you surprised at Christ's leniency toward the adulteress?

Are *you* like the adulterous woman? Do you hang your head when remembering past sins? Adultery is the only sin God allows as a basis for divorce. We've seen it was punishable by death in the Old Testament. But here is the real question: Are your personal sins so horrible, so grievous, that God can't forgive you in just five words and send you out into the world clean and radiant? *Go and sin no more!*

Might Christ's admonition to the adulteress indicate what his view is of *our* past sins? Our present reality? Our future?

How long a period of time do you think Christ expects us to supplement his grace and forgiveness by harboring our own personal feelings of guilt and anguish for our sins?

How does Christ's response to the Pharisees rebut the criticism that Christianity is a religion of men—a religion prejudiced against or unfavorable to women?

_____

_____

_____

What might her secret, unnamed partner have learned after hearing about this drama? Do you think he may have been one of the Pharisees?

_____

_____

_____

Remember, there was another group of people present in the temple courtyard besides the Pharisees. Do you think any of those men and women, who had been listening raptly to Jesus, actually reached out to help this woman 'go, and sin no more'? Would you have waited outside the temple for her and taken that risk?

_____

_____

_____

Can you think of another instance in the Gospels like this? What was Christ's response in that situation? The woman's? (Read Luke 7:36–50.)

_____

_____

_____

THREE

RIGHTEOUS BLOOD IS RED

IN MATTHEW 23:35, WHY DID CHRIST CITE ZECHARIAH SON OF BERECHIAH AS HAVING BEEN MURDERED BETWEEN THE TEMPLE AND THE ALTAR WHEN IT WAS REALLY ZECHARIAH SON OF JEHOIADA?

Read the story of Zechariah's murder in 2 Chronicles 24:17–22. Who was Zechariah, specifically? What message did he have for his king and his people? Where, specifically, was he murdered?

_____

_____

_____

Now read Matthew 23:29–39. Here Jesus was castigating the teachers of the law and the Pharisees. What discrepancies can you pick out? How was Jesus' message (verse 37) different from that of Zechariah son of Jehoiada?

_____

_____

_____

Please read Zechariah 13:2–6. What do you think Zechariah was foretelling here?

_____

_____

_____

Please read 2 Chronicles 30:6–9. What is the theme of this passage?

_____

_____

_____

Please read Nehemiah 1:9. What is the theme of this verse?

_____

_____

_____

Please read Hosea 6:1. What is the theme of this verse?

_____

_____

_____

Please read Malachi 3:7. What is the theme of this verse?

_____

_____

_____

Please read Jeremiah 26:2–15. What similarities do you see between Jeremiah's message and Christ's from Matthew 23:29–39? Where did the Lord tell Jeremiah to stand to deliver his charge against the Israelites? What did the people want to do to Jeremiah?

_____

_____

_____

Please read Zechariah 1:2–6. What similarities do you see between Zechariah's message and the various ones you just read? How does this message sound like Matthew 23?

_____

_____

_____

Please read Joel 2:12–13. What was God's message here?

_____

_____

_____

Connections

How do you feel about publicly standing up for Christ or proclaiming the Lord's message, having seen the consequences for *both* Zechariahs? Are you concerned that proclaiming Christ will cost you something—family, friends, or job?

_____

_____

Have you ever doubted the Scriptures because you couldn't explain something or because it seemed too far-fetched?

_____

_____

As with the Jewish leaders, are there clear scriptural commands (or those heart-burnings kindled by the Holy Spirit) that you find difficult to abide by?

_____

_____

Do you feel there is distance between you and God? What might be the cause? Who was it that moved, you or God, to cause this distance?

_____

_____

How can the fledgling Jewish nation, just returning from exile, commit the same sin against Zechariah son of Berechiah that their forefathers did against Zechariah son of Jehoiada?

_____

_____

Have you ever sensed the Lord pleading with you, "Return to Me"? Is he doing so now? What do you think he requires of you to stop your harmful cycle of behavior and return?

_____

_____

_____

_____

FOUR

THE DEVIL'S ENTERPRISE

AFTER THE STORY OF CHRIST'S TEMPTATION, WHAT DID
LUKE MEAN WHEN HE WROTE, "THE DEVIL . . . LEFT HIM
UNTIL [A MORE] OPPORTUNE TIME" (LUKE 4:13 NIV)?

Please read Luke 4:1–13. In what kind of condition was Jesus?
Who led him into this trial?

_____

_____

_____

Christ was tempted three specific times. Each time, before
proceeding, Satan challenged Christ's authority by questioning
his identity. In what way did he do this? (Compare to Genesis 3:1.)

_____

_____

_____

In response to all three temptations, how did Christ preface his reply? Which Old Testament book did he quote each time to parry the devil's temptations? Does this change your view of the applicability of the *Old Testament* for your current problems or temptations?

_____

_____

_____

Please read Genesis 39:1–20 and Job 1:6–2:10. What do these two passages indicate about the timing of the temptations God may authorize in the lives of people he cherishes? Do they come as a test before or after something great is to be accomplished? How did Joseph and Job exemplify Christlikeness in their suffering?

_____

_____

_____

Who was the troublemaker in Job's and Christ's temptation accounts? In the mystery, Sherlock Holmes referred to him as the Accuser. What do these passages further reveal about him?

_____

_____

_____

Please read Hebrews 2:18. What does this tell you about Christ's temptations? Is there a connection between suffering and temptation? Must suffering accompany temptation to be genuine?

_____

_____

Please read Hebrews 4:15. Does this tell you anything about your temptations? Other than suffering, what additional element could connect you to Christ when you are tempted?

_____

_____

_____

Please read 1 Corinthians 10:12–13. What terms are used here that indicate that the Evil One will try the same tactics on us that he used on Christ?

_____

_____

_____

Please read Luke 23:32–43. What pattern coincides with Christ's earlier temptation?

_____

_____

_____

CONNECTIONS

Christ never succumbed to a single temptation. He responded to each one with firmness. Does this compare with your attempts at resistance? What does our reaction to temptation say about our view of God's all-sufficiency?

_____

_____

_____

The concept of rest is closely aligned with temptation. For instance, after Christ's temptation, the angels attended him in the wilderness. On the cross, rest in the form of early death came for Christ. What might the blessed hope of a promised rest stir in us to help us endure?

Please read Hebrews 4:16. What should our frame of mind be when we are tempted?

What does Christ's response to the devil say about the power of using the Scriptures to combat the devil? In light of this, what is your view of the value of memorizing scripture? Has this mystery changed your opinion about the *Old Testament's* applicability to your personal problems or temptations?

What does Christ's temptation reveal about the Holy Spirit? Do you worry about what terrible plans the *Comforter* may have in store for you?

What do you consider as suffering?

Do you ever use the admission "Well, I'm not God," to cajole you into accepting and even continuing your sin?

_____

_____

_____

What well did Sherlock Holmes draw from? What well was Watson referring to?

_____

_____

_____

What did Watson identify as the crux of Holmes' problem?

_____

_____

_____

How was Sherlock Holmes' view of faith, in essence, satanic? (Remember the temptations of Christ.) What do you think of Watson's rebuttal? With whom do you side?

_____

_____

_____

What is your definition of faith? Will it stand up to the scrutiny of your friends or those with whom you work? Do they know about your faith?

_____

_____

_____

FIVE

PAIN, LOCKS, AND ROMANS

WHY DID THE LORD LEAD PAUL TO BEGIN HIS MACEDONIAN MISSIONARY JOURNEY IN SUCH A DANGEROUS PLACE AS PHILIPPI?

Please read Acts 16:11–40. Note where the civic pride of the Philippians was subtle or overt.

_____

_____

_____

_____

Please read Acts 16:6–10. From what vantage point does this passage seem to be taken (ground level or from ten thousand feet)? How does the Holy Spirit surprise you in this text?

_____

_____

_____

Please read Acts 17:1–9. How does Thessalonica compare to Philippi?

_____

_____

_____

Please read Acts 18:1–18. Who were the repeated troublemakers against the spread of the gospel?

_____

_____

_____

CONNECTIONS

Are "vetted" coworkers important for ministry? What effect might they have on your success? How might John Mark have fared on Paul's second missionary journey? (See Acts 15:37.)

_____

_____

_____

In his subsequent beatings and trials, do you think Paul ever recalled his vision of the Macedonian man for reassurance of his mission? Do you ever claim God's promises or recall answered prayer for strength in difficult or trying times?

_____

_____

_____

In Paul's missionary journeys through Asia Minor and Greece, what lay behind the Jews' envy as they stirred up dissention against Paul (also a Jew)? Why did Paul's particular calling or "revealed mystery" so upset them? (Read Colossians 1:26–27; Acts 22:17, 22 for insight.)

_____

_____

_____

What was God's response to the hard-hearted Jews? Do you have any hardness of heart that may be displeasing the Lord?

_____

_____

_____

Christ, as our shepherd, protects and loves us. Is there evidence that Paul, as the leader on this journey, acted protectively toward those serving under him?

_____

_____

_____

Returning to the theme of rest after trials or temptations (see the study questions in chapter 4), what may have been Paul's time of rest and recuperation after Philippi?

_____

_____

_____

_____

SIX

YOU MISS, YOU DIE

WHY DID DAVID CHOOSE FIVE STONES BEFORE GOING OUT TO FIGHT GOLIATH?

Please read 1 Samuel 17:40–50. What is your impression of the character of the young man David? Why do you think he chose five stones?

_____

_____

_____

Review some key verses from 1 Samuel 17, specifically, verses 32, 34–37, 45–47. Given David's clear-mindedness and focus on the situation, is it arbitrary that Scripture states specifically that he picked up five stones? Why or why not?

_____

_____

_____

Please read the backstory of the duel recorded in 1 Samuel 17:1–39. What specific statements of David's indicate a high level of conviction and faith in the Lord?

_____

_____

_____

Please read 2 Samuel 5:22–25. In this passage, David was a new king. How did God continue to show his faithfulness to David and to Israel?

_____

_____

_____

Please read 2 Samuel 22:38–43. By this time King David was old. To whom did he attribute his success? His victories? What examples did he cite?

_____

_____

_____

CONNECTIONS

Has your faith been challenged after discovering the depths of young David's faith?

_____

_____

_____

_____

In what authority did Goliath place his confidence?

_____

_____

In Joshua 1:9 the armies of Israel were approaching the promised land, to conquer it. The Lord said, "Do not be afraid, nor be dismayed [by your enemies]." In 1 Samuel 17:11, in the story of David and Goliath, the words "afraid" and "dismayed" are used again, but this time the Israelites were cowering in fear. What, in your opinion, had happened to the nation of Israel between the time of Joshua and that of King Saul?

_____

_____

_____

List the ironies that come to mind with regard to how the Lord, through David, dealt with Goliath the giant (hint: large versus small stature, type of weapons, etc.). Does this give you insight into how the Lord chooses the people who will accomplish his plans? How might he use you?

_____

_____

_____

Who should receive the real honor and praise for David's victory. Why?

_____

_____

_____

_____

Is it accidental that Holmes' Great Bible happened to be opened to 2 Corinthians 2?

_____

_____

_____

What do you think is the foundation of Sherlock Holmes' unbelief in God? Do you see him wrestling with possible belief? By nature, must fact and faith be mutually exclusive?

_____

_____

_____

Do you ever find yourself falling into Sherlock Holmes' mode, believing that facts speak louder than faith? Do your circumstances speak louder to you about God and his love for you than the Scriptures do?

_____

_____

_____

SEVEN

DEAD MAN WALKING

WHY DID JESUS DELAY IN COMING TO LAZARUS?

Please read John 11:1–44. Take time to revel in this passage's beauty, how it teaches hope in the face of tragedy and reveals a God who cares deeply. Now reread it. Keep an eye out for details that don't quite make sense. List your findings below.

_____

_____

_____

(Also, please read Matthew 9:18–26 and Luke 7:11–15.)

"Actions speak louder than words." Is this always true? Please read the following verses. What connection or contrast do you see between Christ's miracles and his words?

_____

_____

John 14:11

_____

_____

John 15:22–24

_____

_____

John 4:48; 6:30; Matthew 12:39; Mark 8:12

_____

_____

John 10:24–25

_____

_____

John 12:47–50; 17:8

_____

_____

John 20:29

_____

_____

Please read John 7:38–39. What is the actual time gap between these two verses?

_____

_____

_____

_____

Please reread John 11:1–44. Look for a key verse, no matter how seemingly insignificant, that enlarges the context of the Lazarus story by allowing you to branch outside the story. Do you find anything noteworthy?

_____

_____

_____

_____

Please read John 10:37. What might this verse have to do with the Lazarus story?

_____

_____

_____

_____

CONNECTIONS

Picture a young woman in a white dress, sitting on a sunny hillside, plucking white petals, one by one, from a daisy and proclaiming wistfully, "He loves me; he loves me not . . ." Have you ever come to a decision on whether or not God loved you based on circumstances? Have you asked God for a *sign* (for example, that he loves you) instead of taking him at his *word*?

_____

_____

_____

_____

_____

Why do you think Christ emphasized his words over his miracles—his preaching and message over his marvelous works? (See Mark 1:38.)

_____

_____

_____

Does this mystery's deeper explanation of John 11 resonate with you? How has the totality of what Christ endured on the cross changed your view of him as a mediator?

_____

_____

What can be more terrible for a parent than to witness the death of a son or daughter? Has your view of the Father changed in light of what *he* endured during the crucifixion?

_____

_____

Taking the previous question into account, why do you think Jesus wept after arriving at Lazarus's tomb?

_____

_____

_____

Why don't the Scriptures relate any stories told by Lazarus about his time in the realm of the dead? Does this give you any thoughts about the validity of so-called life-after-death experiences?

_____

_____

Have you thought of other plays or pictures in the Bible that might give a deeper understanding of a traditional Bible story?

_____

_____

_____

Has Christ ever delayed in coming to you? In answering an important prayer of yours? Why do you think he delayed with you?

_____

_____

_____

EIGHT

WHO'S YOUR MAMA?

WHY IS JEHOIACHIN'S NAME INCLUDED IN CHRIST'S
GENEALOGY IN MATTHEW 1 WHEN JEREMIAH
HAD PROPHESIED IT WOULD NOT BE?

Please read Luke 1:26–38. What does the second part of verse 32
specifically state will be given to Christ? Over what will he reign?

_____

_____

_____

Please read Matthew 1:1–16. Take note of the kings listed in
Christ's genealogy. (Remember that the New King James Version
renders the name Jehoiachin as "Coniah" and "Jeconiah.")

_____

_____

_____

Please read Jeremiah 22:24–30. What is Jeremiah's prophecy about King Jehoiachin (or Coniah)?

_____

_____

Please read 1 Chronicles 3:17. Who is listed as King Jehoiachin's (Jeconiah's) sons? What effect does this have on the discussion?

_____

_____

_____

Connections

God is portrayed often as possessing unlimited love and forgiveness. It might be uncomfortable, even alarming to realize, but is there a limit to his pity and compassion? What is the main reason he may withhold mercy or grace? Why might he refuse to listen to an individual's prayer? On the aggressive side, why might he attack a nation?

_____

_____

_____

After reading about the different characters portrayed in this study, do you think there are individuals born without souls, whose natures cannot be redeemed?

_____

_____

_____

Is God's meticulous planning of the future confined to large events? Is he interested in your future as well? What evidence do you have of God's planning in your life?

_____

_____

_____

Are you too insignificant for God to notice? Do you have brothers or sisters who outshine you? In thinking about this chapter, what appreciation should we have for Nathan, the quiet brother?

_____

_____

_____

In 561 BC, Evil-Merodach became king of Babylon. He removed Jehoiachin from prison (where he'd been held for thirty-seven years) to his royal palace. Jehoiachin was honored and ate regularly at the king's table. What might this indicate had happened in fifty-five-year-old Jehoiachin's heart? (See 2 Kings 25:27–30.) Do God's mercies ever fail for those who seek him, no matter how late? Can you think of other vile kings for whom God extended mercy? (See 1 Kings 21:25–29 and 2 Chronicles 33:10–19 for clues.)

_____

_____

_____

NINE

RUN FOR YOUR LIFE

WHY WERE CHRIST'S BIRTH AND DEATH CONSIDERED TO BE "AT THE RIGHT TIME"?

Please read Matthew 2:1–12. What do you think of God's timing here? What do you think of Herod?

_____

_____

Please read Matthew 2:13–23. What disturbs you about this part of the story?

_____

_____

Please read Galatians 4:4 and Romans 5:6. What do these two passages say about the times chosen for Christ's birth and death? About God's sovereignty?

_____

_____

Please read Mark 1:15; Ephesians 1:9–10; 2 Thessalonians 2:6; and Titus 1:3. Does God seem concerned with timing? Read 1 Peter 1:10–11. Have people tried to decipher God's providential timetable? According to verses 12 and 13, what should we do instead?

_____

_____

_____

Are you ready for a marathon? Please read Acts 8:1–4; 9:13, 29–30; 15:3, 30, 36; 16:1–12. What do these passages have in common?

_____

_____

_____

CONNECTIONS

How does God's sovereign timing affect your relationship with him? How might you, as a parent of one of the little boys in Bethlehem, have initially reacted to God? And later?

_____

_____

Have you personalized God's sovereignty? Do you believe God knew when you would be born, where you would live, and when you will die? (See Acts 17:26.)

_____

_____

_____

It is a terrible truth about life, but sometimes, only by looking back on a turbulent event in our lives can we clearly see God's sovereign planning. Are you currently going through trials which make you question God's wisdom or love?

_____

_____

_____

Do you wonder about the wisdom in the timing of Christ's birth? Have you ever looked at circumstances alone to try to discern what God is doing in your life?

_____

_____

_____

Does the answer to this mystery give you any insight into how God formulates solutions to problems?

_____

_____

_____

Do you ever wonder if God really cares about your trials? Why doesn't he relieve our difficulty? (After all, he *is* God.) How might our timing not be God's timing?

_____

_____

_____

TEN

HUMPTY DUMPTY

WHY WERE THE ISRAELITES INSTRUCTED TO MARCH
ABOUT JERICHO ONE TIME FOR THE FIRST SIX
DAYS, BUT SEVEN TIMES ON THE LAST DAY?

Please read Joshua 6:1–25. The number seven plays heavily in the
strict procedure the Lord laid out for the army of Israel to follow.
Why do you think this is?

_____

_____

_____

Please read the whole of Joshua 2. Where was Rahab's house
located? What gives you a clue as to its size? (See verse 6.)

_____

_____

_____

Please read the following verses: Genesis 7:17; Deuteronomy 9:18; Numbers 14:33–34; Genesis 2:2–3; Joshua 6:8; Revelation 1:20. What significance do you attach to the numbers used in these verses?

_____

_____

_____

CONNECTIONS

What walls in your life need to fall down? Think of relationships that might be damaged by such emotions as pride, envy, or anger.

_____

_____

_____

What walls in your life need to be built up or patched? Think of personal weaknesses or sins that so easily entangle you. How do you plan to strengthen your walls?

_____

_____

_____

The order to destroy Jericho, Joshua's first command from God after the death of Moses, might have spawned misgivings about God's strange plan of attack. If so, did Joshua let those feelings show?

_____

_____

_____

Read Matthew 1:5 and Hebrews 11:30–31. What was the only portion of the wall left standing? What hope is there for "enemies" in this life, such as Rahab, of participating significantly in God's plan?

_____

_____

_____

Read Hebrews 11:30. What did God require, besides his own raw power, to bring down Jericho's walls? What might this imply about God's growth plan for you? How might this awareness help you with building up or tearing down your walls?

_____

_____

_____

In the mystery itself, Watson's failed cake led to solving the puzzle. Can the failures of others in our lives somehow hold the key to helping us realize what we should really be focusing on in life? Instead of berating someone for his or her stupidity or shortcomings, might we realize that God looks kindly and with much patience on our and others' failings?

_____

_____

_____

SIX CUPS OF TEA

CONNECTIONS

Watson imperils the comforts of his friendship with Holmes for the sake of sharing the gospel. Have you ever risked a friendship in order to communicate the life-giving gospel message? Is someone coming to your mind right now who may need your boldness?

_____

_____

_____

Have you ever sensed that the Bible was reading you or perhaps that a sermon was meant just for you? To what do you attribute this?

_____

_____

_____

In what does Sherlock Holmes place his trust? What rationale does he give?

_____

_____

_____

What examples does Watson give when criticizing Holmes' theory of morality?

_____

_____

_____

Why is Mrs. Hudson so proud of the venerable but skeptical Sherlock Holmes?

_____

_____

_____

NOTES

FOREWORD
1. Arthur Conan Doyle, *A Study in Scarlet* (n.p.: Empire Books, 2011), 22.

THE NEEDLE'S EYE (INTRODUCTION)
1. A cigar of exceptionally dark tobacco grown in a city of southern India of that same name.
2. In *Valley of Fear* Holmes states he had been in Professor Moriarty's rooms on at least three occasions.
3. A grand paddle steamer hit by the collier *Bywater Castle* at Tripcock Point on the River Thames, September 3, 1878. Nearly seven hundred men, women, and children drowned.

CHAPTER 1: THE HANGING MAN
1. 2 Samuel 17:1–14, 23.
2. 2 Samuel 23:8, 13, 24, 34.
3. 2 Samuel 17:23.
4. London's daily newspaper, which maintained a reputation for accurate news and high literary standards.
5. 2 Samuel 13:1–38.
6. 2 Samuel 15:1–37.
7. The official name for a four-wheeler, enclosed carriage.
8. 2 Samuel 16:20–22.

CHAPTER 2: DIGNIFIED HARLOTS

1. Holmes should have known this, being in the poorer part of town: barley for the poor, wheat for the rich. In keeping with the seasonal cycle, barley would have been harvested four to five months before.
2. Wealthy homes possessed chimneys. In others, smoke escaped through high windows, blackening the ceiling.
3. Mark 7:1–13.
4. Ibid.
5. Philippians 3:4–6.
6. John 7:45–52.
7. Mark 7:6–13.
8. John 8:5.
9. John 8:4.
10. Hosea 4:14.
11. John 5:39–40.
12. James B. Pritchard, *Ancient Near Eastern Texts* (Princeton, NJ: Princeton University Press, 1969), 196.
13. Matthew 23:5–6.
14. Hosea 5:4.

CHAPTER 3: RIGHTEOUS BLOOD IS RED

1. A vast bronze laver measuring forty-five feet around, supported by twelve bronze bulls in four groups of three, and able to hold almost eighteen thousand gallons.
2. Mary Morstan, Watson's second wife.
3. From the Sherlock Holmes short story "The Adventure of the Solitary Cyclist," in which Holmes blundered by not taking an earlier train.
4. Nevill owned and operated many London bathhouses, as this one at Northumberland Avenue, Charing Cross.
5. The King Lud restaurant was world renowned for its Welsh rarebit, smoked from early morning until late.
6. Jeremiah 19:14–15.
7. Jeremiah 26:2–6.
8. Latin: "completely secure."

Chapter 4: The Devil's Enterprise

1. The Olympic, a theater on Wych Street, was connected to the Strand by a long, dark, odorous, and extremely dangerous passageway.
2. A disease caused by wild rodents.
3. Latin for "the untrodden paths of life."
4. An expensively tailored suit.
5. Luke 4:3.
6. Luke 4:4.
7. Luke 4:8.
8. Luke 4:9–11.
9. Luke 4:12.
10. Hebrews 2:18.
11. Hebrews 4:15.
12. Mark 14:50–52.
13. Deuteronomy 8:3; 6:13; 6:16.
14. Charles H. Dyer, *Thirty Days in the Land with Jesus* (Chicago: Moody Publishers, 2012), 49.
15. Matthew 7:9.
16. Charles H. Dyer, *Thirty Days in the Land with Jesus* (Chicago: Moody Publishers, 2012), 51.
17. Ibid., 50.
18. Luke 23:33–39.
19. John 4:1–42.
20. William Winwood Reade's *Martyrdom of Man*, strongly anti-theological, had influenced Holmes greatly.
21. John Carey, *John Donne* (Oxford, UK: Oxford University Press, 1991), 260.
22. Luke 23:46.
23. Luke 23:42.
24. Lamentations 1:12.

Chapter 5: Pain, Locks, and Romans

1. Much like our modern locks. A key is turned and bypasses obstructions to unlock the door.
2. Greco's *Primo Modo del Gioco de Partito* was a treatise on chess published in 1625.
3. Acts 16:17.

4. Cicero had said of Octavian Augustus, "That young man should be lauded, glorified, and eliminated."
5. Sir Joseph Paxton (1803–65) designed Crystal Palace's waterworks, fountains, and cascades.
6. 2 Cor. 11:24–25.

Chapter 6: You Miss, You Die

1. 1 Samuel 17:1–54.
2. The most thief-infested thoroughfare in London, the haunt of ruffians, pickpockets, parasites snoozers, and hardened criminals.
3. Mondollot's *gazogène-briet* was a wire and nickel-plated glass apparatus resembling an hourglass. It produced seltzer, carbonated water used in many fizzy drinks of the day, such as soda, fizzy lemonade, Vichy, etc.
4. 1 Samuel 17:32, 36.
5. 1 Samuel 17:26.
6. 1 Samuel 17:45–46.
7. Joshua 1:9.
8. 1 Samuel 17:11.
9. 2 Samuel 5:17–20.
10. 2 Samuel 5:22–25.
11. 2 Samuel 23:20.
12. The foremost architect of the era.
13. A potato, onion, and cabbage pancake browned lightly in bacon fat.
14. 2 Samuel 21:15–22.
15. Exodus 20:7; Leviticus 24:16.
16. 2 Samuel 22:38–43.

Chapter 7: Dead Man Walking

1. John 11:1–44.
2. Manager of the Savoy Theatre, London, mere yards from Simpson's Divan, a popular London restaurant.
3. The Gaiety Theatre, as opposed to the Savoy, still operated with gaslights.
4. A play on words. On a rainy night, the open-fronted hansom cab would be inconvenient, cold, and messy, necessitating the hire

of the larger, glass-enclosed four-wheeler carriage, nicknamed a "growler."

5. Luke 8:41–56.
6. Luke 7:11–15.
7. NIV.
8. John 14:11.
9. John 20:29.
10. John 11:25.
11. John 10:7, 9; John 10:11; John 14:16; John 15:5.
12. Holmes considered Lestrade, a Scotland Yard inspector, energetic but lacking in originality and vision.
13. John 7:37–39.
14. John 11:25–26: "I am the resurrection and the life. He who believes in Me, though he may die, he shall live. And whoever lives and believes in Me shall never die. Do you believe this?"
15. Luke 10:38–40.
16. A wooden cudgel, about a yard in length, which can be used as a weapon.
17. The luxurious Grand Hotel bordered Trafalgar Square on the southeast.
18. A very large carriage drawn by four horses, with passenger seats inside and on top.
19. A large potato crepe doused with melted butter and brown sugar.
20. Toasted oatmeal stirred into whipped cream and raspberries.
21. John 5:19.
22. ESV.

CHAPTER 8: WHO'S YOUR MAMA?

1. The Darnley Jewel, ordered fashioned by Margaret Douglas for her husband, Matthew Stewart, Regent of Scotland. In 1565, her son, Lord Darnley, married his cousin, Mary Queen of Scots. The richly decorated pendant has, at its center, a luminous blue sapphire in the shape of a heart.
2. Psalm 24:7.
3. Psalm 24:8.
4. Ibid.
5. Luke 1:38.
6. Victoria, Queen of England.

7. *Jehoiachin* is rendered "Coniah" in the New King James Version. Throughout this chapter, wherever Jehoiachin is mentioned, it is this same Coniah to whom the speaker refers (also called Jeconiah in some NKJV passages that are referenced below).

8. Matthew 1:1–16. *Jehoiachin* appears in the NIV rendering of this passage.

9. Jeremiah 22:24–30. Here the name Coniah has been replaced with "Jehoiachin," an alternate name for Coniah (see note 7 above; see also the New King James Version's footnote for verse 24).

10. Jeremiah 11:14.

11. Jeremiah 13:14.

12. Jeremiah 13:18.

13. See chapter 3, "Righteous Blood Is Red."

14. Nehemiah 7:61–65.

15. 1 Chronicles 3:17–19.

16. Ezra 3:2; 5:2; Nehemiah 12:1.

17. 2 Kings 18:4.

18. Hadrian's Wall, separating Roman Britain from the hostile Scottish north country.

19. Luke 3:23–38.

20. Bruce M. Metzger, *The Text of the New Testament* (New York: Oxford University Press, 1992), 194–95.

CHAPTER 9: RUN FOR YOUR LIFE

1. Units composed of a mix of cavalry and infantry, usually organized as the need arose.

2. The smallest unit of cavalry, consisting of thirty-two troops.

3. Chrestus is a common slave-name; Junius, the uncle of Sejanus, was the first member of his family to gain entrance into Roman nobility.

4. Synonymous with Victoria Tower.

5. Johannes Zuckertort, brilliant Prussian grandmaster, winner of the London 1883 chess tournament.

6. Galatians 4:4.

7. Matthew 2:13–23.

8. A city in India where, in June 1857, the European inhabitants were treacherously butchered by Nana Sahib upon the approach of the relieving British force.

9. A single blast upon a cab-whistle summoned a large four-wheeler carriage; two, a two-wheeled hansom.
10. Alexander and Aristobulus, his two sons by Mariamne, and Antipater.
11. Mark 6:14–28; Luke 13:31.
12. Acts 12:20–23.
13. Acts 25:13–26:32.
14. Jeremiah 31:15.
15. 1 Peter 1:10–11.
16. Ephesians 1:10; 2 Thessalonians 2:6; Titus 1:3.
17. Acts 8:1, 4; 9:29–30; 15:3, 30, 36; 17:1.
18. Acts 9:13–14.
19. Luke 3:5–6.
20. British slang for the hired driver of a cab.

CHAPTER 10: HUMPTY DUMPTY
1. Joshua 6:1–21.
2. Mrs. Hudson was proficient at whist, referenced in chapter 4.
3. Watson served in India with the Fifth Northumberland Fusiliers as assistant surgeon.
4. Genesis 7:4, 12, 17; Numbers 14:33–34; Matthew 4:2; Mark 1:13; Luke 4:2; 1 Samuel 17:16.
5. Genesis 2:2–3; Revelation 1:20; Joshua 6:8; 1 Kings 19:18.
6. Luke 11:26.
7. Proverbs 6:16.
8. Jonah 1:17; Matthew 12:40.
9. Chaim Herzog and Mordechai Gichon, *Battles of the Bible* (New York: Random House, 1978), 27.
10. Shadwell Police Station, Stepney, was in a poorer part of London east of New Scotland Yard.
11. Joshua 2:9.

BIBLIOGRAPHY

Baring-Gould, William S. *The Annotated Sherlock Holmes*. Vols. 1 and 2. New York: Clarkson N. Potter, Inc., 1967.

———. *Sherlock Holmes of Baker Street*. New York: Clarkson N. Potter, Inc., 1962.

Bayard, Tanya. *A Medieval Home Companion*. New York: HarperPerennial, 1992.

Carey, John. *John Donne*. Oxford: Oxford University Press, 1991.

Douglas, J. D. *The Illustrated Bible Dictionary*. Vols. 1–3. Leicester, UK: Inter-Varsity Press, 1980.

Dyer, Charles H. *Thirty Days in the Land with Jesus*. Chicago: Moody Publishers, 2012.

Gower, Ralph. *The New Manners and Customs of Bible Times*. Chicago: Moody Press, 1987.

Harrison, Michael. *The London of Sherlock Holmes*. New York: Drake Publishing, Inc., 1972.

Herzog, Chaim and Mordechai Gichon. *Battles of the Bible*. New York: Random House, Inc. 1978.

Lockyer, Herbert Sr. *Nelson's Illustrated Bible Dictionary*. Nashville: Thomas Nelson Publishers, 1986.

Marshall, Alfred. *The Interlinear NASB-NIV Parallel New Testament*. Grand Rapids: Zondervan, 1993.

Matthews, Victor H. *Manners and Customs in the Bible*. Peabody, MA: Hendrickson Publishers, 1988.

Metzger, Bruce M. *The Text of the New Testament, Its Transmission, Corruption, and Restoration*. New York: Oxford University Press, 1992.

Price, Randall. *Rose Guide to the Temple*. Torrance, CA: Rose Publishing, Inc., 2012.

Pritchard, James B. *Ancient Near Eastern Texts*. Princeton: Princeton University Press, 1969.

Shipley, Joseph T. *Dictionary of Early English*. Totowa, NJ: Littlefield, Adams & Co., 1968.

Tracy, Jack. *The Encyclopedia Sherlockiana*. Garden City, NY: Doubleday & Company, Inc., 1977.

Vine, W. E. *Vine's Expository Dictionary of New Testament Words*. Peabody, MA: Hendrickson Publishers.

Viney, Charles. *Sherlock Holmes in London*. Surrey, UK: Colour Library Books, 1995.

ABOUT THE AUTHOR

LEN BAILEY is a professional radio commercial and voiceover actor and bagpipe player. He attended high school at Markoma Bible Academy in Tahlequah, Oklahoma, and earned a BA in history from Trinity College in Deerfield, Illinois, as well as a journalism scholarship. He lives with his wife, Denise, and their three sons in suburban Chicago.